Property and the Pursuit of Happiness

Property and the Pursuit of Happiness

Locke, the Declaration of Independence, Madison, and the Challenge of the Administrative State

Edward J. Erler

Published in cooperation with Claremont Institute

ROWMAN & LITTLEFIELD
Lanham • Boulder • New York • London

Published in cooperation with Claremont Institute

Published by Rowman & Littlefield
An imprint of The Rowman & Littlefield Publishing Group, Inc.
4501 Forbes Boulevard, Suite 200, Lanham, Maryland 20706
www.rowman.com

6 Tinworth Street, London SE11 5AL, United Kingdom

British Library Cataloguing in Publication Information Available

Library of Congress Cataloging-in-Publication Data

ISBN 9781538130865 (cloth : alk. paper)
ISBN 9781538130872 (electronic)

∞™ The paper used in this publication meets the minimum requirements of American National Standard for Information Sciences—Permanence of Paper for Printed Library Materials, ANSI/NISO Z39.48-1992.

Dedicated to the Memory
of
Frances Abigail Erler
1942–2016
Wife, Mother, Friend

Edward, lo! to sudden fate
(Weave we the woof. The thread is spun.)

* * * * * * *

(The web is wove. The work is done.)

—Thomas Gray, "The Bard," 1756

Contents

Introduction

The Declaration of Independence is listed in Title I of the United States Statutes at Large as the first of the "Organic Laws of the United States." The other three organic laws in Title I are the Articles of Confederation, the Northwest Ordinance, and the Constitution. The phrase "organic law" was not commonly used during the founding, but the founders were clear about the relation of the Declaration to the Constitution: the Declaration served as the authoritative source of the principles of the Constitution. This is today a disputed point, but I have taken some care to argue the accuracy of this statement.

Article VI of the Constitution assumes all obligations incurred under the Articles of Confederation, which means that, in effect, the Articles became a part of the Constitution. This accounts, I believe, for the Articles being listed as one of the organic laws of the United States. The Northwest Ordinance was passed under the Articles of Confederation and was actually under consideration at the same time that the Constitution was being debated in the Constitutional Convention. It was re-passed under the new Constitution and was the first act of Congress concerning territory that belonged to the United States that was not a part of any state. The act proclaimed that "there shall be neither slavery nor involuntary servitude" in the territory. Since Congress had no authority to act on the issue of slavery in any state, this is the only place where Congress could decide the issue free from constitutional encumbrances. The act must therefore be considered an attempt to set the future course of the Constitution with respect to the issue of slavery in the territories and thus a part of its organic law.

"Organic law" was frequently used during the Reconstruction debates, and members of the Thirty-Ninth Congress were animated by the single-minded purpose of completing the founding by bringing the Constitution into harmony with the principles of the Declaration of Independence, a founding that had been impossible to complete in 1789 because of the necessity of compromising on the issue of slavery. This is also a disputed point that I have argued in detail and hope to have carried to the satisfaction of thoughtful readers.

In April 1859, Abraham Lincoln wrote what still stands today as the best account of American exceptionalism. In the peroration to his famous letter to Henry L. Pierce, Lincoln recited this paean to the author of the Declaration of Independence:

> All honor to Jefferson—to the man who, in the concrete pressure of a struggle for national independence by a single people, had the coolness, forecast, and capacity to introduce into a merely revolutionary document, an abstract truth, applicable to all men and all times, and so to embalm it there, that to-day, and in all coming days, it shall be a rebuke and a stumbling block to the very harbingers of reappearing tyranny and oppression.

What distinguishes the Declaration from "a merely revolutionary document" was that it relied on "an abstract truth, applicable to all men and all times." A mere revolution would have signaled an exchange of rulers; it would have resembled the many revolutions that have agitated politics throughout history, but it would not have been, as the American Revolution surely was, a world-historical event. What was unique about the American Revolution was that for the first time in history, a nation was founded dedicated to a universal principle—the principle that "all men are created equal." This was said to be a "self-evident truth" derived from the "Laws of Nature and of Nature's God." Nature and natural right would become the foundation of the nation, replacing the historical rights and prescription that had animated British constitutionalism. Natural right and natural law provided the ground for a new kind of constitutionalism.

The other major accomplishment of the Declaration of Independence resides in the fact that it derived its principles from both reason and revelation, giving equal claims to both. The American founding was exceptional in that events transpired in such a way that there were no theological-political disputes that rendered political agreement impossible. America seemed to have been favored by a providential dispensation that allowed a resolution of the theological-political question (at least on a moral and political level), so that no differences involving the ultimate ends or purposes of government or the role of religion stood in the way of founding a new regime. Reason and revelation, of course, ultimately disagree with respect to the question of what perfects and completes human life, but reason and revelation can agree on a political and moral level, as the sermons analyzed in chapter 2 illustrate. That agreement was signified by the Declaration's reliance on the "Laws of Nature and Nature's God," where both reason and revelation are given equal claims. Later this idea would be reflected in the First Amendment to the Constitution, where free exercise of religion is protected equally with freedom of speech. Both reason and revelation have equal claims under America's exceptional founding. Reason and revelation are themes that are explored throughout this book, and I have done my utmost to treat them seriously and with appropriate depth.

The English philosopher John Locke had a profound influence on the American founding, and I have endeavored to explore the ways in which he is justly regarded as "America's philosopher." At the same time, I have tried to understand where the American founders made important innovations and, in my view, improvements on Locke. They saw Locke with the eyes of wise statesmen and, as such, were not as impressed as some seem to be today with the rigid distinction that has been drawn between ancient and modern philosophy. The founders understood Locke in a commonsense way and traced his teachings, in one way or another, in an unbroken line to Aristotle, either unmindful or unaware of the ancients-and-moderns dichotomy. I trust that I have made something of a credible argument on that score.

The theological-political problem is unique to Christianity; Aristotle and the classical philosophers did not have to confront the conundrum that challenged Locke and other modern philosophers, although I believe that Aristotle would have understood the issue in much the same way that Locke did had he been writing in the late seventeenth century. The American founders resolved the problem based on the separation of church and state, a political solution that was fully endorsed by theologians at the time of the founding based on their reading of biblical texts. This agreement between theology and politics was made possible, in large measure, by Locke's writings, which I have attempted to analyze in some depth.

I test the patience of the reader on some occasions by restating crucial arguments when necessary to advance the overall theme of this work that centers on the importance of the comprehensive right to property for the American founding. This is a complex subject, and explanations beginning from the center lead to the periphery and inevitably back to the center by a variety of paths. Each time the center is reached anew, a recounting of its importance is necessary, although the recounting is always undertaken from a different point of view. The right to property was understood by the founders as the comprehensive right that included all other rights. Understood in this manner, the right to property was described in our most authoritative document as the "pursuit of happiness," which was considered not only a natural right but also a moral obligation. I trust that I have made a reasonable attempt to articulate this vital but neglected component of the Declaration of Independence.

The right to property has almost disappeared today from the Bill of Rights. It is the only "fundamental right" in the pantheon of rights that does not receive strict judicial scrutiny against legislative and executive encroachment. This development came about as the result of the advent of the administrative state and what has been called post-constitutionalism. The private right to property stands as a barrier to the developing doctrine that all property is held in public trust and that the rightful owner, to be chosen by government, is the one who can best serve a "public purpose." Once the Supreme Court amended the original language of the Fifth Amendment's Takings Clause from "public use" to the more expansive "public purpose," constitutionalists should have taken alarm at this first innovation on the right to property. The right to property was always regarded as the "fence to liberty," and once that fence was breached, liberty would be in danger. The fence to liberty has in fact been breached, and the right to property, as I argue, has been restored to something like a feudal basis where government has become the "universal landlord." Liberty is indeed under attack by an administrative state that is fast evolving into a post-constitutional state, where administration is deemed to have replaced the Constitution and politics. I take up this controversy in chapter 5 and the conclusion, always with constant reference to the principles of the founding and the Declaration of Independence.

Thomas Klingenstein, chairman of the board of directors of the Claremont Institute, gave his support and encouragement throughout the writing of this book, as did Ryan Williams, president of the Institute. Many thanks are due to John Marini of the University of Nevada, Reno, for reading parts of the manuscript and engaging in valuable and exhaustive conversations on subjects covered in the book. Indispensable help was provided by Gary Wood of Andrews University, who read the entire manuscript and made helpful suggestions for revisions. Mickey Craig of Hillsdale College read the first three chapters and offered his advice, as did Douglas Jeffrey of Hillsdale College, who read chapter 1. David Sonenstein, Esq., read chapters 4 and 5 and provided timely criticism. Richard Reeb of Barstow College read chapter 2 and responded with suggestions. Philip Munoz of the University of Notre Dame read the entire manuscript and reported valuable criticism of the work as a whole.

1

The Declaration of Independence, the Constitution, and "Strictly Republican" Government

"[The Declaration of Independence was] the genuine effusion of the soul of our country."

—Thomas Jefferson[1]

"[I am] convinced that the republican is the only form of government which is not eternally at open or secret war with the rights of mankind."

—Thomas Jefferson[2]

In the summer of 1787, the delegates to the Constitutional Convention met in Philadelphia to design a constitution that was intended to put into motion those principles of constitutional government that had been enunciated in the Declaration of Independence. As Madison later wrote in the *Federalist*, the principles of the Constitution were derived from "the transcendent law of nature and nature's God, which declares that the safety and happiness of society are the objects at which all political institutions aim and to which all such institutions must be sacrificed."[3] Everyone of course would have recognized this passage as a paraphrase of the Declaration of Independence. Madison aptly noted that the Declaration posits the "safety and happiness of society" as the end and purpose of government. This is the central of three explicit references to the Declaration in the *Federalist* and it is mentioned in the central number of the eighty-five papers. The first reference recounts "the transcendent and precious right of

---

1. Thomas Jefferson, Letter to Dr. James Mease, September 26, 1825, in *The Life and Selected Writings of Thomas Jefferson*, ed. Adrienne Koch and William Peden (New York: Modern Library, 1944), 722.
2. Thomas Jefferson, Letter to William Hunter, March 11, 1790, in ibid., 493.
3. Alexander Hamilton, James Madison, and John Jay, *The Federalist Papers*, introduction and notes by Charles R. Kesler, ed. Clinton Rossiter (New York: Signet Classics, 1999), 43:276 (further references in the text by paper number and page).

the people to 'abolish or alter their governments as to them shall seem most likely to
effect their safety and happiness'" (40:249). This reference to the Declaration is the
only one in the *Federalist* that has a footnote giving the source as the Declaration of
Independence. This is rather curious since the quoted portion is inaccurate: the words
"alter" and "abolish" have been transposed, and two clauses indicating the people's right
to reestablish government ("to institute new Government, laying its foundation on
such principles and organizing its powers in such form") have been elided. The citation
seems designed to call attention to this transposition of the terms "abolish or alter" and
the elision of the central clauses. The object of the convention, Madison seems to say,
was to "abolish" rather than to "alter" the Articles of Confederation, and the convention had assumed the people's role in instituting "new Government."[4] The third reference, penned by Hamilton, likewise invoked the right of revolution, "that fundamental
principle of republican government which admits the right of the people to alter or
abolish the established Constitution whenever they find it inconsistent with their happiness" (78:468). Hamilton also clearly implies that the purpose of government is the
"happiness" of the people, and in an earlier number he had noted "the importance of
the Union" for the "safety and happiness" of the people (15:100). Thus it seems evident
that the two principal authors of the *Federalist* believed that the Declaration posited the
"safety and happiness of the people" as the end and purpose of government.

This analysis would seem to belie the argument of those who claim that the
"Declaration unequivocally asserts that the purpose of government is the securing
of rights, and only the securing of rights."[5] Madison seems insistent, however, that

---

4. In *Federalist* 40, Madison answers the allegation that the Convention had exceeded its authority
in proposing a new constitution when it had been charged with "the sole and express purpose of revis-
ing the articles of Confederation . . . [to] render the federal Constitution adequate to the exigencies of
government and the preservation of the Union" (40:244). Madison argued that the instructions to the
Convention were contradictory: no revision of the Articles could make them adequate precisely because
the principles upon which the Articles rested were defective. As Hamilton remarked, the Articles had
created "the political monster of an *imperium in imperio*" that "cannot be amended otherwise than by an
alteration in the first principles and main pillars of the fabric" (15:103). It would be of little avail for the
"safety and happiness" (40:249) of the people to build a new structure on a defective foundation since
the new superstructure would partake of the deficiencies of the foundation itself. Madison argued that
a sound principle of legal construction required those who were faced with contradictory commands to
choose the most important. Obviously it was more important to have a constitution that was adequate to
meet the exigencies facing the Union than one that was inadequate but adhered strictly to the command
that the Articles be revised. In any case, Madison concluded, since "the plan to be framed and proposed
was to be submitted to *the people themselves*, the disapprobation of this supreme authority would destroy
it forever; its approbation blot out antecedent errors and irregularities" (40:249). In submitting the proposed constitution directly to the people, the Convention also subverted its charge to submit the revisions
to Congress, which would, upon approval, submit them to the state legislatures. A unanimous concurrence of the state legislatures was required under the Articles for ratification. Madison argues, however,
that "the establishment of a government adequate to the national happiness was the end at which [the
Articles of Confederation] themselves originally aimed, and to which they ought, as insufficient means,
to have been sacrificed" (40:245). In other words, Madison clearly intimates that the Constitution itself
resulted from an act of revolution appealing to the supreme authority of the people! See 20:133–34;
22:147–48; 30:186–87; 45:285–86; 46:292–93; 84:517.

5. Michael P. Zuckert, *The Natural Rights Republic* (Notre Dame, IN: University of Notre Dame Press,
1996), 26, 28–30, 206.

the purpose of government as understood by "the leaders of the Revolution" was the security of "private rights and public happiness" (14:99). The protection of private rights for Madison was a necessary but not sufficient condition for securing public happiness.

During a particularly contentious session of the Virginia ratifying convention, Madison remarked that "professions of attachment to the public good, and comparisons of parties, ought not to govern or influence us now. We ought . . . to examine the constitution on its own merits solely: we are to enquire whether it will promote the public happiness: its aptitude to produce this desirable object ought to be the exclusive subject of our present researches."[6] Security of private rights thus appears to be only a part of the calculus; the other and—if we are to credit Madison—the more important part is public happiness. Public happiness cannot be understood as simply the aggregate of private rights; it also includes the civic obligations that form the basis for friendship, which in turn is the basis for citizenship. Madison's argument here is reminiscent of Aristotle's argument in the first book of his *Politics* that the *polis* is established for the sake of mere life but continues for the sake of the good life—that is, for the sake of human happiness.

THE *FEDERALIST* AND PUBLIC HAPPINESS

In the *Federalist*, happiness is most frequently mentioned as the end or purpose of government. The most succinct statement was made by Madison: "A good government implies two things: first fidelity to the object of government, which is the happiness of the people; secondly, a knowledge of the means by which the object can be best attained" (62:378; see 30:187; 40:245; 41:252; 71:430). Madison also wrote, in an oft-quoted passage,

> Justice is the end of government. It is the end of civil society. It ever has been and ever will be pursued until it be obtained, or until liberty be lost in the pursuit. In a society under the forms of which the stronger faction can readily unite and oppress the weaker, anarchy may as truly be said to reign as in a state of nature, where the weaker individual is not secured against the violence of the stronger; and as, in the latter state, even the stronger individuals are prompted, by the uncertainty of their condition, to submit to a government which may protect the weak as well as themselves; so, in the former state, will the more powerful factions or parties be gradually induced, by a like motive, to wish for a government which will protect all parties, the weaker as well as the more powerful (51:321–22).

Here Madison clearly posits liberty as the means to justice—justice is not possible without liberty, and liberty is always in the service of justice. Justice seems to

---

6. Robert A. Rutland et al., eds., *The Papers of James Madison* (Chicago: University of Chicago Press, 1962–), 11:78.

be comprehensive since it is the end of both civil society and government. Madison accepts the distinction between civil society and government and, by doing so, certainly implies the social compact origins of civil society and government.[7] Society is formed by the unanimous consent of those who wish to end the "anarchy" of the state of nature and establish security for natural rights. Anarchy is a threat to the weak, but even the strong are aware that the anarchy of the state of nature is contrary to their interests. The security of rights in civil society serves the common good of both the strong and the weak. Each individual who consents to become a member of civil society for the equal protection of his equal rights incurs at the same time equal obligations—the obligation to protect the rights of other members of civil society. Rights and obligations thus form the core of civil society. Once the people form a government, the rights and interests of minorities are exposed to the depredations of majority factions in the same way that the weak are prey to the strong in the state of nature. A just government will be one that protects against majority factions—majorities actuated by common interests or passions that are adverse to the rights or interests of minorities or individuals—while at the same time preserving the form of republican government. In the extended republic, Madison argues, "a coalition of a majority of the whole society could seldom take place on any other principles than those of justice and the general good" (51:322). Madison clearly connects "justice" to the "general good" in this summary of his famous argument in *Federalist* 10.

In *Federalist* 10, Madison rehearsed the "complaints . . . heard from our most considerate and virtuous citizens" who are "equally the friends of public and private faith and of public and personal liberty." These complaints lodged by prominent citizens were that the state administrations "are too unstable, that the public good is disregarded in the conflicts of rival parties, and that measures are too often decided, not according to the rules of justice and the rights of the minor party, but by the superior force of an interested and overbearing majority" (10:72; see 80:476). Madison vouches for the veracity of the complaints, but only in a qualified sense: "they are in some degree true" (10:72). Here the "rules of justice" are associated with the "rights of the minor party." The situation is the same as in the state of nature, where the rights of the weaker are not secured against the violence of the stronger. The "rules of justice" are viewed in the context of an overarching "public good." Instability caused by "rival factions" opposes the stability demanded by the public good. It was "the instability, injustice, and confusion introduced into the public councils" that proved to be "the mortal diseases under which popular governments have everywhere perished" (10:71–72). And if we are to believe "our most considerate and virtuous citizens," this is precisely the politics that dominated the states.[8]

---

7. David F. Epstein, *The Political Theory of* The Federalist (Chicago: University of Chicago Press, 1984), 163.

8. An example of a complaint from a "considerate and virtuous" citizen might be George Washington's letter to Madison, November 5, 1786, in *Papers of James Madison*, 9:161–62.

In *Federalist* 45, Madison once again takes up the question of the "vicissitudes" of the administration of the several states, this time with considerably less reserve. The "adversaries to the plan of the convention," Madison says, have questioned whether the power granted to the federal government was "absolutely necessary" in light of "the possible consequences of the proposed degree of power to the government of the particular States" (45:285). This, of course, was a common anti-federalist theme that evoked few sympathies in Madison. His reply barely concealed his contempt:

> If the Union be essential to the happiness of the people of America, is it not preposterous to urge as an objection to a government, without which the objects of the Union cannot be attained, that such a government may derogate from the importance of the governments of the individual States?

Madison's queries continued: Was the Revolution fought—"was the precious blood of thousands spilt"—to maintain the sovereignty of the states? Another provocative question struck even deeper: opponents of the proposed constitution refused to accept the greatest achievement of the revolution, the sovereignty of the people; they still adhered to the old notion that government, not the people, was the legitimate sovereign. Madison remarks,

> We have heard of the impious doctrine in the old world, that the people were made for kings, not kings for the people. Is the same doctrine to be revived in the new, in another shape—that the solid happiness of the people is to be sacrificed to the views of political institutions of a different form? It is too early for politicians to presume on our forgetting that the public good, the real welfare of the great body of the people, is the supreme object to be pursued; and that no form of government whatever has any other value than as it may be fitted for the attainment of this object. Were the plan of the convention adverse to the public happiness, my voice would be, Reject the plan. Were the Union itself inconsistent with the public happiness, it would be, Abolish the Union. In like manner, as far as the sovereignty of the States cannot be reconciled to the happiness of the people, the voice of every good citizen must be, Let the former be sacrificed to the latter. How far the sacrifice is necessary has been shown. How far the unsacrificed residue will be endangered is the question before us (45:285–86).

For Madison, of course, energetic government was the key to securing the ends contemplated by the Constitution: the public good and public happiness of the people. Sovereignty lodged in the states would be irreconcilable with both the "public good" and "the happiness of the people." "An irregular and mutable legislation," Madison asserts, "is not more an evil in itself than it is odious to the people; and this country, enlightened as they are with regard to the nature, and interested, as the great body of them are in the effects of good government, will never be satisfied till some remedy be applied to the vicissitudes and uncertainties which characterize the State administrations" (37:223). Thus one of the important ingredients of "public happiness" or "the public good" is the "repose and confidence" that is produced by good laws and the steady administration of justice. The "vicissitudes and uncertainties which characterize State administrations" can only be remedied by a "well constructed Union" (10:71). Hamilton had almost the last word on this subject when he remarked that

> the great bulk of the citizens of America are with reason convinced that Union is the basis of their political happiness. Men of sense of all parties now with few exceptions agree that it cannot be preserved under the present system, nor without radical altera- tions; that new and extensive powers ought to be granted to the national head, and that these require a different organization of the federal government (84:517).

An extended discussion of "public happiness," or of the relation between the "public good" and "public happiness," to say nothing of the relation of "justice" or the "rules of justice" to "public happiness," would have been out of place in the *Federalist*. The principal task of Publius was to convince the people of the utility of a firm and energetic union. But from the discussion that is scattered throughout, it can hardly be doubted that for Madison and Hamilton and, in all likelihood, the Federalist supporters of the Constitution generally, the purpose of government was not exhausted by the simple idea of protecting private rights, nor did they believe that public happiness could be understood as merely the aggregate of private rights without any sense of the public or common good. When Madison makes his famous assertion that "justice" is the end of both government and civil society, he clearly al- ludes to the social compact origins of civil society and government. In civil society, there are no rights without correspondent responsibilities. In this sense, justice refers to the reciprocity of rights and obligations that rest at the core of civil society. Madi- son clearly implied that the social compact served a common good: in its primitive form, the common advantage between the weaker and the stronger for the protection of equal natural rights. Public happiness seems to have a more extensive signification and is more frequently associated with the "public good," although we saw in *Federal- ist* 10 the "rules of justice" understood as the protection of rights were considered the primary ingredient of the "public good."

There are three unequivocal expressions of the ends or purposes of government in the *Federalist*, all made by Madison: "the public good," "justice," and the "happiness of the people." It would undoubtedly be too simple to equate these three, as all seem to be essential to good government as understood by Publius, although the "hap- piness of the people" seems to be, almost by definition, the comprehensive good. As one careful commentator notes, "Publius frequently identifies happiness as the proper end of political deliberations. In these references, happiness seems to have the character of a final end, which sets limits to human striving, and also of a collective or public end, which cannot be reduced to calculations of immediate self-interest."[9]

---

9. Eugene F. Miller, "What Publius Says About Interest," *Political Science Reviewer* 19 (1990): 34. Professor Miller's remarks are directed against Martin Diamond's view that the *Federalist* displays "a fundamental reliance on ceaseless striving after immediate interest." See Martin Diamond, "Democracy and *The Federalist*: A Reconsideration of the Framers' Intent," *American Political Science Review* 53, no. 1

The most authoritative statement of Publius is undoubtedly the central reference to the Declaration in *Federalist* 43, which identifies the Declaration as the principled source of the Constitution and adopts the ends of government specified in the Declaration as the "safety and happiness" of the people.

SAFETY AND HAPPINESS: THE
DECLARATION OF INDEPENDENCE

Professor Harry Jaffa comments on the ends of government contemplated in the Declaration of Independence:

> After speaking of our unalienable rights, to secure which governments are instituted, the Declaration of Independence goes on to say that "whenever any form of government becomes destructive of these ends, it is the right of the people to alter or abolish it, and to institute new government, laying its foundations on such principles and organizing its powers in such form, as to them shall seem most likely to effect their safety and happiness." Notice that in the second institution, or reinstitution of government, "rights" become "ends." And these ends are now said to be "Safety" and "Happiness," the alpha and omega of political life in Aristotle's *Politics*.

In a statement that is not entirely hyperbolic, Jaffa asserts that "in one form or another, this metamorphosis of Lockean 'rights' into Aristotelian 'ends' (or vice versa) recurs in many of the documents of the Founding."[10] It might seem strange that Jaffa conflates Locke and Aristotle in an attempt to discover Aristotelian elements in the Declaration. Jefferson himself suggested such a conflation when he wrote in 1826 that "the object of the Declaration of Independence" was "to place before mankind

---

(March 1959): 52–68, at 67. This statement is fully in accord with Diamond's view that "*The Federalist* is almost wholly silent" about "the ends of government" (64). Where Publius states that "justice is the end of government," Diamond is compelled to dismiss it as a modern view—"low but solid"—referring "primarily to the protection of economic liberties" (62). Similarly, while admitting that happiness "is the most frequently occurring definition of the 'object of government,'" Diamond discounts these references as having "little in common with traditional philosophic or theological understanding of them." Rather, happiness for the *Federalist* seems more concerned with "the comforts afforded by a commercial society" (63). Diamond's analysis of the *Federalist* was driven by his unreflective adherence to the ancients-moderns paradigm. Diamond was therefore compelled to ignore or discount any evidence (however obvious or commonsensical) of premodern influence. Since modernity eschewed ends in favor of beginnings, any evidence that Publius might have articulated the ends of the new regime had to be obfuscated. Publius, however, is anything but "silent" on ends or purposes of government, as has already been amply demonstrated. And those ends become fully intelligible only upon the realization that the American founding seems to have stood against the storms of modernity, sheltered by its still intelligible attachment to classical natural right. See Leo Strauss, *City and Man* (Chicago: Rand McNally, 1964), 89; and Edward Erler, "Aristotle, Locke and the American Founding," *Interpretation* 40, no. 3 (Winter 2014): 346 n. 10; 348–52; 354–55; 358–63; 368–75.

10. Harry V. Jaffa, "Aristotle and Locke in the American Founding," in *The Rediscovery of America: Essays by Harry V. Jaffa on the New Birth of Politics*, ed. Edward J. Erler and Ken Masugi (Lanham, MD: Rowman & Littlefield, 2019), 6.

the common sense of the subject, in terms so plain and firm as to command their assent, and justify ourselves in the independent stand we are compelled to take." "It was intended," Jefferson continued, "to be an expression of the American mind. . . . All its authority rests then on the harmonizing sentiments of the day, whether expressed in conversation, in letters, printed essays, or the elementary books of public right, as Aristotle, Cicero, Locke, Sidney, &c."[11] Jefferson undoubtedly read the "elementary books of public right" with the eyes of what Aristotle called a *phronimos*—a "practically wise statesman." He read the history of political philosophy largely unmindful of the philosophic dispute between ancients and moderns. As a statesman, Jefferson's primary concern was the history of politics, not the history of philosophy; he certainly understood Locke's natural law as a reflection or adaptation of Aristotle.[12]

Two years before the Declaration of Independence, James Wilson, a signer of the Declaration, a prominent member of the Constitutional Convention, and a Supreme Court justice, published *Considerations on the Nature and Extent of the Legislative Authority of the British Parliament*. In this work, Wilson claimed that he, too, endeavored to express the "common sense of the subject" as it was understood by the "American mind." "All men are, by nature, equal and free," Wilson wrote,

> no one has a right to any authority over another without his consent: all lawful government is founded on the consent of those who are subject to it: such consent was given with a view to ensure and to increase the happiness of the governed, above what they could enjoy in an independent and unconnected state of nature. The consequence is, that the happiness of the society is the *first* law of every government.[13]

In a footnote, Wilson states that "the right of sovereignty is that of commanding finally—but in order to procure real felicity; for if this end is not obtained, sovereignty ceases to be a legitimate authority."[14]

At about the same time that Wilson was composing his treatise, Jefferson was writing *A Summary View of the Rights of British America*, a work that was to have significant influence in the year before the Revolution. *A Summary View* was in the form of instructions to Virginia delegates to the general Congress in Philadelphia. Although it was never acted on, *A Summary View* was published and widely circulated. Jefferson wrote,

> Our ancestors, before their emigration to America, were the free inhabitants of the British dominions in Europe, and possessed a right, which nature has given to all men, of

11. Thomas Jefferson, Letter to Henry Lee, May 8, 1825, in *Jefferson: Writings*, ed. Merrill Peterson (New York: Library of America, 1984), 1501.

12. See Leo Strauss, *Natural Right and History* (Chicago: University of Chicago Press, 1953), 165.

13. James Wilson, *Considerations on the Nature and Extent of the Legislative Authority of the British Parliament* (1774), in *The Works of James Wilson*, ed. Robert McCloskey (Cambridge, MA: Harvard University Press, 1967), 2:723.

14. Ibid.

departing from the country in which chance, not choice has placed them, of going in quest of new habitations, and of there establishing new societies, under such laws and regulations as to them shall seem most likely to promote public happiness.[15]

"Our ancestors" exercised the natural right of emigration, which allows men to leave the country where "chance" and not "choice" has placed them. Choice, of course, implies reason, and reason is the foundation of natural right. If the quest for new societies that are better calculated to serve "public happiness" is a natural right, then we must conclude that "public happiness," the end or purpose of these societies, is also according to reason and therefore a natural right.[16] This was the same "universal law" that impelled—"in like manner"—"their Saxon ancestors" to leave "their native wilds and woods in the North of Europe" and to establish on "the island of Britain . . . that system of laws which has so long been the glory and protection of that country."[17] Their descendants who came to America exercised this same natural right to expatriate themselves in their quest for "public happiness."

Jefferson, of course, was well aware that the natural right of expatriation was in conflict with English common law. Blackstone gave a summary of the common law of "birthright subjectship," which had been first described by Sir Edward Coke in his famous opinion in *Calvin's Case* (1608). The common law never recognized citizenship, describing only the allegiance due from "subjects." Here is Blackstone:

Natural allegiance is such as is due from all men born within the king's dominions immediately upon their birth [citing *Calvin's Case*]. For, immediately upon their birth, they are under the king's protection. . . . Natural allegiance is therefore a debt of gratitude; which cannot be forfeited, cancelled, or altered, by any change of time, place or circumstance. . . . For it is a principle of universal law, that the natural-born subject of one prince cannot by any act of his own, no, not by swearing allegiance to another, put off or discharge his natural allegiance to the former: for his natural allegiance was intrinsic, and primitive, and antecedent to the other; and cannot be devested without the concurrent act of that prince to whom it was first due.[18]

What Blackstone describes here as "natural allegiance" is purely conventional, as is the term "natural-born subject." The allegiance due from a "natural born subject" is perpetual because it is "intrinsic" and "primitive." "Allegiance is the tie, or *ligamen*, which binds the subject to the king, in return for that protection which the

15. Thomas Jefferson, *A Summary View of the Rights of British America*, in *Jefferson: Writings*, 105–6. These instructions were never acted on by either the Virginia delegates or the Congress. *A Summary View* was undoubtedly considered too radical. As Jefferson's biographer Dumas Malone stated, "as a contemporary indictment of British policy it bordered on recklessness, but it was distinctive in its emphasis on philosophical fundamentals and its prophetic quality" (*Jefferson: The Virginian* [Boston: Little, Brown, 1948], 182).

16. See Thomas Jefferson, *Autobiography*, in *Jefferson: Writings*, 36 ("natural right of expatriation").

17. Jefferson, *A Summary View*, 106.

18. William Blackstone, *Commentaries on the Laws of England* (1765–1769; repr., Chicago: University of Chicago Press, 1979), I:357–58.

king affords the subject. The thing itself, or a substantial part of it, is founded in reason and the nature of government." But Blackstone concedes that the concept is an inheritance from the "feodal system"—it derives from the "mutual trust or confidence subsisting between the lord and vassal," and "by an easy analogy the term of allegiance was soon brought to signify all other engagements, which are due from subjects to their prince."[19] One could hardly imagine a doctrine further removed from the "natural right to expatriation."

Jefferson emphasizes that no obligations were created by the free exercise of this "natural right of expatriation" by "our ancestors." No claim of dependence had ever been levied against the Saxons by the "mother country from which they had migrated." Similarly, no claim of dependence can rightfully be made against their descendants. "America was conquered, and her settlements made and firmly established, at the expence of individuals," Jefferson claims, "and not of the British public. Their own blood was spilt in acquiring lands for their settlement, their own fortunes expended in making that settlement effectual. For themselves they fought, for themselves they conquered, and for themselves alone they have right to hold."[20] Once arrived in America, it was only to be expected that these expatriates would adopt a system of laws and government to which they were accustomed. But this was a matter of deliberate choice, and the king's authority now derived from the consent of the governed.[21] If the king's authority now rested on the consent of his "subjects," this surely represented a radically new view of monarchical authority.[22]

Proclaiming that his address would be "penned in the language of truth, and divested of those expressions of servility" that would only serve to "persuade his majesty that we are asking favors and not rights," Jefferson invites King George to reflect on the fact "that he is no more than the chief officer of the people . . . and consequently subject to their superintendence."[23] Jefferson even had the ill grace to remind the king of "those sacred and sovereign rights of punishment reserved in the hands of the people for cases of extreme necessity, and judged . . . unsafe to be delegated to any other judicature."[24] Rights are derived from "the laws of nature" and are not "the gift of their chief magistrate." Those who assert "the rights of human nature" "know, and will therefore say, that kings are the servants, not the proprietors of the people."[25] Jefferson goes to such lengths to argue that the king is, in effect, only a chief executive officer of the people, serving for their benefit and under their

19. Ibid., I:354–55.

20. Jefferson, *A Summary View*, in *Jefferson: Writings*, 106.

21. Ibid., 107.

22. See Edward Erler, "From Subject to Citizens: The Social Compact Origins of American Citizenship," in *The American Founding and the Social Compact*, ed. Ronald J. Pestritto and Thomas G. West (Lanham, MD: Lexington Books, 2003), 163–97.

23. Jefferson, *A Summary View*, in *Jefferson: Writings*, 105. Jefferson probably drew his inspiration for this argument from Locke's *Two Treatises of Government*, II.205 (fin.). I have used John Locke, *Two Treatises of Government*, ed. Peter Laslett (New York: New American Library, 1965). Further references will be in the text by treatise and paragraph number.

24. Jefferson, *A Summary View*, in *Jefferson: Writings*, 107.

25. Ibid., 121.

direction because it would have been illegitimate—against the principles of natural right—to have consented to the rule of a monarch, or to any other non-republican form of rule. Jefferson's history is retrospective. Americans consented not to a king but to a king who had been transmogrified into a republican executive, serving at the pleasure of the sovereign people! But under these circumstances, the only check the people have on the "chief executive's" power is the right of revolution. It was the Constitution that substituted free elections for revolution as the means of holding government responsible. But elections as a substitute for revolution are only effective if there are constant reminders—a "frequent recourse to fundamental principles," in the oft-expressed phrase of the founding generation—of the people's ultimate sovereignty. The requirement that the "just powers" of government can only be authorized by the consent of the governed was the decisive moment when subjects were transformed into citizens. The idea of citizenship, of course, was impossible in the feudal regime. And, as Blackstone readily admitted, the common law of perpetual allegiance was a feudal inheritance. Neither Coke nor Blackstone ever used the term "citizen." The feudal relation was that of master and subject, in which subjects never gained the elevated status of citizens who not only freely accept obligations but also have the obligation to assert rights. James Wilson almost certainly had Blackstone in mind when he noted, in 1793, that "under the Constitution of the United States there are citizens, but no subjects."[26]

The historical accuracy of Jefferson's account in *A Summary View* has often been questioned. Dumas Malone, his sympathetic biographer, wrote that "the presuppositions" of *A Summary View* "may be questioned, and there were flaws in his historical presentation, but morally his case was strong."[27] Another commentator has noted that

> the problem with Jefferson's reliance on the Ancient Constitution as a basis for legitimizing American independence was the questionable historical validity of that Saxon precedent and the consequences of basing his arguments on historical inaccuracies. . . . To the extent native Saxons possessed any organized society and government, it was tribal and chieftain rather than the ideal liberal order of John Locke.[28]

---

26. *Chisholm v. Georgia*, 2 U.S. (2 Dall.) 419, 456 (1793). David Ramsay made a similar remark in 1789 when he said,

A citizen of the United States, means a member of this new nation. The principle of government being radically changed by the revolution, the political character of the people was also changed from subjects to citizens. . . . Subjects look up to a master, but citizens are so far equal, that none have hereditary rights superior to others. Each citizen of a free state contains, within himself, by nature and the constitution, as much of the common sovereignty as another. In the eye of reason and philosophy, the political condition of citizens is more exalted than that of noblemen. Dukes and earls are the creatures of kings, and may be made by them at pleasure: but citizens possess in their own right original sovereignty (*A Dissertation on the Manner of Acquiring the Character and Privileges of a Citizen of the United States* [published as a widely circulated pamphlet in 1789, probably in Charleston, South Carolina], 3).

27. Malone, *Jefferson: The Virginian*, 184.
28. Garrett W. Sheldon, *The Political Philosophy of Thomas Jefferson* (Baltimore, MD: Johns Hopkins University Press, 1991), 34–35.

This criticism scarcely reaches the heart of the matter. For Jefferson and the revolutionary generation, what was essential was natural right, not history. *A Summary View* barely conceals—if it does so at all—its appeal to the right of revolution, the ultimate ground and foundation of all rights of nature, including the right of expatriation.[29]

Jefferson's argument here would indeed have been familiar to any reader of Locke—but no reader of Locke in the revolutionary generation (or perhaps any other) would have thought that his *Second Treatise of Government* contemplated "the ideal liberal order." For Locke, the rightful origin of civil society is consent—"the only way whereby any one devests himself of his Natural Liberty" (II.95). According to Locke, only compact "did, or could give *beginning* to any *lawful Government* in the World." In answer to the objection that history has never furnished an example of government based on consent, Locke asserts that "as far as we have any light from History, we have reason to conclude, that all peaceful beginnings of Government have been *laid in the 'Consent of the People'*" (II.112). While Locke seems to admit the scarcity of historical evidence to support his position, nevertheless there is "reason to conclude" that consent is at least the peaceful origin of all government. Whether any government has in fact had a peaceful beginning is a question that does not deter Locke from adumbrating the rightful origins of civil society by reference to natural right any more than the historical evidence deterred Jefferson.

Another objection Locke answers is that since all men are born under one form of government or another, "it is impossible any of them should ever be free, and at liberty to unite together, and begin a new one, or ever be able to erect a lawful Government." Taken to its conclusion, this objection would mean that no lawful government is ever possible if in fact lawful government proceeds from the consent of the governed, because men are not born in the state of nature but in civil society. Against this argument, Locke denies that there is such a thing as "natural subjection." By nature, men are "free, equal and independent," and no one can be "subjected to the Political Power of another, without his own *Consent*" (II.95). Consent is the only legitimate method of exchanging natural liberty for civil society. No one is born owing allegiance. Birth-right subjectship, which incurs perpetual allegiance to a prince without consent, is a violation of "the Law of right Reason" (II.118) and, as such, a violation of natural right or the law of nature. History supports these conclusions of reason. In a passage that must have been all too familiar to Jefferson, Locke writes, "For there are no Examples so frequent in History, both Sacred and Prophane, as those of Men withdrawing themselves, and their Obedience, from the Jurisdiction they were born under . . . and *setting up new Governments* in other places. . . . All

---

29. Jefferson often referred to the natural right of expatriation. When he was a member of the committee to revise the legal code for Virginia, appointed in 1776, he proposed a bill proclaiming the "natural right, which all men have of relinquishing the country, in which birth, or other accident may have thrown them, and, seeking subsistence and happiness wheresoever they may be able, or may hope to find them" (Julian P. Boyd et al., eds., *The Papers of Thomas Jefferson* [Princeton, NJ: Princeton University Press, 1950–], 2:477). See also *Jefferson: Writings*, 9.

which are so many Testimonies against Paternal Sovereignty" (II.115). The natural right of expatriation announced by Jefferson at the beginning of *A Summary View* was a right in the service of the "pursuit of happiness," which we learn from Locke "is our greatest good."[30] There is little doubt that the founders derived a great deal of their understanding of the "pursuit of happiness" from Locke, and this accounts for the fact that there is no extended discussion of the topic in any of the founding documents: the doctrines of "America's philosopher" had become ingrained in "the American mind."

THE GENIUS OF THE AMERICAN PEOPLE

Another connection between the *Federalist* and the Declaration of Independence should be acknowledged. Madison announces that *Federalist* 39 begins "a candid survey of the plan of government reported by the convention." "The first question that offers itself," he asserts,

> is whether the government be strictly republican. It is evident that no other form would be reconcilable with the genius of the people of America; with the fundamental prin-ciples of the Revolution; or with that honorable determination which animates every votary of freedom to rest all our political experiments on the capacity of mankind for self-government. If the plan of the convention, therefore, be found to depart from the republican character, its advocates must abandon it as no longer defensible (39:236).

The central reason that the Constitution must be "strictly republican" is to conform to the "fundamental principles of the Revolution"—that is, the principles of the Declaration of Independence. This statement is further proof, if any were needed, that for the framers there was an indefeasible connection between the Declaration and the Constitution. The connection was a "strictly republican" form of govern-ment as a means of securing the ends posited by the Declaration—the "safety and happiness" of the people.

The first reason Madison gave for the necessity of a "strictly republican form of government" was "the genius of the people of America"—their habits, manners, character—which would tolerate nothing less than a strictly republican form of government, one having no admixture of oligarchical, aristocratical, or monarchi-cal principles even where some admixture might prove useful in promoting the ends of republican government (see 63:382–83). A large part of the "genius of the people of America" is its "vigilant and manly spirit"—a "spirit," Madison says, that "actuates the people of America" (57:350). It was this spirit that animated the Revolution "for which a precedent could not be discovered." Based on that unique precedent, the American people were asked to approve a constitution that had no

---

30. John Locke, *An Essay Concerning Human Understanding*, ed. Peter H. Nidditch (Oxford: Claren-don Press, 1975), II.xxi.51–58.

example in the annals of history. "To this manly spirit," Madison avers, "posterity will be indebted for the possession, and the world for the example, of the numerous innovations displayed on the American theatre in favor of private rights and public happiness" (14:99). The manly spirit of the people of America is thus "a spirit which nourishes freedom, and in return is nourished by it" (57:350).[31] It is true that Americans had lived under monarchical rule, but at the same time they had been accustomed to a considerable degree to the privileges of self-rule. Republican habits, manners, morals, and, above all, a sense of self-sufficient independence had been formed by many years of self-government. This was the republican character, the "genius of the American people." It was a character fit only for citizens and could no longer tolerate subjectship. At the Constitutional Convention, James Wilson remarked, "The British Government cannot be our model. We have no materials for a similar one. Our manners, our laws, the abolition of entails and of primogeniture, the whole genius of the people, are opposed to it."[32] Before the mid-eighteenth century, Americans had begun to chafe at all manifestations of monarchical rule—and parliamentary tyranny. In 1787, America's "manly spirit" made it impossible to accept any form of government that was not "strictly republican." The "genius of the people" made freedom and republican government fated, if not inevitable.

THE CAPACITY OF MANKIND FOR SELF-GOVERNMENT

The third reason proffered by Madison for adhering to a "strictly republican" form of government was the "honorable determination which animates every votary of freedom to rest all our political experiments on the capacity of mankind for self-government." Self-government is an "experiment" that must be undertaken for the honor of human nature. In 1783, Congress appointed a committee, consisting of Madison, Hamilton, and Oliver Ellsworth, to draft an "Address to the States" on the newly adopted plan for restoring public credit. Madison was its principal author, although in later years he claimed that he did not agree with some of the recommendations and regretted that others had been omitted. Nevertheless, Madison's handiwork is evident throughout the address. One revealing passage is quintessential Madison and deserves quotation at length:

> Let it be remembered finally that it has ever been the pride and boast of America, that the rights for which she contended were the rights of human nature. . . . No instance has heretofore occurred, nor can any instance be expected hereafter to occur, in which the unadulterated forms of Republican Government can pretend to so fair an opportunity

---

31. See Edmund Burke, "Speech on Conciliation with America" (1775), in *The Works of the Right Honorable Edmund Burke* (Boston: Little, Brown, and Company, 1899), 2:120–22, 125, 133.

32. Max Farrand, ed., *Records of the Federal Convention of 1787* (New Haven, CT: Yale University Press, 1966 [orig. pub. 1911]), I.153.

of justifying themselves by their fruits. In this view the Citizens of the U.S. are responsible for the greatest trust ever confided to Political Society. If justice, good faith, honor, gratitude & all the other Qualities which ennoble the character of a nation, and fulfill the ends of Government, be the fruits of our establishments, the cause of liberty will acquire a dignity and lustre, which it has never yet enjoyed; and an example will be set which can not but have the most favorable influence on the rights of mankind. If on the other side, our Governments should be unfortunately blotted with the reverse of these cardinal and essential Virtues, the great cause which we have engaged to vindicate, will be dishonored & betrayed; the last & fairest experiment in favor of the rights of human nature will be turned against them; and their patrons & friends exposed to be insulted & silenced by the votaries of Tyranny and Usurpation.[33]

Although putatively an address to the states, the argument is directed to the "Citizens of the U.S." and describes "the character of a nation." The rhetorical movement is from states to nation—from the many to the one. American citizens are "responsible for the greatest trust ever confided to Political Society," the trust of conducting "the last & fairest experiment in favor of the rights of human nature." A failure will be a victory for "the votaries of Tyranny and Usurpation." But the "character of the nation," its virtue, predicts success. And if the nation's justice, good faith, honor, gratitude, and other "ennobling" qualities—in sum, "the genius of the American people"—lead to the success of the experiment, "the cause of liberty will acquire a dignity and lustre" that has never before been achieved. And this "genius" demands "unadulterated forms of Republican Government," which is to say government that is "strictly republican." If republican government fails, "the votaries of Tyranny and Usurpation" will have survived their greatest challenge, a challenge that will, in all likelihood, never be renewed. The votaries of freedom, however, look to "strictly republican" government for their salvation.

Hamilton writes in *Federalist* 36 that "every sincere and disinterested advocate for good government" will have no doubt as to "the propriety and expedience of adopting" the proposed constitution. And in the rousing peroration, Hamilton declaims, "Happy will it be for ourselves, and most honorable to human nature, if we have wisdom and virtue enough to set so glorious an example to mankind!" (36:220). The experiment itself is grounded in the principles of human nature or natural right—its success will be a vindication of those principles and thus "most honorable to human nature." Still, the outcome of the experiment is uncertain and every "votary of freedom" should pray for its success. "As there is a degree of depravity in mankind which requires a certain degree of circumspection and distrust," Madison writes, "so there are other qualities in human nature which justify a certain portion of esteem and confidence. Republican government presupposes the existence of these qualities in a higher degree than any other form." If "there is not sufficient virtue among men for self-government," Madison concludes, "nothing less than the chains of despotism can restrain them from destroying and devouring one another" (55:343). The choice

33. Madison, *Papers of James Madison*, 6:493–94.

is stark: strictly republican government or despotism. The American experiment will determine whether "reflection and choice" can be the ground of "good government." To say almost the same thing, the question is whether "wisdom and virtue" can be the foundation of republican government.

In order to become part of a self-governing people, each member of the body politic must be capable of governing himself—that is, he must be capable of guiding himself by reason. Republican virtue means possessing those qualities that lead men to be independent, capable of deliberation, and willing to assert rights as well as accept obligations. As Madison noted, "the aim of every political constitution is, or ought to be, first to obtain for rulers men who possess most wisdom to discern, and most virtue to pursue, the common good of the society; and in the next place, to take the most effectual precautions for keeping them virtuous whilst they continue to hold their public trust." And the "characteristic policy of republican government . . . for obtaining" such rulers is the "elective mode" (57:348). The rulers are charged with deliberating about the public good, and this is a peculiar public trust that requires wisdom. The core of republican virtue for the individual citizen is to determine his private interest by deliberation, recognizing that individual interest is intimately connected to the interest of society as a whole or to the public good—this is what some have called self-interest rightly understood. In order for an individual to become a member of a self-governing people, he must first be able to govern himself; once an individual can deliberate about his own interest in a way that shows awareness of the common good or public happiness, then he can judge the fitness of those who are charged with the more complicated task of deliberating about the public good and national happiness.

In "Vices of the Political System of the United States," compiled in preparation for the Constitutional Convention, Madison pondered the question of how republican government might deal with the problem of majority faction. One of the "motives" that might be used to lessen the effects of majority faction, he writes, is to inculcate "a prudent regard" in the citizens as "to their own good as involved in the general and permanent good of the Community." Madison was quick to add, however, that "this consideration although of decisive weight in itself, is found by experience to be too often unheeded."[34] Under the proper form of republican government, the idea of self-interest rightly understood can be of decisive importance in forming public opinion.

Republican government seeks to honor human nature, and it does so by creating the conditions for the rule of reason over passion in government and in individual citizens. Reason, rather than passion, is the basis for republican virtue. "It is the reason alone, of the public," Madison writes, "that ought to control and regulate the government. The passions ought to be controlled and regulated by the government" (49:314). Aristotle presents the rule of law as "reason [*nous*] unaffected by desire."[35] Insofar as the rule of law was central to the Constitution and its principles, the prospect of success depended on the extent to which adherence to the rule of law could

---

34. Ibid., 9:355.
35. Aristotle, *Politics*, 1287a30.

supply both the crucial element of reason demanded for self-government by the people and responsibility in government. As Professor Thomas G. West has aptly noted,

> the rule of law . . . is a governmental practice designed to make as likely as possible the coincidence of the two requirements of just government: that it be by the consent of the people, and that it secure the safety and happiness of society. The law aims to embody the public's reason by requiring the men who govern to act in conformity, at least in principle, to reasoned discussion and a rule of universal application.[36]

The rationality of the law is embodied in its universal character, and it is this feature of the rule of law that fosters rationality in the public. Everyone can see the benefit of the law's universality, and therefore every law-abiding citizen becomes habituated to understanding his particular interests in the light of a general good or in terms of self-interest rightly understood. It is the rule of law that makes it possible for government to rely on the reason of the public while at the same time controlling and regulating the passions of the public through legislation.

The "reason of the public" or "the deliberate sense of the community" (71:430) is demanded by "republican principles" because republican government must be a matter of "reflection and choice" rather than "accident and force." Reflection and choice not only require reason but also imply natural right. Choice, of course, ultimately begins with will, but as a prominent commentator notes,

> although choice begins from a will, it is a reasoned will with inconsistencies and momentary inclinations refined out. Government by choice is settled and stable; when it changes, it does so deliberately by design and for a definable purpose. . . . The work of reason is to give direction and solidity to the insistence of will, both to elevate it above whim and to settle it into determination. In this view the American Constitution does after all attempt to improve men's souls, but the method peculiar to it is to elicit reason from the people rather than to impose it on them.[37]

Reason is not in the service of the passions, as Hobbes would have it; rather, the passions, instructed and refined by considerations of the public good, are in the service of "the reason of the public." And this reason is called upon to "deliberate and decide" (14:100; 1:27) the fate of a new Constitution, a decision that will undoubtedly decide the fate of republican government itself. Never before in human history has the reason of the public been put to such a test—and never before has so much rested on the outcome. The capacity for deliberation and decision is the epitome of self-government, both for the individual and for the polity—it is the "genius of the American people." And it is self-government that does in fact "improve men's souls" by uniting liberty and republican virtue.

---

36. Thomas G. West, "The Rule of Law in *The Federalist*," in *Saving the Revolution:* The Federalist Papers *and the American Founding*, ed. Charles R. Kesler (New York: Free Press, 1987), 153–54.

37. Harvey C. Mansfield Jr., "Social Science and the Constitution," in *Confronting the Constitution*, ed. Allan Bloom (Washington, DC: AEI Press, 1990), 414.

PUBLIC OPINION

But for all of the discussion of republican virtue and the rule of law consisting in the rule of reason over passion, we know that in the realm of politics, opinion is the common currency. A republican regime must depend on sound public opinion. The entire scheme of government envisioned by the founders makes it improbable that the passions of the public will ever control the government. The extended republic, with a multiplicity of competing factions and interests, makes it unlikely (but not impossible) that a "majority of the whole" will be "united and actuated by some common impulse of passion, or of interest" so as to become a "majority faction" (10:72). When interest is pitted against interest and passion against passion, no one interest or passion is likely to dominate the majority, and in the "equipoise of these passions, reason is free to decide for the public good."[38] Besides, if a majority faction were to form, the genius of the constitutional system, the separation of powers—its "auxiliary precautions"—would allow the government to resist until the "cool and deliberate sense of the community" could be restored and "reason, justice, and truth can regain their authority over the public mind" (63:382).

In a republican form of government, the manner in which government controls and regulates passions may not be principally through laws but through the formation of public opinion. In an essay published in the *National Gazette* in 1791, Madison wrote,

> Public opinion sets bounds to every government, and is the real sovereign in every free one.
>
> As there are cases where the public opinion must be obeyed by the government; so there are cases, where not being fixed, it may be influenced by the government. This distinction, if kept in view, would prevent or decide many debates on the respect due from the government to the sentiments of the people.[39]

The most difficult task of republican statesmen is, of course, reconciling wisdom and consent (public opinion). In a regime based on the active consent of the governed, statesmanship must always work within the constraints of public opinion at the same time that it attempts to lead public opinion in the direction of wise policies. As Madison indicates, when public opinion is ambiguous or neutral, statesmen have relative freedom to act on particular issues. Most of the time republican statesmen must work incrementally, and often by indirection, in their attempt to persuade the public to accept wise policies. On many occasions it may be necessary to advocate merely expedient policies that are part of a larger plan that will result in the establishment of wise policies only in the remote future; at other times it may be necessary to conceal the ultimate reach of some policies so that they might be accepted in the

---

38. James Madison, "Universal Peace," *National Gazette*, January 31, 1792, in *Papers of James Madison*, 14:208.

39. "Public Opinion," December 19, 1791, in ibid., 14:170; see "Charters," January 18, 1792, in ibid., 14:192, and "British Government," January 28, 1792, in ibid., 14:201.

present without disturbing the opinions that are necessary to support future progress. As Madison noted, "the objects of government may be divided into two general classes: the one depending on measures which have singly an immediate and sensible operation; the other depending on a succession of well-chosen and well-connected measures, which have a gradual and perhaps unobserved operation. The importance of the latter description to the collective and permanent welfare of every country needs no explanation" (63:381–82).

If Madison's expectations were to become something more than utopian speculations, an active politics of public opinion would have to become the core of American political life. In a well-known passage that commands quotation at length, Madison writes,

> If it be true that all governments rest on opinion, it is no less true that the strength of opinion in each individual, and its practical influence on his conduct, depend much on the number which he supposes to have entertained the same opinion. The reason of man, like man himself, is timid and cautious when left alone, and acquires firmness and confidence in proportion to the number with which it is associated. When the examples which fortify opinion are *ancient* as well as *numerous*, they are known to have a double effect. In a nation of philosophers, this consideration ought to be disregarded. A reverence for the laws would be sufficiently inculcated by the voice of an enlightened reason. But a nation of philosophers is as little to be expected as the philosophical race of kings wished for by Plato. And in every other nation, the most rational government will not find it a superfluous advantage to have the prejudices of the community on its side (49:311–12).

A nation of philosophers would be ruled by reason and an attachment to truth alone. The rule of law, as we have already intimated, supplies a kind of imitation reason for non-philosophers. Philosophers, of course, because they live a life of reason, would be a law unto themselves. But a nation of philosophers is "little to be expected"—and even the rule of philosophers, as Plato amply demonstrated in *The Republic*, is impossible (or highly unlikely). All free governments resting on the principles of natural right require the rule of law supported by opinion—in the best case, numerous and ancient opinion.

If that opinion is supported or generated by a philosophic cause, then it might become "enlightened" opinion or "true opinion." Enlightened opinion would not be genuine or philosophic knowledge. It would reach the same result although it would not be possessed or held with the same firmness that it would be if it were genuine knowledge. In 1860, Lincoln argued that whenever the slavery "question shall be settled, it must be settled in some philosophical basis. No policy that does not rest upon some philosophical public opinion can be permanently maintained."[40] The philosophic cause in the American regime is natural right— the "Laws of Nature and of Nature's God"—and the political opinion animating

---

40. Abraham Lincoln, "Speech at New Haven, Connecticut," March 6, 1860, in *The Collected Works of Abraham Lincoln*, ed. Roy P. Basler (New Brunswick, NJ: Rutgers University Press, 1953), 4:27.

political life is ultimately derived from those philosophical principles. Given the prominence of the Declaration, there can be little doubt that the opinion that supported the founding principles was "numerous."

That opinion, however, could hardly have been "ancient" since the Declaration had been adopted only twelve years previously. In the *Politics*, Aristotle made the revolutionary statement that political philosophy seeks "not the traditional [*patrion*] but the good [*agathon*]."[41] The good, discovered by political philosophy, necessarily challenges the old or the traditional and deprives it of its reverence, an ingredient that Madison noted is necessary to the stability of political opinion. Aristotle, of course, realized that the distinction between the ancestral and the good was fundamental for political science; therefore, caution in the form of prudence must be applied in recommending political change. The art of politics is not like the other arts in which change is essential to development. Professor Harry Jaffa cogently remarks that "politics is not an art like medicine and gymnastics, for the law has no power to persuade other than that derived from custom or habit, and these are formed only over a long period of time. Changing laws weakens their power, it loosens the bonds of the community, and requires the greatest circumspection."[42]

Madison understood the central role of political prudence as well as any statesman. In the argument of *Federalist* 49 that we have been discussing, Madison criticized Jefferson's proposal to revise the Virginia Constitution by including a provision that would allow disputes concerning the separation of powers to be appealed directly to the people for resolution. Madison's main complaint was "an objection inherent in the principle that as every appeal to the people would carry an implication of some defect in the government, frequent appeals would, in great measure, deprive the government of that veneration which time bestows on everything, and without which perhaps the wisest and freest governments would not possess the requisite stability" (49:311). This argument was muted somewhat by the fact that the fate of the proposed constitution was to be decided by an appeal to the people. Perhaps only its principles, the principles of natural right, could claim the venerable status that time bestows on everything because nature and natural right are older than any convention.

As Madison wrote in 1792 with understandable hyperbole, "a government, deriving its energy from the will of the society, and operating by the reason of its measures, on the understanding and interest of the society . . . is the government for which philosophy has been searching . . . from the most remote ages."[43] Although natural right is a ground that is older than any tradition, the American founding was the first attempt to establish a government that was explicitly based on the "Laws of Nature and of Nature's God." The principles may be ancient, but

---

41. Aristotle, *Politics*, 1269a3–4.

42. Harry V. Jaffa, "Aristotle," in *History of Political Philosophy*, ed. Leo Strauss and Joseph Cropsey, 2nd ed. (Chicago: University of Chicago Press, 1972), 88.

43. James Madison, "Spirit of Governments," *National Gazette*, February 18, 1792, in *Papers of James Madison*, 14:234.

the regime generated by those principles was admitted on all sides to be a novel experiment. Madison deals with this issue in a manner that is not without amusement in *Federalist* 14.

In perhaps the most exaggerated rhetoric in the *Federalist*, Madison urges his readers not to listen to the "unnatural voice" of "the advocates for disunion":

> Hearken not to the voice which petulantly tells you that the form of government recommended for your adoption is a novelty in the political world; that it has never yet had a place in the theories of the wildest projectors; that it rashly attempts what is impossible to accomplish. No, my countrymen, shut your ears against this unhallowed language.

Madison then turns the argument of novelty against the opponents of union:

> And if novelties are to be shunned, believe me, the most alarming of all novelties, the most wild of all projects, the most rash of all attempts, is that of rending us in pieces in order to preserve our liberties and promote our happiness.

The greatest of innovators are now those who oppose the new union. But the next sentences still come as something of a surprise:

> But why is the experiment of an extended republic to be rejected merely because it may comprise what is new? Is it not the glory of the people of America that, whilst they have paid a decent regard to the opinions of former times and other nations, they have not suffered a blind veneration for antiquity, for custom, or for names, to overrule the suggestions of their own good sense, the knowledge of their own situation, and the lessons of their own experience?

Don't reject the proposed constitution because it is new! It should be approved because it is a departure from the old! Madison attributes the ability to reject "a blind veneration for antiquity" and "custom" to the "manly spirit" of the American people, a spirit that we have already argued is an important element of the "genius of the American people." "Posterity," Madison avers, will be "indebted," and the world will find "the example" "of the numerous innovations played on the American theatre." Next, Madison portrays the newly proposed constitution as an attempt to perpetuate the work of the "leaders of the Revolution":

> Happily for America, happily we trust for the whole human race, they pursued a new and more noble course. They accomplished a revolution which has no parallel in the annals of human society. They reared the fabrics of governments which have no model on the face of the globe. They formed the design of a great Confederacy, which it is incumbent on their successors to improve and perpetuate. If their works betray imperfections, we wonder at the fewness of them. If they erred most in the structure of the Union, this was the work most difficult to be executed; this is the work which has been new modeled by the act of your convention, and it is that act on which you are now to deliberate and to decide (14:99–100).

The Declaration had been adopted slightly more than eleven years before, and the Articles of Confederation—approved by Congress in November 1777 but not ratified until March 1781—had only been in force for six years at the time Madison wrote this passage. The Articles did not deserve to be venerated; they did not deserve to be perpetuated. The leaders of the Revolution made their greatest mistakes in the "structure of the Union"—that is, in the only thing that mattered. This mistake undermined the very possibility of a successful regime. Madison did not believe for one moment—any more than Hamilton or the other Federalist supporters of the Constitution—that the Articles should be "perpetuated." Rather, all agreed that the Articles urgently needed to be "new modeled" as a matter of principle—and this "new modeling" is portrayed by Madison as an act of ancestral piety! This points to an omnipresent political problem: everything novel must be characterized as a perpetuation of something old or something traditional. The problem with all new regimes is finding a source for the veneration that is needed for stability.

Madison had said in *Federalist* 49 that even "the most rational government will not find it a superfluous advantage to have the prejudices of the community on its side." These prejudices are not necessarily irrational attachments to the regime; in the United States they will proceed most likely from a veneration of the Declaration and the Constitution, a veneration derived not from their antiquity but from the fact that those documents belong to the people as "the most sacred part of their property"—"the immediate work of their own."[44] The people will undoubtedly take pride in protecting the regime they have created and will surely engage "the manly spirit of liberty" that is generated by that pride. If the principles are sound, then the opinions and prejudices generated by those principles provide sound support for the regime. The most "rational government" can not only use them to advantage but also cultivate them with reasonable assurances.

THE POLITICS OF PUBLIC OPINION

Yet there is only so much "enlightened statesmen" can do in forming public opinion, and we must also contend with the sobering fact that "enlightened statesmen will not always be at the helm." Statesmen and founders have to work within the circumstances as they find them—they do not create ex nihilo. As Madison said during the Virginia Ratifying Convention, a sentiment he had expressed a few months earlier in the *Federalist*,

> I go on this great republican principle, that the people will have virtue and intelligence to select men of virtue and wisdom. Is there no virtue among us? If there be not, we are in a wretched situation. No theoretical checks—no form of government can render us secure. To suppose that any form of government will secure liberty or happiness without

---

44. "Government of the United States," February 4, 1792, in ibid., 14:218.

any virtue in the people, is a chimerical idea. If there be sufficient virtue and intelligence in the community, it will be exercised in the selection of these men [to the Congress]. So that we do not depend on their virtue, or put confidence in our rulers, but in the people who are to choose them.[45]

Virtue requires intelligence, which in this context means the ability to recognize and be persuaded by reason. This is the primary virtue of a self-governing people. In the *Politics*, Aristotle casually noted that it was advances in the art of rhetoric that facilitated the revolution from tyranny to democracy even as the art of rhetoric alone proved insufficient for the rule of democracy.[46] And what we learn from Aristotle's *Rhetoric* is that persuasive arguments in all forms of rhetoric, particularly deliberative and forensic rhetoric, depend upon the extent to which the rhetorician can render the passions of his audience capable of listening to reason. Deliberative rhetoric addresses the future, contesting questions of what policies are best calculated to serve the public good in the immediate and long-term future. This is the kind of rhetoric most closely associated with political life, and it is the kind of rhetoric that dominates legislative politics. Forensic rhetoric also plays a role in legislative politics insofar as the determination of the justice or injustice of past actions might bear on future policies. As quoted above, in his critique of Rousseau's "Perpetual Peace," Madison wrote that in the equipoise of the passions, reason is free to decide. This is precisely what Aristotle had in mind: rhetoric in all its forms disposes the passions so as to make them capable of accepting reasonable arguments. When passions and interests have been placed in equipoise— balanced, as it were—then reason is more likely to be effective. As Madison noted, "The best provision for a stable and free Govt. is not a balance in the powers of the Govt. tho' that is not to be neglected, but an equilibrium in the interests & passions of the Society itself, which can not be attained in a small Society."[47] For Madison, the whole constitutional scheme—the extended republic encompassing a multiplicity of different competing interests and passions, with separation of powers—is an attempt to create an equipoise of interests and passions so that "a coalition of the majority of the whole society could seldom take place on any other principles than those of justice and the general good."[48] Presumably "justice and the general good" will be the result of the "reason of the public," which in turn will control government.

Deliberative rhetoric, of course, is applicable to politics—shaping and forming the "public mind"—no less than to legislative politics; it is essential for "the politics of public opinion."[49] Eugene Miller writes that "within the deliberative framework

---

45. Ibid., 11:163.

46. Aristotle, *Politics*, 1305a10–12, but see 1269a19–24; compare with *Federalist*, 49:311–12.

47. James Madison, "Notes on Government," in *Papers of James Madison*, 14:158. I owe this reference to Colleen A. Sheehan, *James Madison and the Spirit of Republican Self-Government* (New York: Cambridge University Press, 2009), 83. Throughout her book, Professor Sheehan presents a valuable thematic analysis of "Madison's conception of the politics of public opinion." See *Federalist* 63:385.

48. *Federalist* 51:322. This important passage is, I believe, the key to understanding "the politics of public opinion." See 63:383.

49. Sheehan, *James Madison*, 80, 82–83, 92, 100, 112.

that is natural to political life, a basic distinction is made between the ultimate end of action, which is happiness, and the instrumental goods that are chosen as a means to this end." This distinction, Miller explains, is not only "natural to political life" but also "central to the deliberative rhetoric of *The Federalist*."[50] If it is true that Publius posits happiness as the comprehensive end of government, then deliberation must always be about the best or most advantageous means of securing public happiness. The idea that the end of government is merely the protection of private rights and liberties—or the idiosyncratic pursuit of happiness—is unsupported by any fair-minded reading of the *Federalist*. The predisposition to categorize Publius as a "wholly modern" author incapable of formulating government in terms of ends or purposes, much less in terms of public happiness, makes it impossible to understand the authors of the *Federalist* as they understood themselves. As Miller notes,

> Publius takes a much broader view of the place of "interest" in the political realm than one would judge to be the case from the dominant interpretation of *The Federalist*. . . . We see that Publius conceives of "interest" as something broader than the mere pursuit of material gain and more comprehensive than the individual's self-interest. When he calls on Americans to regard their "interest," he invests the term with all those lofty connotations that are appropriate to deliberative rhetoric, especially those that relate to the common good.[51]

The public, of course, is incapable of deliberating en masse; it is not called upon to deliberate about the public good but to judge the deliberation of those who occupy constitutional offices. It is possible to judge the deliberation of others without being able to perform the elevated kind of deliberations required of republican statesmen. The flute-player is the ultimate judge of flute-making even though he lacks the expertise of the flute-maker. The deliberations informing political decisions are considerably more complex than flute-making, and it is thereby more difficult for the public to hold accountable those who hold deliberative offices. But in a general sense, the standards for accountability are not overly complex; they comprise the ends for which government is created: the "safety and happiness of the people." An active citizenry animated by the "politics of public opinion" and possessed of the "manly spirit" that is part of the "genius of America" will always be competent judges of those who occupy the deliberative offices of government.

DELIBERATION AND REPRESENTATION

In book 3 of the *Politics*, Aristotle states that "the citizen simply is defined by nothing other than having a share in judging [*kriseōs*] and ruling [*archēs*],"[52] adding that

---

50. Miller, "What Publius Says About Interest," 34.
51. Ibid., 45, 47.
52. Aristotle, *Politics*, 1275a22–23.

this definition of the citizen is exemplified above all in democracies.[53] Aristotle did not, of course, have in mind citizens of a representative democracy but those of a democracy in which citizens serve in offices (*archēs*). The characteristic way that citizens in a democratic republic deliberate and judge is not through holding office but through elections judging the performance of their representatives and holding them to account.

The principal difference between American republicanism and classical republicanism was, in Hamilton's terms, the "*ENLARGEMENT* of the orbit within which such systems are to revolve" (9:67). Classical republicans, including Montesquieu, had argued that a republic must be small so that a common good could be identified and a concord of opinion and interests could form the basis of republican unity. The framers of the American Constitution, however, in advocating its greatest innovation, argued the necessity of a large and diverse nation with a multiplicity of competing interests. A small republic would be more likely to be dominated by majority faction because of its unity of interests and opinions. The result would be fatal to republican liberty and the rule of law. Small republics, as Hamilton pointedly argued in *Federalist* 9, were perpetually vibrating between the extremes of political life—anarchy and tyranny. A large republic embracing and encouraging diversity of interests and opinions was the remedy for the defects of small republicanism. If it was true that majority faction was the rock upon which all previous attempts to establish republics had foundered, then a scheme that produced majority coalitions that changed from election to election would seem to be an eligible remedy. But would this diversity be fatal to the public good?

A republic large enough to embrace sufficient diversity would have to be one in which a "scheme of representation takes place" (10:76). "If Europe has the merit of discovering this great mechanical power in government," Madison avers, "by the simple agency of which the will of the largest political body may be concentrated and its force directed to any object which the public good requires, America can claim the merit of making the discovery the basis of unmixed and extensive republics" (14:95–96). Representation provides for "the delegation of the government . . . to a small number of citizens elected by the rest." This process may serve "to refine and enlarge the public views by passing them through the medium of a chosen body of citizens, whose wisdom may best discern the true interest of their country and whose patriotism and love of justice will be least likely to sacrifice it to temporary or partial considerations." Under such a scheme, "it may well happen that the public voice, pronounced by the representatives of the people, will be more consonant to the public good than if pronounced by the people themselves, convened for the purpose." But since representation is only a "great mechanical power," "the effect may be inverted. Men of factious tempers, of local prejudices, or of sinister designs, may, by intrigue, by corruption, or by other means, first obtain the suffrages, and then betray the interests of the people" (10:76–77). But when representation is employed

---

53. Ibid., 1275b-5–6.

in a large, diverse republic, a mechanical device becomes intrinsically valuable for republican ends. The representatives in a large republic will be elected by a greater number of citizens, and it will therefore "be more difficult for unworthy candidates to practise with success the vicious arts by which elections are too often carried; and the suffrages of the people being more free, will be more likely to center on men who possess the most attractive merit and the most diffusive and established characters" (10:77). These men of merit and of "diffusive and established characters" to be chosen from the extensive republic are most likely to have the necessary wisdom and patriotic motives to serve the public good.

The people won't deliberate on the public good as such, but they will judge those who are charged by the Constitution with serving the public weal. Even though we have already seen Madison's claim that the principle of representation was the discovery of "modern Europe," he admits that "it is clear that the principle of representation was neither unknown to the ancients nor wholly overlooked in their political constitutions" (63:385).

In the American example, the advantage over the ancient examples "lies in the *total exclusion of the people in their collective capacity*" from any share in the government, giving "a most advantageous superiority in favor of the United States." "But to insure to this advantage its full effect," Madison concludes, "we must be careful not to separate it from the other advantage, of an extensive territory. For it cannot be believed that any form of representative government could have succeeded within the narrow limits occupied by the democracies of Greece" (63:385). Combined with an extended territory encompassing a multiplicity of competing interests, the principle of representation is transmogrified from a mere mechanical contrivance to a vital principle of republican government. In a large republic, representation results from the reason of the public, and representatives are thereby given the freedom to represent the public good.

If the people do not have the capacity to judge—if the "politics of public opinion" and elections cannot replace the right of revolution in the ordinary course of politics[54]—then the great experiment in self-government will fail; it will fail, as Madison notes,

---

54. In his second inaugural, Jefferson referred to "the reflecting character of our citizens at large, who, by the weight of public opinion, influence and strengthen the public measures; it is due to the sound discretion with which they select from among themselves those to whom they confide the legislative duties; it is due to the zeal and wisdom of the characters thus selected, who lay the foundations of public happiness in wholesome laws." Jefferson offered his "sincere congratulations" to the people for the "union of sentiment now manifested so generally, as auguring harmony and happiness to our future course" (*Jefferson: Writings*, 521). In his first inaugural, Jefferson had stated that "the preservation of the General Government in its whole constitutional vigor [was] the sheet anchor of our peace at home and safety abroad." He emphasized that it was of utmost moment to preserve "a jealous care of the right of election by the people—a mild and safe corrective of abuses which are lopped by the sword of revolution where peaceable remedies are unprovided" (*Jefferson: Writings*, 494–95). Jefferson seemed to have accepted as an accomplished fact that elections as manifestations of the "public mind" could supersede revolution in the ordinary course of politics. Harry Jaffa writes that "not until his inaugural address in 1801 would Jefferson see the right of free election as the normal and peaceful fruit of the right of revolution" (*New Birth of Freedom: Abraham Lincoln and the Coming of the Civil War* [Lanham, MD: Rowman & Littlefield, 2004], 8).

because no institutional devices will ever be a substitute for republican virtue. Whether it was possible for deliberative rhetoric to become the basis for a "politics of public opinion" remained to be seen. But this is what Madison and the other leading framers thought would become the center of the American experiment in self-government.

LINCOLN'S STATESMANSHIP AND THE AMERICAN MIND: THE LIMITS OF POLITICAL RHETORIC

Abraham Lincoln's political philosophy was Jeffersonian, and as a Whig, Lincoln in his economic thought followed that of Alexander Hamilton. But no one understood Madison's (or Jefferson's) "politics of public opinion" better than Lincoln. In 1856, he famously remarked, "Our government rests in public opinion. Whoever can change public opinion, can change the government, practically just so much."[55] And in his first debate with Douglas, Lincoln argued,

> In this and like communities, public sentiment is everything. With public sentiment, nothing can fail; without it nothing can succeed. Consequently he who moulds public sentiment, goes deeper than he who enacts statutes or pronounces decisions. He makes the statutes and decisions possible or impossible to be executed.[56]

Lincoln viewed the contest with Douglas as a struggle to shape the "American mind." Douglas, in Lincoln's view, was preparing the nation to accept the opinion that slavery was not a moral issue but merely a matter of interest. Once that view was accepted—and Douglas was well on his way to success—the public mind would be prepared to reject the principles of the Declaration and the idea that rights have an objective ground in the "Laws of Nature and Nature's God." The idea that rights and liberties have no other basis than interest would be fatal to liberty because it would mean that rights exist only at the sufferance of government—or of interested majorities.

There is no doubt that Lincoln's statesmanship with regard to the slavery issue epitomized Madison's view of republican statesmanship. Lincoln noted in his Dred Scott speech in 1857 that the framers did not have the power to abolish slavery all at once: they could have done so only in opposition to the consent of the governed, thus purchasing the freedom of the slaves at the price of subjecting the nation to tyranny. Lincoln took great pains to refute Chief Justice Taney's argument in *Dred Scott* that the Declaration's central tenet that "all men are created equal" was not intended to include blacks of African descent. Taney, Lincoln says,

> admits that the language of the Declaration is broad enough to include the whole human family, but he . . . argue[s] that the authors of that instrument did not intend to

---

55. Abraham Lincoln, "Speech at a Republican Banquet," December 10, 1856, in *Collected Works of Abraham Lincoln*, 2:385.

56. Ibid., 3:27; 2:552–53; 2:281–82; 3:424; 3:442; 4:17.

include negroes, by the fact that they did not at once, actually place them on an equality with the whites. Now this grave argument comes to just nothing at all, by the other
fact, that they did not at once, *or ever afterwards*, actually place all white people on an
equality one with another.

Lincoln deftly points out the illogic of Taney's argument: he has "proven" that the
Declaration did not include whites by the mere fact that not all whites were equalized all at once! Lincoln continued,

> I think the authors of that notable instrument intended to include *all* men, but they did
> not intend to declare all men equal in *all* respects. They did not mean to say all men were
> equal in color, size, intellect, moral developments, or social capacity. They defined with
> tolerable distinctness, in what respects they did consider all men created equal—equal in
> "certain inalienable rights, among which are life, liberty, and the pursuit of happiness."
> This they said, and this meant. They did not mean to assert the obvious untruth that
> all were then actually enjoying that equality, nor yet, that they were about to confer it
> immediately upon them. In fact they had no power to confer such a boon. They meant
> simply to declare the *right*, so that the *enforcement* of it might follow as fast as circum-
> stances should permit. They meant to set up a standard maxim for free society, which
> should be familiar to all, and revered by all; constantly looked to, constantly labored for,
> even though never perfectly attained, constantly approximated, and thereby constantly
> spreading and deepening its influence, and augmenting the happiness and value of life
> to all people of all colors everywhere.[57]

Taney's argument wholly misunderstood the founders' view of statesmanship. Lincoln argued that the "abstract truth" at the core of the Declaration served no practical
purpose in effectuating independence from Great Britain. In fact, Lincoln says, it
was not placed in the Declaration for that reason but for future use as a "standard
maxim" or a goal to be attained. Once it was accepted, the Declaration placed moral
demands on all Americans. How those demands were to be met and at what speed
had to be determined by wise statesmen, and Lincoln's principle of statesmanship
was that of the founders: eliminate as much evil as possible while it is possible without destroying the basis in public opinion from which further evil can be eliminated.
In a regime based on the consent of the governed, statesmanship must always operate
within the constraints of public opinion at the same time that it attempts to lead
public opinion ever closer to the fulfillment of its highest aspirations.

Lincoln certainly followed Madison in insisting that the Constitution was intended by the framers to put the principles of the Declaration into practice. But, as
in all things political, it is rarely possible to translate principles directly into practice. Insofar as the Constitution allowed the continued existence of slavery, it was
an incomplete expression of the Declaration's principles. Madison argued that the
compromises with slavery were necessary to secure the adoption of the Constitution—otherwise, the slave-holding states would have bolted from the Constitutional

57. "Speech at Springfield, Illinois," June 26, 1857, in ibid., 2:405–6.

Convention.[58] And, as the most thoughtful of the Federalists understood, without a strong national government, the prospect of ever ending slavery was remote.[59] Thus the prudential compromises regarding slavery in the Constitution were actually in the service of eventual emancipation. As Lincoln always maintained, the Constitution, when understood in the light of the principles of the Declaration, put slavery "in the course of ultimate extinction."[60] Those provisions in the Constitution protecting slavery were no part of the Constitution's principles; they were compromises of principle designed to allow the ultimate fulfillment of the Constitution's principles. The Constitution treated slavery as in principle wrong—a necessary evil—to be tolerated only as long as necessary and to be eliminated as soon as politically expedient. Slavery could not be abolished all at once, but the "public mind," according to Lincoln, had been convinced that slavery had been put "in the course of ultimate extinction" by the Constitution. Resist the spread of slavery by constitutional means and prepare the public mind for its eventual demise. This is republican statesmanship.

In his first inaugural, Lincoln made a plea to the seceding states to listen to reason. Lincoln argued there was no cause for them to leave the Union since no "plainly written" constitutional right had been violated. In *Dred Scott*, the Supreme Court ruled that the Constitution gave Congress "the power coupled with the duty" to pass a slave code for the territories, but one could hardly argue that it was a "plainly written" command of the Constitution or a "plainly written" constitutional right belonging to the slave-holding states.[61] Chief Justice Taney had held that "the right of property in a slave is distinctly and expressly affirmed in the Constitution."[62] Lincoln had utterly refuted Taney's claim by demonstrating that slavery could hardly be "distinctly and expressly affirmed" if the word "slave" or "slavery" never appeared in the Constitution, nor was the word "property" ever used in connection with any of the circumlocutions used for slavery. Lincoln averred that these circumlocutions ("three fifths of all other persons"; "the migration or importation of such persons"; "person held to service or labor") were "employed on purpose to exclude from the Constitution the idea that there could be property in man. To show all this is easy and certain."[63] Even though Lincoln repeatedly assured the South that he had no

---

58. See Madison's speech at the Virginia Ratifying Convention, June 17, 1788, in *Papers of James Madison*, 11:150–51.

59. See, for example, James Wilson's speech at the Pennsylvania Ratifying Convention, December 4, 1787, in John McMaster and Frederick Stone, eds., *Pennsylvania and the Federal Constitution 1787–1788* (Indianapolis, IN: Liberty Fund, 2011 [orig. pub. 1888]), 311–12.

60. Lincoln, *Collected Works of Abraham Lincoln*, 2:461, 492, 498, 501, 514, 520–21; 3:18, 78, 87, 92–93, 117, 180–81, 254–55, 276, 307, 312–13, 333, 404, 406–7, 439, 483, 488, 489, 498, 535, 537–38, 550–51, 553; 4:17–18, 21–22.

61. *Dred Scott v. Sandford*, 60 U.S. (19 How.) 393, 452 (1857) (Taney, C. J.).

62. Ibid. at 451. In a lecture on February 21, 2014, titled "The Four Words That Caused the Civil War," delivered at California State University, San Bernardino, Harry Jaffa argued that "distinctly and expressly affirmed," the language of Taney in *Dred Scott*, was the proximate cause of the Civil War because, for the first time, it provided the South with a constitutional reason—endorsed by the Supreme Court—for secession.

63. Abraham Lincoln, "Address at Cooper Union," February 27, 1860, in *Collected Works of Abraham Lincoln*, 3:545; see also "Fifth Debate," 3:231. During the Constitutional Convention, Madison remarked

intention of interfering with slavery where it already existed and that in fact there was no constitutional power to do so, the slave-holding states believed that the *Dred Scott* decision had given them an unambiguous constitutional basis for secession. By 1861, the South had become deaf to the voice of reason and Lincoln's unassailable logic. The greatest logic—indeed, the greatest rhetoric—is impotent when the audience is unwilling to listen. This is the lesson of the opening scene of Plato's *Republic*. All of Lincoln's greatest speeches—Peoria, Dred Scott, House Divided, Cooper Union, his first inaugural—were rhetorical masterpieces but political failures. Lincoln demonstrated both the vital importance of "the politics of public opinion" and its limitations.

Harry Jaffa notes,

> In the presence of Lincoln's arguments [in his first inaugural], no sane person would have opted, as the South did, for secession, slavery, and war. Lincoln knew when he spoke these lines that they would have no effect upon the actions or passions of his antagonists. Were it possible for them to have been persuaded, tragedy might have been averted. But it was not possible, because slavery had engendered passions that were immune to reason.[64]

In the debate over slavery, no equipoise of the passions was possible, and reason was therefore impotent. No compromise was possible on the issue of slavery. Slavery had been tolerated as a necessary evil, but it could never be allowed as a "positive good" without repealing the principles of the Declaration of Independence.

Lincoln accepted Madison's vision of the role of public opinion in constitutional democracy. Madison could not have described his own handiwork in more concise terms than Lincoln did in his first inaugural:

> A majority, held in restraint by constitutional checks, and limitations, and always changing easily, with deliberate changes of popular opinions and sentiments, is the only true sovereign of a free people. Whoever rejects it, does, of necessity, fly to anarchy or to despotism. Unanimity is impossible; the rule of a minority, as a permanent arrangement, is wholly inadmissible; so that rejecting the majority principle, anarchy, or despotism in some form, is all that is left.[65]

---

that he "thought it wrong to admit in the Constitution the idea that there could be property in men" (*Papers of James Madison*, 10:157). See also "Vices of the Political System," in ibid., 9:351.

64. Jaffa, *New Birth of Freedom*, 280, 168.

65. Lincoln, *Collected Works of Abraham Lincoln*, 4:268; see James Madison, "Veto Message," January 30, 1815, in *The Writings of James Madison*, ed. Gaillard Hunt (New York: G.P. Putnam's Sons, 1908), 8:327, 330; and James Madison, Letter to M. Lafayette, November, 1826, in *Letters and Other Writings of James Madison* (Philadelphia, PA: J.B. Lippincott & Co., 1867), 3:542. Madison wrote to Lafayette, "I have been charged with inconsistency in not putting a veto on the last act of Congress establishing a Bank . . . a word of explanation may not be improper." He averred that his view of the constitutionality of the bank had not changed, but he "regarded the reiterated sanctions given to the power by the exercise of it through a long period of time, in every variety of form, and in some form or other under every administration preceding mine, with the general concurrence of the State authorities, and acquiescence of the people at large, and without a glimpse of change in the public opinion" should be "regarded as a

The slave states refused to acquiesce in the "majority principle," and their obstinate refusal to listen to reason led to secession and war. The appeal to reason was insufficient to avoid tragedy because in the grip of passion, the slave states were rendered incapable of listening to the voice of reason. Lincoln had begun his first inaugural by referring to custom ("In compliance with a custom") and ended with nature ("the better angels of our nature"). The ascent from custom to nature is the epitome of Socratic dialectic. But Lincoln's appeal to the slave states was a failure not as an example of Socratic reasoning or philosophic rhetoric but as an example of political rhetoric. No mere speech—no reasoning—could have been effective in the conditions that prevailed in March 1861. The human political condition, it seems, will always exist within a tragic horizon. Lincoln was not unaware of this, despite the fact that he appeared too optimistic in his first inaugural. What alternative did he have? He was obliged to appeal to reason and constitutional government. He did not make the same mistake in his second inaugural.[66]

Lincoln followed the founders in regarding the American constitutional system as a great experiment, but he believed that its success had not yet been established. The Revolutionary War had vindicated the principle of consent for most, but not all, of the governed. Insofar as the Constitution allowed the continued existence of slavery, the founding was only a partial expression of the principles of the Declaration. Lincoln undoubtedly viewed the Civil War as the second phase of the Revolutionary War, fought for the vindication of the same principle of consent, this time for all the governed. Whether the experiment in self-government could ever succeed was still undecided in 1861. Harry Jaffa remarks, with unusual candor, that

> we must face the reality . . . that in the long experience of mankind, the self-evident truths of the Declaration of Independence had never, before 1776, been the basis of the experiment of popular self-government. This in itself is sufficient to raise the question of whether it was utopian to think that mere abstract truth could serve as the basis of an actual political regime. It is to ask the question that Plato himself asked, *but did not answer*, of whether natural right could become political right.[67]

Publius seemed convinced that Americans possessed the capacity for self-government and that the attempt to derive "strictly republican government" from the

---

construction put on the Constitution by the nation, which, having made it, had the supreme right to declare its meaning." See also James Madison, Letter to Mr. Ingersoll, June 25, 1831, in *Letters and Other Writings of James Madison*, 3:186.

66. See Edward Erler, "*Marbury v. Madison* and the Progressive Transformation of Judicial Power," in *The Progressive Revolution in Politics and Political Science*, ed. John Marini and Ken Masugi (Lanham, MD: Rowman & Littlefield, 2005), 216–17, n. 111.

67. Jaffa, *New Birth of Freedom*, 120 (emphasis added); "The intrinsic wrongness of tyranny and the intrinsic rightness of free government, as they are distinguished in the Declaration of Independence, are beacons of truth not affected by circumstances. The question of how, when, and *whether* such truth may be made the ground and basis of government, however, is governed by dictates of prudence, as the Declaration itself says. We must not, then, be misunderstood to say that the cause of legitimate government can be advanced only by the arguments in the Declaration" (125; emphasis added). See Harry V. Jaffa, *American Conservatism and the American Founding* (Durham, NC: Carolina Academic Press, 1984), 138.

"principles of human nature" or natural right could succeed. But if America failed, it would be not just an American tragedy but also "the general misfortune of mankind" (1:27). The reason was simple: the conditions for the success of the experiment in America were so propitious that failure would be taken to mean that republican self-government was impossible or simply utopian, and, in all likelihood, no one would be foolish enough to try the experiment again. The enemies of free government would simply point to America's failure and proclaim, "If it could not succeed there, it cannot succeed anywhere. Any attempt to establish republican government will only repeat the American failure." It is little wonder that Madison appealed to "every votary of freedom" for support.

STRICTLY REPUBLICAN GOVERNMENT AND THE FUNDAMENTAL PRINCIPLES OF THE REVOLUTION

Madison's central reason that the proposed constitution must be "strictly republican" was, we recall, because it was the only form of government reconcilable "with the fundamental principles of the Revolution." This statement of Madison's should settle the question of whether the framers of the Constitution believed they derived any guidance with respect to the form of government required from the principles of the Declaration. Still, one accomplished commentator argues to the contrary. It might "seem that only a republican form of government is strictly in accordance with 'the transcendent law of nature and nature's God.' But this Publius never says," our commentator avers. "He seems much more certain that republican government is dictated by the 'genius of the American people,' and even by the 'fundamental principles of the Revolution,' than that it is dictated by nature or natural law."[68] But how is it possible not to conclude that the "fundamental principles of the Revolution"—the Declaration of Independence—are not a dictate of "nature or natural law"? Surely no one would argue that the Declaration, grounded as it is in the "Laws of Nature and of Nature's God," is not an expression or "dictate" of natural law or natural right. Another prominent observer of the founding, Professor Harvey Mansfield, while recognizing that the Declaration was intended to be an expression of natural law, argues,

> The Declaration specifies that governments derive their just powers by consent but it does not specify which governments do that best. It does not even rule out any forms of government, though absolute monarchy seems to be rejected by implication. Limited monarchy, however, such as the existing British government, is apparently included among governments that *could* gain the consent of a people. Otherwise it would have made no sense to list "a long train of abuses and usurpations" in the longest part of the

68. Thomas L. Pangle, *The Spirit of Modern Republicanism* (Chicago: University of Chicago Press, 1988), 118. It is curious that Pangle notes only two of the three reasons Madison gives for adhering to a "strictly republican" form of government, omitting "the capacity of mankind for self-government."

Declaration; it would have been enough to say that monarchy is illegitimate in itself. Apparently all governments must rule by consent, but there is some leeway not only in the details of free government but even in the character or form of the government as a whole.[69]

The claim here that limited monarchy might be consistent with the principles of the Declaration if it received the consent of the governed seems to be wholly at odds with Madison's judgment that the form of government must be "strictly republican." Would it have sufficed for the Declaration to have issued an *ipse dixit* that monarchy is inherently illegitimate and leave it at that? The Declaration was not a logical treatise but an example of philosophic rhetoric of the highest level. It was meant to convince by argument and to marshal evidence in support of argument. Surely the part of the world still held in the grip of divine right monarchy would be shocked and repelled by the fact that the American colonies proclaimed themselves "absolved from all Allegiance to the British Crown." Allegiance was a sacred obligation that could only be dissolved with the permission of the king. As we have seen, under divine right kingship there are no citizens—only subjects owing perpetual allegiance. It is only on the basis of the arguments of the Declaration that subjects become citizens, and once the natural right basis for rule is discovered in the consent of the governed, subjects become citizens and thereby not only acquire a right to become active participants in their own governance but also assume a duty to do so. This is the essence of self-government. Elective monarchy seems excluded almost by definition. The examples of King George's perfidy, the "long train of abuses pursuing invariably the same Object"—to reduce "these States" to "Absolute Tyranny"—were necessary to complete the rhetorical argument; they were part of the enthymeme that was meant to persuade a skeptical world that self-government resting on the sovereignty of the people—not the divine right of kings—was the just and rightful form of government.

The signers of the Declaration were undoubtedly aware that they were participating in a world-historical event; they knew that the success of the American Revolution, upon which they pledged their "Lives, Fortunes and sacred Honor," would change the course of human events. For the first time in the history of the world, the "Laws of Nature and of Nature's God" would become the foundation of an actual government. Principles derived from natural right and natural law would replace government based on "force and fraud." Force and fraud were the way of the world, and the divine right of kings was only a particular kind of fraud. The American

---

69. Harvey C. Mansfield Jr., "Thomas Jefferson," in *American Political Thought: The Philosophic Dimensions of American Statesmanship*, ed. Morton J. Frisch and Richard G. Stevens (Itasca, IL: F.E. Peacock, 1983), 27, 25. See Harvey C. Mansfield Jr., *The Spirit of Liberalism* (Cambridge, MA: Harvard University Press, 1978), 76. See Zuckert, *The Natural Rights Republic*, 206, 234. Zuckert claims that Jefferson later abandoned his earlier "flexible and prudential" standards with respect to regime forms and came to consider that "democracy" was "the only legitimate form of government." See also Michael P. Zuckert, *Launching Liberalism: On Lockean Political Philosophy* (Lawrence: University Press of Kansas, 2002), 228, 231.

experiment in self-government would test whether good government could in fact be derived from reflection and choice. But the deeds of the Revolution could not be left to speak for themselves: those deeds would become an example to the world only through an account of its philosophic cause, and the virtue of that account would be its candor. Why monarchy—and the British monarchy in particular—was a violation of the principles derived from "the Laws of Nature and of Nature's God" needed examples by way of proof.

The signers of the Declaration surely understood its rhetorical function. Jefferson made an important statement on the rhetorical purpose of the Declaration in the last letter he ever wrote:

> May it be to the world, what I believe it will be (to some parts sooner, to others later, but finally to all) the signal of arousing men to burst the chains under which monkish ignorance and superstition had persuaded them to bind themselves, and to assume the blessings and security of self-government. That form which we have substituted, restores the free right to the unbounded exercise of reason and freedom of opinion. All eyes are opened, or opening, to the rights of man. The general spread of the light of science has already laid open to every view the palpable truth, that the mass of mankind has not been born with saddles on their backs, nor a favored few booted and spurred, ready to ride them legitimately, by the grace of God. These are grounds of hope for others. For ourselves, let the annual return of this day forever refresh our recollections of these rights, and an undiminished devotion to them.[70]

The argument that some men had been born with boots and spurs was the argument for the divine right of kings. But the self-evident truth about the human species is that no human being occupies a position with respect to other human beings that any human being occupies with respect to a horse. The inequality between human beings and horses makes every human being by nature the ruler of every horse. From a slightly different point of view, one could say that the inequality between God and man is so great that whatever inequalities exist between human beings would be insignificant (indeed nonexistent) in the eyes of God. Thus the doctrine of the Declaration is one of natural law as well as divine law. Lincoln understood the radical core of Jefferson's meaning when he asserted that the argument for the divine right of kings and the argument for slavery "were precisely alike."[71] Both stood in opposition to the central principle of the Declaration that "all men are created equal"—the first axiom in the calculus of self-government. Not since the promulgation of the New Testament has a document had such a profound influence on world opinion as the Declaration of Independence.

The principal error of Professor Mansfield's argument, I say, is in thinking that consent is required only to establish government, whereas the Declaration clearly specifies that it is necessary to operate government as well. It is true that the first ap-

---

70. Thomas Jefferson, Letter to Roger C. Weightman, June 24, 1826, in *Jefferson: Writings*, 1517.
71. Lincoln, *Collected Works of Abraham Lincoln*, 2:278; 2:500; 3:313.

pearance of consent in the Declaration specifies no form of government other than the fact that its just powers be derived from the consent of the governed. But the word "consent" appears on two subsequent occasions, both implying that consent must be an active agency in the operation of government. Mansfield would have us believe, to use Lincoln's words, that the government of the Declaration should be of and for the people, but not necessarily by the people. But one of the usurpations adduced by the Declaration to demonstrate the attempt to establish tyranny is the fact that the king "has kept among us, in times of peace, Standing Armies without the Consent of our legislatures." Whether to have standing armies in times of peace is a policy question; it has nothing to do with founding a regime. Here, it seems, consent is required to answer a question that arises subsequent to founding, implying the active agency in the administration of the regime. The consent of the legislatures in a representative form of government is the equivalent of the consent of the people.

Another specific complaint against the king is that he has imposed "taxes on us without our consent." This, of course, was the rallying cry of the American Revolution: "No taxation without representation." But the matter of taxes, what kind, what rates, and so on, is not involved in founding; it is a matter of administration or policy. Again, the clear implication is that consent must be a part of the administration as well as the establishment of a regime.

It seems clear from these latter two uses of the word "consent" in the list of usurpations that some form of government that actively solicits the consent of the governed on a regular basis is required by the principles of the Declaration. This would be a government that has regularly scheduled elections, one in which each election is considered a renewal of the people's consent to be governed. Each election, in effect, would draw the regime back to its first principles and serve as a reminder that elections serve as a substitute for revolution. In sum, a popular form of government is a requirement of the Declaration, and any form of government not grounded on the active consent of the governed is excluded by the principles of the Declaration. This conclusion seemed to be ratified by Jefferson when he wrote in *Notes on the State of Virginia*, "Civil government being the sole object of forming societies, its administration must be conducted by common consent."[72] Government required by the principles of the Declaration must be "by the people," as well as "of the people" and "for the people." Lincoln's gloss on the Declaration in the Gettysburg Address was eminently correct!

A government whose just powers are derived from the consent of the governed is necessarily limited government. It can exercise only those powers that are delegated to it, and whatever is not delegated is retained by the people. By the terms of the Declaration, government is limited to the exercise of the "just powers" of government—the only powers that can be authorized by consent. Thus constitutional government is necessarily limited government, and constitutional government excludes

---

72. Jefferson, *Notes on the State of Virginia*, in *Jefferson: Writings*, query viii, 211.

plebiscitary democracy or any kind of direct democracy. One particularly perceptive author, the late professor George Anastaplo, without engaging in too much hyperbole, remarked that "we see in the Declaration's references to divinity an oblique anticipation of the separation of powers established in the Constitution." "The first reference to God," he notes, is in the "Laws of Nature and Nature's God." This is a reference to "God as *legislator*: it is He that orders things, ordaining what is to be. He first comes to sight as the law-giver or law-maker." God next appears as the "Supreme Judge of the world," to whom the signers of the Declaration appeal "for the rectitude of [their] intentions." Lastly, God as "divine Providence" is "revealed as *executive*, as One Who extends protection, enforcing the laws that have been laid down (with a suggestion as well of the dispensing power of the executive)." "Thus," our commentator concludes, "the authors of the Declaration of Independence created even the Government of the World in the image of their political institutions."[73] It is true that the Creator is represented in the Declaration as having legislative, executive, and judicial powers, but what is crucial is that the Creator exercises all these powers *in propria persona*. In other words, since the Creator possesses infinite wisdom, it is only natural to conclude that there is no need for a separation of powers of government. The Creator is omniscient and omnipotent (or omnipotent because omniscient) and his rule is infinitely wise and just.[74] But, as Madison cautioned, when "framing a government which is to be administered by men over men," "experience has taught mankind the necessity of auxiliary precautions" (51:319). Separation of powers is a recognition of the limitations of human wisdom—and the role of passion in human affairs—that requires limited government. In any case, there can be little doubt that the authors of the Declaration and the framers of the Constitution—as well as the entire founding generation—considered separation of powers as intrinsic to the very idea of limited constitutional government.

STRICTLY REPUBLICAN GOVERNMENT AND THE SEPARATION OF POWERS

Hamilton announced in *Federalist* 22 that "the fabric of American empire ought to rest on the solid basis of THE CONSENT OF THE PEOPLE. The streams of national power ought to flow immediately from that pure, original fountain of all legitimate authority" (22:148; 49:310). In *Federalist* 39, however, Madison seems to qualify Hamilton's statement when he defines republican government as "government which derives all its powers directly or indirectly from the great body of the people, and is administered by persons holding their offices during pleasure for a limited period, or

73. George Anastaplo, "The Declaration of Independence," *St. Louis University Law Journal* 9 (1964–1965), 404–5.
74. See Theophilus Parsons, "The Essex Result" (1778), in *American Political Writing during the Founding Era*, ed. Charles S. Hyneman and Donald S. Lutz (Indianapolis, IN: Liberty Press, 1983), I:489.

during good behavior." Madison continues, "It is *essential* to such a government that it be derived from the great body of the society, not from an inconsiderable proportion or a favored class of it. . . . It is *sufficient* for such a government that the persons administering it be appointed, either directly or indirectly, by the people" (39:237). What is noteworthy is that the sufficient condition of republican government allows its constitutional officers to be derived either *directly* or *indirectly* from "the original fountain of all legitimate authority." Indirect derivation of power would seem to provoke questions as to whether Madison's definition was "strictly republican." We learn, however, that the different modes for electing constitutional officers—both directly and indirectly—are intimately connected with the separation of powers.

Even though there was agreement during the founding period that limited government rested on the foundation of separated powers, there was considerable debate about the precise configuration the separated powers would assume in the Constitution. Since the Constitution contemplates an "unmixed" regime, the crucial check-and-balance function of the separation of powers could not rely on class motives. In a mixed regime, the natural class antagonisms that exist in society would be reflected on the level of government and thus provide the interests and motives for checks and balances. But in a "wholly popular" government, class motives would be unavailable; they would be replaced by "personal motives" (51:319). Some republican substitute for the mixed regime had to be discovered if separation of powers was to operate in a republican government, and that substitute was found in the different methods of election. All of the branches are ultimately derived from "the great body of society," but by different electoral modes. These different modes allow different interests to be represented in government that are not class interests or derived from class motives. As M. J. C. Vile has noted, "the division of functions between agencies of government who will exercise a mutual check upon each other *although both are elected, directly or indirectly, by the same people*, is a unique American contribution to modern constitutional theory."[75]

All government power will be derived from the "original fountain of power," but at different times and from different constituencies. Hamilton spoke of this as

the dissimilar modes of constituting the several component parts of the government. The House of Representatives being to be elected immediately by the people, the Senate by the State legislatures, the President by electors chosen for that purpose by the people, there would be little probability of a common interest to cement these different branches in predilection for any particular class of electors (60:366).[76]

The role that class would have played in the mixed regime is replaced by "dissimilar modes" of election. This is the republican method—direct and indirect derivation of power—of introducing different interests into the various branches of government.

---

75. M. J. C. Vile, *Constitutionalism and the Separation of Powers* (Oxford: Clarendon Press, 1967), 125, 122, 134.
76. See James Madison, Letter to George Nicholas, May 17, 1788, in *Papers of James Madison*, 11:48.

The *Federalist* thus presents the first genuinely republican account of the separation of powers.[77]

However parsed, the executive and judicial branches were designed to exist at the very limits of republican theory—to be as little connected with the direct influence of the "great body of society" as possible. We must always bear in mind that the separation of powers was designed not just to prevent tyrannical government but also to promote "good government," and it almost goes without saying that non-tyrannical government is not the same as good government. Madison had famously written that "the accumulation of all powers, legislative, executive, and judiciary, in the same hands, whether of one, a few, or many, and whether hereditary, self-appointed, or elective, may justly be pronounced the very definition of tyranny" (47:298; 22:148). Creating a separation of powers in which the different branches of government would be independent of one another and armed with defensive powers would ensure non-tyrannical government. The functional specialization of the separation of powers contributes to good government: the multi-member legislature is well suited to deliberation; the unitary executive is best for execution of the laws; and the Supreme Court, with its exclusive membership isolated from the pressures of ordinary politics, is free to make independent decisions in defense of the Constitution.

Without some mixing and blending of the various powers, however, there can be no separation of powers in practice because in a republic, the legislative branch, being closest to the people and practiced in the arts of electoral politics, has a natural advantage over the other branches. As Madison notes in *Federalist* 48, "some . . . adequate defense is indispensably necessary for the more feeble against the more powerful members of the government. The legislative department is everywhere extending the sphere of its activity and drawing all power into its impetuous vortex" (48:305–6; 49:312; 71:432).[78] Hamilton concurred, arguing that "on the credit of historical examples as from the reason of the thing . . . the most *popular* branch of every government partaking of the republican genius, by being generally the favorite of the people, will be as generally a full match, if not an overmatch, for every other member of the government" (66:401–2). The founders of the state constitutions "seem never for a moment to have turned their eyes from the danger, to liberty, from the overgrown and all-grasping prerogative of an hereditary magistrate, supported and fortified by an hereditary branch of the legislative authority." In doing so, "they seem never to have recollected the danger from legislative usurpations, which, by assembling all power in the same hands, must lead to the same tyranny as is threatened by the executive usurpations" (48:306).[79] Thus the founders of the state

77. See W. B. Gwyn, *The Meaning of the Separation of Powers* (New Orleans, LA: Tulane University Press, 1965), 27; and Edward Erler, *The American Polity: Essays on the Theory and Practice of Constitutional Government* (New York: Taylor & Francis, 1991), 39–57.

78. See *Records of the Federal Convention*, II:35; 74.

79. At the Constitutional Convention, James Wilson made this remarkable statement: "The prejudices ag[ain]st the Executive resulted from a misapplication of the adage that the parliament was the palladium of liberty. Where the Executive was really formidable, *King* and *Tyrant*, were naturally associated in the minds of people; not *legislative* and *tyranny*. But where the Executive was not formidable, the two last

constitutions—and the anti-federalist opponents of executive power—have not paid sufficient attention to regime forms.

In monarchy, executive power is the most dangerous; in republics, legislative power assumes prominence. This is simply a result of the form of the regime, and it is of little avail to apply an analysis of monarchical government to a "representative republic where the executive magistracy is carefully limited, both in the extent and the duration of its power." This being the case, it is the legislative branch

> which is inspired by a supposed influence over the people with an intrepid confidence in its own strength; which is sufficiently numerous to feel all the passions which actuate a multitude, yet not so numerous as to be incapable of pursuing the objects of its passions by means which reason prescribes; it is against the enterprising ambition of this department that the people ought to indulge all their jealousy and exhaust all their precautions (48:306).

In the case of legislative tyranny, as in the case of all tyranny, reason is subordinated to the rule of the passions.

"But it is not possible," Madison avers,

> to give to each department an equal power of self-defense. In republican government, the legislative authority necessarily predominates. The remedy for this inconveniency is to divide the legislature into different branches; and to render them, by different modes of election and different principles of action, as little connected with each other as the nature of their common functions and their common dependence on the society admit.

Madison concludes, "As the weight of the legislative authority requires that it should be thus divided, the weakness of the executive may require, on the other hand, that it should be fortified" (51:319–20). The attempt to fortify the executive was based on the recognition that, in Hamilton's words, "energy in the executive is a leading character in the definition of good government." Hamilton added, however, that "there is an idea, which is not without its advocates, that a vigorous executive is inconsistent with the genius of republican government" (70:421; 1:29). The opponents of the proposed Constitution were appealing to "the aversion of the people to monarchy" (67:405) in order to cast aspersions on the "energetic executive" as the "foetus of monarchy."[80] Publius nevertheless pressed executive power "as far as republican principles will admit" (77:462), arguing that republican government, properly understood, is impotent without an energetic executive.

---

were most properly associated. After the destruction of the King in Great Britain, a more pure and unmixed tyranny sprang up in the parliament than had been exercised by the monarch. We had not guarded ag[ain]st the danger on this side by a sufficient self-defensive power either to the Executive or Judiciary department" (ibid., II:300–301).

80. Ibid., I:66 (Edmund Randolph). See also Patrick Henry's speech at the Virginia ratifying convention, June 5, 1788, in Jonathan Elliot, ed., *The Debates in the Several State Conventions* (Washington, DC: U.S. Congress, 1836), III:58 ("Your President may easily become king."). Despite its rhetorical excesses, Henry's speech probably reflected the dominant view of the anti-federalists on executive power.

The principal defensive "weapon" in the executive's arsenal was veto power. The framers rejected the absolute veto, although it might appear to be "the natural defense," as "neither altogether safe, nor alone sufficient." The absolute veto provision had to be avoided because it might remind those suspicious of executive power too much of the kind of royal prerogative that could be "perfidiously abused" (51:320).[81] The real reason the framers settled on the qualified veto (which can be overridden by a two-thirds majority in both houses), however, was that it was likely to be used more frequently and "with the requisite firmness" (51:320) than the absolute veto, which carried such a weight of finality that a republican executive might hesitate to use it. Thus the president's active agency or energy was aggressively solicited by the choice of the qualified veto.

Madison was more likely to speak of "energy in government" than energy in the executive. He noted that "among the difficulties encountered by the convention, a very important one must have lain in combining the requisite stability and energy in government with the inviolable attention due to liberty and to the republican form." If this combination proved impossible, there would be no hope that the American experiment would succeed. "Energy in government," Madison asserts,

> is essential to that security against external and internal danger and to that prompt and salutary execution of the laws which enter into the very definition of good government. Stability in government is essential to national character and to the advantages annexed to it, as well as to that repose and confidence in the minds of the people, which are among the chief blessings of civil society (37:222–23).

The "very definition of good government" for Madison is "energetic government" without any specification about which part of government should play the leading role in providing energy. An "irregular and mutable legislation" is an "evil" that subjects the people to intolerable "vicissitudes and uncertainties." This had been the situation, by and large, in the state governments. The "remedy" in Madison's mind was an energetic national government, and he was convinced that weak government, incapable of decisive action, was the greatest danger to the rights and liberties of the people—and a danger to republican government itself. Mutable legislation undermines the very notion of the rule of law and invites political corruption at every turn. An irregular or arbitrary administration is no less a threat to the peace and tranquility that every civil society strives to maintain.

Hamilton argued that energetic government and the benefits that resulted from it were principally due to energy in the executive, which he said

> is essential to the protection of the community against foreign attacks; it is not less essential to the steady administration of the laws, the protection of property against those irregular and high-handed combinations which sometimes interrupt the ordinary course

---

81. See "Essays by William Penn," in *The Complete Anti-Federalist*, ed. Herbert Storing (Chicago: University of Chicago Press, 1981), 3.12.15–17.

of justice; to the security of liberty against the enterprises and assaults of ambition, of faction, and of anarchy.

He concludes with the oft-quoted statement that "a feeble executive implies a feeble execution of the government. A feeble execution is but another phrase for a bad execution; and a government ill executed, whatever it may be in theory, must be, in practice, a bad government" (70:421). Energetic government is centered in the unitary executive; decision, dispatch, and responsibility are the hallmarks of presidential government. But energy is most needed in the case of emergencies. In foreign affairs especially, constitutional restraints are difficult to construct because the exigencies that face nations are unpredictable. As Hamilton had noted earlier in the *Federalist*, "no precise bounds could be set to the national exigencies; that a power equal to every possible contingency must exist somewhere in the government" (26:165–66). In fact, Hamilton cautioned, it would be unwise to impose constitutional restrictions on government's ability to meet exigencies because it was inevitable that these restrictions would be violated. All measures must be employed in a nation's defense when it is threatened by foreign invasions or domestic insurrections. In these circumstances, constitutional restrictions would be ignored under the pressure of events. Hamilton notes,

> Wise politicians will be cautious about fettering the government with restrictions that cannot be observed because they know that every breach of the fundamental laws, though dictated by necessity, impairs that sacred reverence which ought to be maintained in the breast of rulers towards the constitution of a country, and forms a precedent for other breaches where the same plea of necessity does not exist at all, or is less urgent and palpable (25:163).

It is inevitable that restraints in the fundamental law attempting to restrict the government's power of meeting "national exigencies" will be violated "*because it is impossible to foresee or to define the extent and variety of national exigencies, and the correspondent extent and variety of national means which may be necessary to satisfy them*" (23:149). The only possible conclusion is that the "power" to meet these emergencies "ought to exist without limitation." Restrictions in the fundamental law on the right of self-defense would inevitably be violated, and every violation of the fundamental law under exigent circumstances would invite a breach under circumstances that might not be "exigent." In any case, citizen confidence in the organic law and the rule of law would be impaired by frequent innovations.

Dealing with exigencies is best left to the executive. An energetic and unified executive can act in the face of national emergencies with decision and dispatch—precisely those qualities that are needed most. "In the conduct of war," Hamilton proclaims, "the energy of the executive is the bulwark of the national security" (70:425). The president will be the commander in chief of the armed forces, and this will give him the power and the flexibility to deal with military emergencies—as well as domestic insurrection.

CONSTITUTIONAL MEANS AND AMBITION
IN THE SEPARATION OF POWERS

In dealing with "national exigencies," particularly those involving foreign affairs, presidential power equips the executive with one of the greatest advantages of monarchy, and here the presidency most resembles monarchy. But it is the motivations and virtues required of the executive under the Constitution that distinguish it from monarchy—monarchical power is republicanized by the separation of powers operating in an "unmixed" regime. As Professor Mansfield has acutely noted, executive power is a modern invention that "has a natural basis in monarchy which it both reflects and attempts to repress." In the context of the American Constitution, "the task of political science in *The Federalist* was to show that an energetic executive could be republicanized."[82]

Still the question of what motivates the "republicanized" and "energized" executive remains. What ends does the executive pursue? And what virtues or qualifications are required to pursue those ends? When Publius advocates "energy in government" and "energy in the executive," we must keep in mind that "energy" is a neutral term, having been imported into political discourse from physics. Energy can be used for republican ends or non-republican ends. For Publius, what drives "energy in government"—and particularly "energy in the executive"—is "ambition." But ambition too is ambiguous; it can be used for well or ill. How can ambition and energy, along with executive power, be "republicanized"? The answer is that ambition exercised within the context of separated powers will ensure that energy will be used in the service of republican ends. Madison famously said that "the great security against a gradual concentration of the several powers in the same department consists in giving to those who administer each department the necessary constitutional means and personal motives to resist encroachments of the others" (51:318–19). The "constitutional means," as we have seen, are the various intermixed and blended powers assigned to the executive and legislative branches. Since the Supreme Court possesses neither force nor will, merely "judgment," the framers apparently didn't think it was necessary to construct "constitutional means" for the judicial branch—judgment, it seems, does not require energy. What Madison means by "personal motives" is revealed in his famous declaration that "ambition must be made to counteract ambition. The interest of the man must be connected with the constitutional rights of the place" (51:319). As previously mentioned, it is not class motives that drive the separation of powers in the "unmixed" regime of the Constitution but personal motives and interests. What interests are connected to constitutional offices? Professor Mansfield rightly says that these interests are not determined by the constitutional place but are "connected." To understand the well-known passage of *Federalist* 51, Mansfield contends, "one must not only consider office in the light of interest but

---

82. Harvey C. Mansfield, *Taming the Prince: The Ambivalence of Modern Executive Power* (Baltimore, MD: Johns Hopkins University Press, 1993), 250, 251, 256, 265, 271, 276, 295.

also interest in the light of office. Publius does not appeal to virtue, wary as he is of virtue in both republican and aristocratic form. But he also avoids reliance on the base motives of greed and vanity as well as common gain."[83] And with only the slightest hyperbole, Mansfield suggests that Publius "returns to Aristotle's promotion of ambition. Publius differs from Aristotle, however, in connecting ambition to interest rather than calling it a virtue," and "he seems to want to teach Americans that outstanding men of ambition are not so far from ordinary men as traditional republican suspicion supposes."[84] In Publius's account, the source of ambition, the love of honor, has its origins in interest, but ambition understood as the love of honor can only manifest itself as a force for the public good. Self-interest ("personal motives") is transformed into public interest when those who occupy constitutional offices realize that the love of honor is best served by subordinating short-term interests to long-term interests. The honor that accrues to those who serve the public good is the most valuable self-interest. In this manner, self-interest is transformed into public-regarding virtue. A rivalry for public honor will gratify private ambition at the same time that it will serve the public good; this will elevate "the private interest of every individual" to become "a sentinel over the public rights." Madison concludes that the "opposite and rival interests" supply "the defect of better motives" by serving as "inventions of prudence" (51:319). The ambiguity of energy will be resolved by the rivalry for public honor—ambition. The rivalry may supply "inventions of prudence" by grounding honor in interest, but the virtue that results is genuine.

In *Federalist* 57, Madison discusses "the relation between the House of Representatives and their constituents." The representatives "will be bound to fidelity and sympathy," Madison asserts, by "chords" of "duty, gratitude, interest, [and] ambition itself." It is possible, Madison cautions, that this will "be insufficient to control the caprice and wickedness of man. But are they not all that government will admit, and that human prudence can devise? Are they not the genuine and the characteristic means by which Republican Government provides for the liberty and happiness of the people?" (57:350–51). If prudential decisions in the service of the public weal are the habitual and secure means of public recognition, prudence will become a public virtue and be recognized as such. Prudence is the core of the kind of deliberation that is in the service of the public good, and service to the public good is the object of ambition and honor. Prudence—practical wisdom—rules the sphere of politics. It is essential to political life. As such, it cannot be supplied simply by institutional arrangements or constitutional mechanisms; it depends on virtue. Ambition solicits genuine prudence—wise deliberation and decision—because the rivalry of interests will leave reason free to deliberate about the public good, and it is service to the public good that brings the greatest recognition and public honor. If republics depend on virtue more than any other form of government, then republics must

---

83. Ibid., 263.
84. Harvey C. Mansfield, "Liberty and Virtue in the American Founding," in *Never a Matter of Indifference: Sustaining Virtue in a Free Republic*, ed. Peter Berkowitz (Stanford, CA: Hoover Institution Press, 2003), 18–19 (understanding Aristotle's *philotimos*, the lover of honor, to be a man of ambition).

encourage whatever inspires or calls forth virtue. Self-interest rightly understood guides individual choice among republican citizens, but it is also the motive force for those ambitious officeholders in pursuit of honor—a genuine virtue that is closely connected to the public good. Self-interest rightly understood will apply, Professor Mansfield observes, "to the whole society over which the Constitution will preside" and will supply "a *new principle* connecting virtue to liberty."[85]

Hamilton expressed no qualifications about the virtues that would be called forth by the Constitution's highest office, the executive. This is the sole office of government that stands alone and the one that bears the greatest responsibility. That presidential government became the core of the Constitution's republican system was largely due to Hamilton's efforts. He famously wrote that "the love of fame [is] the ruling passion of the noblest minds." It is the "love of fame" that will inspire the "noblest minds" to "undertake extensive and arduous enterprises for the public benefit" (71:436). Hamilton's statement is remarkably bold; generally speaking, Publius avoids extended discussions of virtue—to say nothing of nobility—because of the likelihood it will be misrepresented as evidence of aristocratic tendencies.

Hamilton steadfastly defends republican choice, but in the case of the executive it is republican choice that stretches to the limits of strict republicanism. It is only indirect choice: state legislatures choosing members of the Electoral College, who in turn elect the president. This "process of election," Hamilton asserts,

> affords a moral certainty that the office of President will seldom fall to the lot of any man who is not in an eminent degree endowed with the requisite qualifications. Talents for low intrigue, and the little arts of popularity, may alone suffice to elevate a man to the first honors in a single State; but it will require other talents, and a different kind of merit, to establish him in the esteem and confidence of the whole Union. . . . It will not be too strong to say that there will be a constant probability of seeing the station filled by characters preeminent for ability and virtue (68:412; 75:451; 76:454).

It is almost startling that Hamilton—who was not loath to express cynicism about human nature—would say that the mode of electing the executive would "afford the moral certainty" of returning an eminently qualified candidate. Hamilton seemed satisfied that the people would always use their freedom to choose virtue—but only if the choice of the most energetic constitutional officer were refined and disciplined by the indirect mode of election specified by the Constitution.

COURAGE AND MAGNANIMITY IN THE EXECUTIVE

"It is a just observation," Hamilton notes, "that the people commonly INTEND the PUBLIC GOOD." It almost goes without saying that only in a republican form of government does the ruling element "commonly intend the public good." In a mixed

---

85. Ibid., 18 (emphasis added).

regime, for example, the public good would result, if at all, only from a balancing of interests where none of the interests were actuated by an intention to promote the public good. We have already seen Madison's argument that indirect election of constitutional officers is compatible with the republican form of government and is essential to the maintenance of the separation of powers. Popular election of the president, according to Hamilton, would risk engaging "talents for low intrigue and the little arts of popularity," rendering the executive office incapable of serving the public good on those occasions when the people "intend the public good" but do not "reason right about the means of promoting it" (71:431). But even here, "the good sense" of the people "would despise the adulator" who would flatter their pretension to know in each case what is required for the public good and the best means of securing it. It is the role of "energetic" and "ambitious" executives to be guardians of the public good when "the interests of the people are at variance with their inclinations." Presidents must be able

> to withstand the temporary delusion in order to give them time and opportunity for more cool and sedate reflection. Instances might be cited in which a conduct of this kind has saved the people from very fatal consequences of their own mistakes, and has procured lasting monuments of their gratitude to the men who had courage and magnanimity enough to serve them at the peril of their displeasure (71:431).

Thus the method of electing the president is designed so that he will be willing to take risks—to become unpopular—when required by considerations of the public good. The indirect means of deriving executive power from the people allows the president to take the long view of the public good, to see further than the public but not differently from the public. The office of the president is designed to look further into the future than is possible for the legislative branch, whose members are more immediately connected to the "great body of the people." It is notable that while the president looks to the future, the Supreme Court—the other branch that stretches the limits of what constitutes a "strictly republican" form of government—was designed to keep the nation solidly anchored to the past, to the Constitution and the intentions of the framers.

As Hamilton noted, the president must display "courage and magnanimity enough" to serve the public good at the "peril" of displeasing the people. It is this "courage and magnanimity," the alpha and omega (so to speak) of Aristotelian moral virtue, that will earn "lasting monuments" of the people's gratitude. Thus the highest virtue solicited by ambition is magnanimity, itself the highest moral virtue, but a virtue that ultimately does not depend upon fame or recognition but only the self-satisfaction of having served a noble cause.[86] And while ambition solicits magnanimity, not every holder of the executive office will prove to be magnanimous.

---

86. This is the only appearance of the word "magnanimity" in the *Federalist*. It is the English translation of the Latin *magnanimus* which in turn is the translation of the Greek *megalopsychia*, meaning "greatness of soul."

Presidents without greater ambition than to hold the highest office will often be elected. As Madison says, "enlightened statesmen" will not always be at the helm, but they sometimes will be, and they will serve as examples for the less ambitious. Professor Mansfield seems to indicate that there is an Aristotelian element in the regime described by Publius: "'the genius of republican government' consists of two things: a due dependence on the people, and a due responsibility to them. But as the argument proceeds, due dependence is elevated to due responsibility."[87] It is true that as the argument for executive power progresses, the executive becomes manifestly less dependent on the people and more responsible to the people. And, Mansfield adds, "a political science capable of discerning responsibility . . . is essentially Aristotelian, opposed to the Machiavellian political science that invented the modern executive. A responsible political science joins the form of government to its end so that it can see how well the form performs."[88] According to Mansfield, it was essential for responsibility to adapt monarchical power to republican ends—"to republicanize the executive." This had already been accomplished in theory by Jefferson in *A Summary View*, but it was also necessary to constitutionalize the "chief officer of the people," an officer who was wholly a fiction of Jefferson's imagination, into a republican executive. Above all, it was necessary to ensure that in constitutional government, elections—the judgment of the people—could be a practical substitute for the sovereign prerogative of the people, the right of revolution.

---

87. Mansfield, *Taming the Prince*, 270.
88. Ibid., 291.

2

The Declaration of Independence and Social Compact: The Theological-Political Problem

"It is proper to keep in mind that all power in just & free Govt is derived from compact."

—James Madison[1]

"The people are in the habit and exercise of liberty, when they resort to the first principles of government, and trace their rights up to God the Creator: when they exercise their natural power of framing any social compact conducive to the common interest: feel independent of all human power but that which flows from themselves: disdain the subjection of their consciences to any authority but the will of God: refuse to be controuled by the will of any man who claims an independent power of disposing of their lives and estates: recollect that they entered into society to have their natural rights, which are the basis of civil rights, secured. To maintain such principles of original justice, is to stand fast in the righteous liberty of man. True liberty suffers no man to be injured in his person, estate, or character: it encourages and enables him to improve his happiness; and, within the limits of the public good, insures to him every blessing to which imperfect human nature can attain."

—Israel Evans[2]

By 1776, the idea that social compact was the only legitimate ground of civil society had become an established political principle as well as an accepted theological precept. It was just as likely to be extolled in election-day sermons as it was in political

---

1. "On Sovereignty," in *The Writings of James Madison*, ed. Gaillard Hunt (New York: G.P. Putnam's Sons, 1908), 9:569.
2. "A Sermon Delivered at the Annual Election" (Concord, 1791), in *Political Sermons of the American Founding Era*, ed. Ellis Sandoz (Indianapolis, IN: Liberty Fund, 1991), I:1068.

tracts. This remarkable agreement between theology and politics was a significant factor in the success of the American founding. No persistent religious disputes distracted the founders from the serious task of building a new nation. The Reverend Samuel West delivered an extraordinary election-day sermon in Boston in 1776 in which he remarked, "A revelation, pretending to be from God, that contradicts any part of natural law, ought immediately to be rejected as an imposture; for the Deity cannot make a law contrary to the law of nature without acting contrary to himself,— a thing in the strictest sense impossible, for that which implies contradiction is not an object of the divine power." And in a statement that is clearly an echo of a phrase from Locke's *First Treatise of Government*, West asserts that "reason . . . is the voice of God" and "whatever right reason requires as necessary to be done is as much the will and law of God as though it were enjoined us by an immediate revelation from heaven, or commanded in the sacred Scriptures." "Thus," West concludes, "we see that both reason and revelation perfectly agree in pointing out the nature, end, and design of government."[3] West's sermon was not atypical of the many sermons that attempted to harmonize reason and revelation in support of politics. The Declaration's reliance on "the Laws of Nature and of Nature's God" symbolized the agreement between reason and revelation that the New England clergy had promoted for more than one-half century. This agreement, of course, could exist only on a moral and political level. On the question of what ultimately perfects or completes human life, reason or revelation, no resolution seems possible on the basis of either reason or revelation. The question of ultimate perfection must be excluded from political life because it is politically irresolvable, and any attempt at a political resolution would almost certainly result in tyranny. Thus free exercise of religion and separation of church and state are political and theological doctrines that are intrinsic to the idea of the social compact and for the founding generation were dictates of both natural and divine law.

Another remarkable election sermon, profoundly influenced by Locke, was delivered by the Reverend John Tucker in 1771. "Civil and ecclesiastical societies are, in some essential points, different," the reverend declaimed. "Our rights, as men, and our rights, as Christians, are not, in all respects, the same," Tucker continued. It cannot be denied that God's

> subjects stand in some special relation and are under some peculiar subjection to him, distinct from their relation to and connection with civil societies, yet we justly conclude, that as this divine polity, with its sacred maxims, proceeded from the wise and benevolent Author of our being, none of its injunctions can be inconsistent with that love of liberty he himself has implanted in us, nor interfere with the laws and government of human societies, whose constitution is consistent with the rights of men.[4]

---

3. Samuel West, "On the Right to Rebel Against Governors," in *American Political Writings during the Founding Era 1760–1805*, ed. Charles S. Hyneman and Donald S. Lutz (Indianapolis, IN: Liberty Fund: 1983), I:414; I:416; I:431.

4. John Tucker, "An Election Sermon," Boston, 1771, in *American Political Writings*, Hyneman and Lutz, I:161.

Tucker exhibited a common view among New England clergy: the constitution of the "divine polity" cannot be in conflict with any civil government "whose constitution is consistent with the rights of men" and the "love of liberty" that God has implanted in human nature. According to Tucker, the proper constitution of civil government begins with the reflection that

> all men are naturally in a state of freedom, and have an equal claim to liberty. No one, by nature, not by any special grant from the great Lord of all, has any authority over another. All right therefore in any to rule over others, must originate from those they rule over, and be granted by them. Hence, all government, consistent with that natural freedom, to which all have an equal claim, is founded in compact, or agreement between the parties;—between Rulers and their Subjects, and can be no otherwise. Because Rulers, receiving their authority originally and solely from the people, can be rightfully possessed of no more, than these have consented to, and conveyed to them.[5]

Thus compact seems to be the key to reconciling divine polity and civil polity. Reverend Tucker began his sermon with the invocation that "the great and wise Author of our being, has so formed us, that the love of liberty is natural."[6] Liberty is the law of God and nature. The laws of divine polity are prescribed in the Gospel; those of civil polity are derived from social compact. What connects divine polity and civil polity is the liberty that God created as the essential part of man's nature. Social compact is the reasonable exercise of that freedom in the formation of civil society. Thus it seems that the theological-political problem—the problem of potentially conflicting obligations between divine polity and civil polity—is solved by Tucker, at least on the moral and political level, on the basis of social compact, which provides the only rightful basis of government because it is the only origin of government consistent with natural liberty. In fashioning his account of the social compact, the Reverend Tucker readily acknowledges the influence of "the great and judicious Mr. Locke," extensively quoting and citing "Locke on civil Government."[7] I think it is fair to say that "America's philosopher" dominated the pulpit no less than he dominated legislative halls and constitutional conventions. Thus a remarkable providence seemed to have guided the American founding in the form of a dispensation—largely orchestrated by "the great and judicious Mr. Locke"—from theological-political disputes that would have rendered impossible any attempt to establish constitutional government.

---

5. Tucker, *American Political Writings*, Hyneman and Lutz, I:162. On compact, see inter alia Daniel Shute, "An Election Sermon," Boston, 1768, ibid., I:117; Gad Hitchcock, "An Election Sermon," Boston, 1774, ibid., I:282, 289; Levi Hart, "Liberty Described and Recommended: In a Sermon Preached to the Corporation of Freemen in Farmington," Hartford, 1775, ibid., I:308–9; Zabdiel Adams, "An Election Sermon," Boston, 1782, ibid., I:546–47; John Allen, "An Oration upon the Beauties of Liberty," New London, 1773, in *Political Sermons of the American Founding*, Sandoz, I:311; Samuel Sherwood, "Scriptural Instructions to Civil Rulers," New Haven, 1774, in *American Political Writings*, Hyneman and Lutz, I:383; Israel Evans, "A Sermon Delivered at the Annual Election," Concord, 1791, ibid., I:1068.
6. Tucker, *American Political Writings*, I:159.
7. Ibid., I:163–64.

EQUALITY

The Declaration is, of course, the quintessential example of social compact. Compact is the necessary consequence of the fact that "all men are created equal," which is said in the Declaration to be a "self-evident" truth. A self-evident truth is one that contains the proof within the terms of the statement itself and is incapable of any further proof. For example the axiom that things equal to the same thing are equal to each other is a self-evident truth. Anyone who understands the terms "same" and "other" cannot fail at the same time to understand the meaning of "equal" or fail to affirm the truth of the axiom. It is an objective statement of the relation of things in the world. Any person of normal intelligence would recognize the truth of this statement immediately upon hearing it even though he would be unlikely to formulate the axiom in the first instance.[8] This statement was true before the axiom was discovered and will continue to be true even if the axiom is ever forgotten or its truth denied. In other words, its existence or truth is independent of human thought or creation; it is an eternal truth that does not depend on human consent or recognition.

But in what sense is human equality a self-evident truth? Clearly many inequalities exist among human beings, not the least of which are inequalities of strength, beauty, intelligence, and social and moral capacity. It is equally a self-evident truth then that all men are not created equal in all respects. The Declaration addresses the question of political rule, and it is in this regard that the self-evident truth of human equality is applicable. Whatever inequalities exist among human beings—however measured— none are so great as to make one human being (or class of human beings) naturally the rulers of others. The self-evident truth about the human species is that no human being occupies a position with respect to other human beings that every human being occupies with respect to every horse. The inequality between a human being and a horse makes every human being by nature the ruler of every horse. The same inequalities—however great—do not exist within the human species. As Jefferson noted, "because Sir Isaac Newton was superior to others in understanding, he was not therefore lord of the person or property of others."[9] Whatever intellectual superiority Newton displayed over other human beings, it was not equivalent to the difference between a human being of normal intelligence and a horse or any other beast.

LOCKE ON EQUALITY AND SELF-EVIDENT TRUTH

Jefferson, of course, had derived his argument, in large part, from Locke's famous statement in his *Second Treatise* that all men are naturally in a state of

---

8. See John Locke, *An Essay Concerning Human Understanding*, ed. Peter H. Nidditch (Oxford: Clarendon Press, 1975), I.iii.4. Locke gives as an example that "it is impossible for the same thing to be, and not to be."

9. Thomas Jefferson, Letter to Henri Gregoire, February 25, 1809, in *Jefferson: Writings*, ed. Merrill D. Peterson (New York: Library of America, 1984), 1202.

Equality, wherein all the Power and Jurisdiction is reciprocal, no one having more than another: there being nothing more evident, than that Creatures of the same species and rank promiscuously born to all the same advantages of Nature, and the use of the same faculties, should also be equal one amongst another without Subordination or Subjection, unless the Lord and Master of them all, should by any manifest Declaration of his Will set one above another, and confer on him by an evident and clear appointment an undoubted Right to Dominion and Sovereignty.[10]

We presume that "nothing more evident" is the equivalent of "self-evident," and that human equality for Locke, as for Jefferson, was a "self-evident truth." A "manifest Declaration" of God's will that some have the right to assume sovereignty over others would be something like the boots and saddles recounted by Jefferson's metaphor quoted in chapter 1. In the absence of such a sign of God's intention, experience provides evidence that the Almighty's intentions were to the contrary. Locke makes an even more explicit statement in the *First Treatise* when he says that it "is very evident, then Man has a *Natural Freedom* . . . since all that share in the same common Nature, Faculties and Powers, are in Nature equal, and ought to partake in the same common Rights and Privileges, till the manifest appointment of God, who is *Lord over all, Blessed for ever*, can be produced to shew any particular Persons Supremacy, or a Man's own consent subjects him to a Superior" (I.67; see I.81). Reason and scripture thus seem to conspire in supporting the idea that the equality of man is a self-evident truth—a manifest part of God's creation.

A "self-evident truth"—however much it is "perceived immediately by itself" (*An Essay Concerning Human Understanding*, IV.vii.2)—still requires evidence, and like all ideas, self-evident truths are ultimately grounded in the world experienced by sense perception. As Locke relates,

self-evident truths, must be *first* known, which consist of *Ideas* that are *first* in the mind: and the *Ideas first* in the Mind, 'tis evident, are those of particular Things, from whence, by slow degrees, the Understanding proceeds to some few general ones; which being taken from the ordinary and familiar Objects of Sense, are settled in the Mind, with general Names to them (IV.vii.9–10; I.ii.21).

Thus self-evident truths derive from sense perception, where the human mind displays a unique capacity, not possessed by brute creation, to abstract intelligible experiences or ideas from merely sensible experiences (II.xi.i10; IV.xvii.i1).[11] The power

10. John Locke, *Two Treatises of Government*, ed. Peter Laslett (New York: New American Library, 1965), II.4. Further references will be in the text by treatise and paragraph number.

11. At first glance, Locke's description of the mind's capacity to abstract ideas from the sensible particulars appears to resemble the account given by Aristotle (*Posterior Analytics* 100b2–16). Locke, however, disagreed with Aristotle (and the schoolmen) insofar as he argued that the intellectual experience that is abstracted from sensible experiences is not inherent in the substance or matter experienced by the senses but is purely "the workmanship of the understanding." The form or species generated in the mind is not in the object itself but the creative product of the mind, "nominal essences" or abstract definitions created

of abstraction is the faculty of reason and it is reason—inductive reason—that is the foundation of self-evident truths.

The *First Treatise*, of course, was devoted, in large part, to a refutation of Sir Robert Filmer's defense of divine right monarchy, and Locke had the ill grace to ask kings to show the marks of God's designation of divine appointment. But we know that Locke's project was more ambitious than the destruction of divine right monarchy; it was in fact the elimination of the grounds for all non-republican government. But he first had to deal with the widespread and powerful opinions that supported divine right monarchy that putatively derived its authority from scripture.[12] If Filmer was the most authoritative source for divine right monarchy, Locke met him on the ground of scripture and won a clear and decisive victory. Any argument for divine right derived from biblical sources ultimately resulted either in an absolute monarchy that was indistinguishable from tyranny or in anarchy.

Locke's next step, to be executed in the *Second Treatise*, was to destroy not just absolute government but all government that was not derived from the consent of the governed. As one perceptive reader has noted, for Locke, "only a representative government is not absolute, and only government by a legislative in Locke's novel sense is not arbitrary." This commentator concludes that "Locke's constitutionalism is a universal razor to cut away aristocrats and theocrats as well as monarchs, and in general all regimes in which the rulers pretend to a superior authority."[13]

In a much discussed passage Locke argues that in the state of nature all men are "equal and independent" (II.6). Equality by nature and independence by nature seem to be reciprocal aspects of man's natural condition or man's nature. If men are naturally equal and independent, they are, by a parity of reason, born free and equal, or, to say the same thing, all men are created equal.[14] All men, Locke avers in the same passage, are "the Workmanship of one Omnipotent, and infinitely wise Maker; All the Servants of one Sovereign Master, sent into the World by his order and about his business, they are his Property whose Workmanship they are, made to last during his, not one another's Pleasure" (II.6). The act of creation—the workmanship of God (*An Essay Concerning Human Understanding*, IV.x.18)—makes each man equally the property of God, and each being the property of God, no one can be the property of anyone else. Thus each man is "equal and independent" with respect to every other human being, which can only mean that "every Man has a *Property* in

---

by the mind to organize sense experience (*An Essay Concerning Human Understanding*, III.vi.6). The senses are not deceptive; they are simply inadequate to reveal the complexities of matter and motion.

12. See Leo Strauss, *Natural Right and History* (Chicago: University of Chicago Press, 1953), 220.

13. Robert Faulkner, "The First Liberal Democrat: Locke's Popular Government," *Review of Politics* 63, no. 1 (Winter 2001), 18; see John Locke, *Two Treatises of Government*, I.91–93.

14. Harry V. Jaffa, *How to Think About the American Revolution* (Durham, NC: Carolina Academic Press, 1978), 109. Pauline Maier, *American Scripture: Making the Declaration of Independence* (New York: Alfred A. Knopf, 1997), 136, reports that Jefferson's first draft of the Declaration incorporated Locke's phrase "equal and independent."

his own *Person*" (II.27; II.44). To say nothing of a host of other considerations no less important, the transition from the property of God to the property *in propria persona* was necessary to forestall claims to priestly rule. We will, of course, have more to say about the workmanship argument in due course. To paraphrase Locke in a slightly different but not unrelated context, whether we consult reason or revelation, it would be difficult to deny that all men are created equal.

THE ARGUMENT OF THE DECLARATION IS INDUCTIVE REASON FROM THE FACT OF EQUALITY

All of the "self-evident truths" of the Declaration are derived from the "Laws of Nature and of Nature's God." The self-evident truth that "all men are created equal" takes priority because it is the truth that is immediately available to sense perception as an empirical fact. All the other truths in the Declaration are inferences or deductions from the fact of human equality. Equality is a unique feature of the human species. It is an abiding mystery why God created the human species different from every other social species, but it is an observable fact and as much a part of man's experience as the intuitive certainty of his own existence (*An Essay Concerning Human Understanding*, IV.10.1). Among the human species there are no individuals or classes who are so superior by nature as to be the natural rulers of others. As we have seen, God has not marked some with natures so superior as to designate them to be the rulers of others, as He has, for example, marked the queen bee to be the natural ruler of the bee hive, or the male dominant lion to be the ruler of the lion pride. While every other social species has rulers appointed by nature and its form of rule imposed by instinct, the human species seems to have been left free (or at least potentially free) to choose its own form of rule, and it is in this choice that human political freedom resides.

The Declaration speaks of self-evident *truths*, and we know that as a matter of strict logic, a self-evident truth cannot be derived from another prior or antecedent self-evident truth. But to the extent that the argument of the Declaration begins with a self-evident truth and proceeds by necessary inferences dictated by that truth, every step in the argument retains an intrinsic element of the self-evident source. When a self-evident or intuitive truth stands at the beginning of a demonstrative proof, each step of the demonstration participates in the same intuitive certainty as the original proposition. According to Locke, in demonstrative knowledge, intuitive knowledge or self-evident truth is the point of departure, and in every step of the reasoning "*there is an intuitive knowledge* of that agreement or disagreement it seeks with the next intermediate idea, which it uses as a proof." Thus, "it is plain, that every step in reasoning, that produces knowledge, has intuitive certainty, which when the mind perceives, there is no more required, but to remember it to make the agreement or disagreement of the ideas, concerning which we inquire visible and certain" (*An Essay*

Concerning Human Understanding, IV.ii.i7).[15] In this sense, the Declaration's use of the plural "self-evident truths" is fully justified, as long as we understand that natural human equality is the self-evident truth that gives rise to the chain of inferences that forms the inductive reasoning that gives coherence to the argument as a whole, and that each step in the reasoning contains the self-evidence or "intuitive certainty" of the original self-evident truth.

While the founders were certainly familiar with Locke's metaphysical writings, they were more apt to speak of self-evident truths in terms of "commonsense" understanding. Jefferson always claimed that his "object" in writing the Declaration was "to place before mankind the common sense of the subject in terms so plain and firm as to command their assent."[16] Jefferson said he hoped to give expression to the "American mind." That American mind was on display nearly a century later when Senator Charles Sumner, Republican of Massachusetts, argued early in the Reconstruction debates that the Constitution "must be interpreted in harmony with the Declaration of Independence. . . . The promises of the Fathers must be sacredly fulfilled. This is the commanding rule, superseding all other rules." Here is Sumner's commonsense understanding of the train of reasoning that begins with "all men are created equal":

> This is the first of the self-evident truths that are announced, leading and governing all the rest. Life, liberty, and the pursuit of happiness are among inalienable rights; but they are held in subordination to that primal truth. Here is the starting-point of the whole, and the end is like the starting-point. In announcing that Governments derive their just powers from the consent of the governed, the Declaration repeats again the same proclamation of Equal Rights. Thus is Equality the Alpha and the Omega, in which all other rights are embraced.[17]

Senator Sumner undoubtedly expressed Jefferson's understanding of the relation of rights to equality as a self-evident truth. Equality embraces "all the other rights" because it is the "primal truth." After John C. Calhoun had convinced the leaders of the Southern slaveocracy that the Declaration of Independence was "the most dangerous of all political errors," Sumner urged that Reconstruction must ensure that the principles of the Declaration be completed and reaffirmed by amendments to the Constitution.[18]

---

15. Locke described "self-evident truths" and "intuitive knowledge" in identical terms. As we have already seen, a self-evident truth is where the "agreement or disagreement [of ideas] is perceived immediately by itself, without the intervention or help of any other" (*An Essay Concerning Human Understanding*, IV.vii.2). Intuitive knowledge is when "the mind perceives the agreement or disagreement of two ideas immediately by themselves, without the intervention of any other" (IV.ii.1). See also IV.xvii.14, where "intuitive knowledge" is said to be "certain, beyond all doubt, and needs no probation, nor can have any . . . which nobody has any doubt about, but every man (does not . . . only assent to, but) knows to be true, as soon as ever they are proposed to his understanding."

16. Thomas Jefferson, Letter to Henry Lee, May 8, 1825, in *Jefferson: Writings*, 1501.

17. *Congressional Globe*, 39th Cong., 1st Sess., 680 (1866) (Sen. Sumner).

18. Ibid. at 686, 674.

Alexander Hamilton also conveyed the commonsense understanding of political first principles when he wrote in *Federalist* 31,

> In DISQUISITIONS of every kind there are certain primary truths, or first principles upon which upon which all subsequent reasonings must depend. These contain an internal evidence which, antecedent to all reflection or combination, commands the assent of the mind. Where it produces not this effect, it must proceed either from some disorder in the organs of perception, or from the influence of some strong interest, or passion or prejudice (31:189).

Hamilton gives examples from geometry:

> Of this nature are the maxims in geometry that the whole is greater than its parts; that things equal to the same are equal to one another; that two straight lines cannot enclose a space; and that all right angles are equal to each other (31:189).[19]

We have already had occasion to discuss Hamilton's central example. Its cogency for the Declaration resides in the fact that it contains the term "equal." The examples from geometry are easily understood examples of self-evident truths: once the terms are understood, their truth cannot be denied. "Of the same nature," Hamilton proceeds,

> are these other maxims in ethics and politics, that there cannot be an effect without a cause; that the means ought to be proportioned to the end; that every power ought to be commensurate with its object; that there ought to be no limitation of a power destined to effect a purpose which is itself incapable of limitation (31:189).[20]

There are "other truths" in politics and ethics, Hamilton continues, "which, if they cannot pretend to rank in the class of axioms, are yet such direct inferences from them, and so obvious in themselves, and so agreeable to the natural and unsophisticated dictates of common sense that they challenge the assent of a sound and unbiased mind with a degree of force and conviction almost equally irresistible" (31:189). Here Hamilton mentions the necessity of lodging the power of taxation in the national government. This is a simple, commonsense inference from the fact that the national government is entrusted with the common defense, a trust which, as we have already discussed, is an "illimitable power." The national government should not depend on the goodwill of the states to fund those objects—particularly common defense—that are entrusted exclusively to its care. This is a commonsense conclusion that, while not an axiom, carries a "conviction almost equally irresistible."

---

19. It is curious that Hamilton calls these geometric examples "maxims" instead of "axioms." This may reflect the influence of Locke, who designates both maxims and axioms as reflecting self-evident truth in *An Essay Concerning Human Understanding* (IV.vii.1).

20. The first maxim is a rule of reason; the central two maxims concern means-end relations and are used by Madison (44:282) and Hamilton (33:199) to argue in favor of provisions in the proposed Constitution. The fourth maxim, that there cannot be a limitation on the means when the ends themselves are illimitable, was applied to the case of national defense (23:149).

These "maxims of ethics and politics" are easily recognizable as the rules of construction that are intrinsic to a written constitution, especially one that is, in Madison's terms, "partly national, partly federal," but also one that has the separation of powers as its central institutional feature.

We will see in the next chapter that Locke's claim that moral and political questions, beginning "from self-evident propositions, by necessary consequences" can be answered as incontestably as those in mathematics. Hamilton seems to share Locke's confidence in the incontestability of the proofs that proceed from self-evident truths, but he emphasizes more than Locke does the commonsense appeal of the arguments. This, of course, is wholly expected in a regime that is grounded in the politics of public opinion, engendered by the necessity of a frequent recurrence to first principles. Locke promised an entire system of moral and political truths based on mathematical certainty. He failed to deliver on that promise, but, as we will see, he did put forward some instructive examples that have significance for our consideration of the American founding.

EQUALITY IS THE FOUNDATION OF NATURAL RIGHTS

Both Jefferson and Madison described natural rights as "the rights of human nature" because they are a necessary consequence of or conclusion from the "principles of human nature"—the fact that "all men are created equal." Equality and natural rights belong to the first group of "self-evident truths" in the Declaration and they relate to man in the pre-political state of nature. From equal creation, the necessary inference is that human beings are "endowed by their Creator with certain unalienable Rights, that among these are Life, Liberty and the pursuit of Happiness." If among human beings there are no rulers by nature, every individual is by nature his own ruler and has sovereignty over his own being. This is the natural right to life. Individuals also have the natural right to liberty, the right to decide by the same sovereign prerogative what best conduces to the preservation of their lives as well as their liberty. By the same logic, individuals have the right to the pursuit of happiness.

The Declaration notes that "life, liberty and the pursuit of happiness" are "among" the rights possessed by "all men." It is assumed that the right to property is an intrinsic part of the "pursuit of happiness" and must be included "among" the other "unalienable" rights with which men "are endowed by their Creator." The right to property was undoubtedly considered by the founders as a necessary (but not sufficient) condition for the "pursuit of happiness." This is a topic that will be addressed *in extenso* in the next chapter. Other natural rights must be included as "among" those explicitly mentioned. Freedom of speech and the press were necessary for the politics of public opinion that was integral to the American founding. Perhaps even more important, as we will discuss shortly, the right of conscience must be included in the list because it served such an important role in the solution to the theological-political issues that confronted both Locke and the American founders. But another important natural right, the subject of much lively controversy today, is illustrative of the relationship between rights and obligations that is at the heart of social compact: the right to keep and bear arms. This is a right that is clearly implied in the argument of the Declaration.

The last natural right mentioned in the Declaration is the "Right of the People to alter or to abolish" government whenever it becomes destructive of their "Safety and Happiness." We know that social compact in its primitive form is an agreement for the mutual protection of equal natural rights. Each person who consents to be governed agrees to defend the rights of fellow citizens in return for the protection of his own rights. Thus each person who consents to the protection of his rights incurs obligations to civil society. Anyone who is unwilling or incapable of fulfilling his obligation to cooperate in the defense of his fellow citizens cannot be a member of civil society. Rights and obligations are intrinsic to social compact. Since the compact in this first instance is something of a mutual defense pact, the civil society might be described as a militia for the equal protection of equal rights, an idea that later entered American constitutional jurisprudence as "equal protection of the laws" but was integral to social compact from the beginning. If the right of revolution is among the natural rights reserved to the people, then the people also have a natural right to the means to effect that right. Thus the right to keep and bear arms is clearly "among" the "unalienable Rights" "endowed" by the "Creator."

Rights were understood by the American founders to be part of an objective order. A creator and a created universe are clearly specified in the Declaration: "all men are *created* equal, that they are endowed by their *Creator* with certain unalienable Rights." As part of a created—and therefore intelligible—universe, rights cannot be something private or subjective; they are part of an objective—not a subjective—order. Every right has a corresponding duty or obligation; this was essential to the social compact understanding of the American founding.[21] Thus whatever was destructive of the public good or "public happiness," however much it might contribute to one's private pleasures or imagined pleasures, was not a part of the "pursuit of happiness" and could be proscribed by society. Liberty was understood to be "rational liberty," and the pursuit of happiness was understood to be the "rational pursuit of happiness." The founders' understanding of the pursuit of happiness was taken, in large measure, from Locke's *Essay Concerning Human Understanding*. Locke treated the "pursuit of happiness" not as a natural right but as a moral duty. The American founders, however, translated Locke's understanding of the "pursuit of happiness" into both a natural right and a moral duty. This transformation will be explored in the next chapter.

CONSENT AND THE JUST POWERS OF GOVERNMENT

The next group of conclusions from the fact of natural human equality pertains to the establishment of government: "That to secure these rights, Governments are

---

21. See Thomas Jefferson, "Opinion on the French Treaties," 1791, in *Jefferson: Writings*, 423–24; Thomas Jefferson, Letter to Francis W. Gilmer, June 7, 1816, in *The Works of Thomas Jefferson*, ed. Paul Leicester Ford (New York: G.P. Putnam's Sons, 1904–1905), 11:533–34.

instituted among Men, deriving their just powers from the consent of the governed."
Locke assures us that "the *State of Nature* has a Law of Nature to govern it, which
obliges every one: And Reason, which is that Law, teaches all Mankind, who will but
consult it, that being all equal and independent, no one ought to harm another in his
Life, Health, Liberty, or Possessions" (II.6). The intent of the law of nature is the preservation of "the Peace and *Preservation of all Mankind*," and since the state of nature
is "that *State of perfect Equality*, where naturally there is no superiority of jurisdiction
of one, over another, what any may do in Prosecution of that Law, every one must
need have a Right to do" (II.7; II.128). Those who violate the law of nature trespass
against "*reason* and common Equity, which is that measure God has set to the actions
of Men, for their mutual security" (II.8). By abandoning "the right Rule of reason,"
violators of the law of nature "quit the Principles of Human Nature" (II.10) for "the
most excellent part of [God's] workmanship" is reason (*An Essay Concerning Human
Understanding*, IV.xviii.5).

Locke admits that the right of every man to "*be the Executioner of the Law of
Nature*" "will seem a very strange Doctrine to some Men," but it is an inevitable
consequence of the "perfect equality" in the state of nature in which there is "no
jurisdiction of one, over another." While Locke assures us that the law of nature is
"as intelligible and plain to a rational Creature, and a Studier of that Law, as the
positive Laws of Common-wealths, nay possibly plainer," it has been pointed out
often enough that Locke subsequently reveals that the "inconveniences" associated
with the state of nature renders it impossible for there to be studiers of the law of
nature in the state of nature (II.124). The study of the law of nature can take place
only within the peaceful conditions of civil society, and even there the complexities
that surround such investigations make it inevitable that the study will always be
accompanied by substantial controversy, as Locke's own early *Essays on the Laws of
Nature* readily confirms.

Locke unhesitatingly admits that there will be objections to his "strange Doctrine." The principal objection, even granting that the law of nature is plain and
intelligible, is that "it is unreasonable for Men to be Judges in their own Cases,
that Self-love will make Men partial to themselves and their Friends." In addition
to this easily granted objection, Locke comments that "ill Nature, Passion and
Revenge will carry them too far in punishing others," with the consequence that
"nothing but Confusion and Disorder will follow." Locke concludes that "God hath
certainly appointed Government to restrain the partiality and violence of Men. I
easily grant," Locke continues, "that *Civil Government* is the proper Remedy for the
Inconveniences of the State of Nature, which must certainly be Great, where Men
may be Judges in their own Case, since 'tis easily to be imagined, that he who was
so unjust as to do his Brother an Injury, will scarce be so just as to condemn himself
for it" (II.13). God has appointed government, but, as Locke quickly adds, he has
not appointed "*Absolute Monarchs*" because this would simply be a continuation of
the state of nature, where the absolute monarch would have discretion to "Judge
in his own Case, and may do to all his Subjects whatever he pleases" as if he were

still in a state of nature with respect to them. Locke avers that it would be much better for the subjects of such a monarch to remain in the state of nature "wherein Men are not bound to submit to the unjust will of another: And if he that judges, judges amiss in his own, or any other Case, he is answerable for it to the rest of Mankind" (II.13; II.21 fin.). In contrast to Hobbes, Locke maintains that the state of nature, despite its great "inconveniences," is preferable to absolute government. This idea, expressed early in the *Second Treatise*, prepares us for Locke's most radical doctrine, reserved for the final chapter: the dissolution of government, or what has become known as the right of revolution, the ultimate expression of the sovereign prerogative of the people.

The Declaration adopts the Lockean idea that civil government is the remedy for the great inconveniences of the state of nature and that the only basis for the "just powers" of government is derived "from the consent of the governed." Since there are no natural rulers, the only way rule can become legitimate is with the consent of those who are to be ruled. This is where the idea of social compact enters. Consent involves compact; each person who agrees to be ruled executes a compact with every other person who consents to form civil society; civil society in turn will be governed by settled, known laws for the equal protection of equal natural rights. Anyone who does not consent remains in the state of nature with respect to the members of the newly formed civil society. Each member on entering civil society submits to society as a whole the sovereign prerogative he possessed in the state of nature to determine how best to protect his life, liberty, and pursuit of happiness. Strictly speaking, of course, rights cannot be submitted to civil society because rights are "unalienable." What is entrusted to civil society is the determination of how rights are to be *secured*. The executive power to enforce the law of nature that each individual possessed in the state of nature, and that led to "nothing but Confusion and Disorder," is ceded to civil society, which employs the rule of law, "the rule of reason and equity," to determine how rights and liberties are best secured and disputes adjudicated.

It is important to note that the Declaration specifies that consent can authorize only the "just powers" of government, not all powers. We will explore this question in more detail in the next section, but obviously the only powers that can be entrusted to the rule of the community are those that are truly designed to implement the "safety and happiness" of the people. At a minimum, "just powers" endeavor to provide the rule of law understood as the equal protection of equal natural rights. This means, as we discussed in chapter 1, that there are limits on the form of government to which the people can consent. We have already argued that a republican form of government that actively solicits the participation of the people in its own governance was the only form that met the requirements of the framers. Constitutionalism and the rule of law are the means—the "just powers"—that the framers designed to pursue just ends, the "safety and happiness" of the people.

We have already anticipated the last self-evident truth deduced from the principle of natural human equality, the right to "alter or abolish government," which we also know as the right of revolution. Some further reflections, however, are in order. We first notice that the right to "alter or abolish government" is said to be both a right and a duty. And since it is the only duty mentioned in the Declaration, it clearly designates something fundamental. Sovereignty, we know, resides in the people, and however much we speak of the Constitution as "the supreme Law of the Land," or of the government as sovereign, the people can never cede sovereignty. The people can delegate specified powers to government to be exercised for their "safety and happiness," but sovereignty is always retained by the people—it cannot be delegated. And the people have a duty to defend their sovereignty when it is threatened by government. The right of revolution is the ultimate expression of the people's sovereignty. When government exercises force without right—when it exercises powers that have not been authorized or delegated by the people— government places itself in a state of nature with the people, which is the same as to say, following Locke, that government puts itself "into a state of War with the People, who are thereupon absolved from any farther Obedience and are left to the common Refuge, which God hath provided for all Men against Force and Violence." Whenever government endeavors to exercise "*an Absolute Power* over the Lives, Liberties, and Estates of the People," this amounts to a "breach of Trust" whereby the government forfeits the power "the People had put into their hands, for quite contrary ends, and it devolves to the People, who have a Right to resume their original Liberty" (II.222).

As we have already noted, the right to resume "original liberty" in the Declaration is a natural right as well as a (natural) duty. Passive obedience had always been a powerful political doctrine of divine right monarchy, and it was supported by biblical authority. Most commonly cited was Romans 13, which yielded the teaching that all existing government and authority was authorized by God. Obedience to God's representatives on earth was therefore obedience to God, and whoever resisted established rulers disobeyed God and would incur His judgment. As God's representatives, rulers were not a terror to good conduct but only to bad conduct. Passive obedience to established rulers was thus the authoritative doctrinal support for divine right monarchy. Locke's chapter "Dissolution of Government" in the *Second Treatise* emphatically argued, however, that "*the People shall be Judge*" of whether rulers have acted for the good of the ruled and that the people have no duty of passive obedience, "wherein the Appeal lies only to Heaven" (II.243). The cautious Locke never made an explicit reference to Romans 13, but a passage in the *First Treatise* is unambiguous:

> Government being for the Preservation of every Mans Right and Property, by preserving him from the Violence or Injury of others, is for the good of the Governed: for the Magistrates Sword being for a *Terror to Evil Doers*, and by that Terror to inforce Men to observe the positive Laws of Society, made conformable to the Laws of Nature, for the Public good, *i.e.* the good of every particular Member of that Society, as far as by common Rules, it can be provided for; the Sword is not given the Magistrate for his own good alone (I.92 and editor's note; see II.228 fin.).

Locke did not originate the argument that transmogrified the biblical duty of passive obedience to one of a right to resist arbitrary authority. He inherited the argument from earlier writers, perhaps most notably from John Milton,[22] but he gave it a greater force and established it on a broader foundation.

By the time of the American founding, the doctrine of passive obedience was moribund. We have already referred to the Reverend Samuel West's sermon "On the Right to Rebel Against Governors," delivered in Boston in 1776. West described passive resistance as a pernicious principle "industriously propagated by artful and designing men, both in politics and divinity. The doctrine of non-resistance and unlimited passive obedience to the worst of tyrants," he avowed, "could never have found credit among mankind had the voice of reason been hearkened to for a guide, because such a doctrine would immediately have been discerned to be contrary to natural law."[23] This was a sentiment that was frequently expressed in founding era sermons.[24] The right to alter or abolish government in the Declaration expressed itself as a doctrine of both divine and natural law—a dictate of "the Laws of Nature and of Nature's God."

Locke anticipated the criticism that the demise of the doctrine of passive resistance "*lays a foundation for Rebellion*" and "that it may occasion Civil Wars, or Intestine Broils, to tell the People they are absolved from Obedience, when illegal attempts are made upon their Liberties or Properties," and that they "may oppose the unlawful violence of those, who were their Magistrates, when they invade their Properties contrary to the trust put in them" (II.228). In fact, Locke argued that civil wars and intestine disorders were more likely to result from the insolence of rulers and the exercise of arbitrary power over the people than from the disaffection of the people. In a passage that was closely paraphrased in the Declaration, Locke declaimed that "till the mischief be grown general, and the ill designes of the Rulers become visible, or their attempts sensible to the greater part, the

---

22. John Milton, "The Tenure of Kings and Magistrates," in *Areopagitica and Other Political Writings of John Milton* (Indianapolis, IN: Liberty Fund, 1999), 64–65, 93; John Milton, "Defence of the People of England," ibid., 162–67.

23. Tucker, *American Political Writings*, Hyneman and Lutz, I:414.

24. See inter alia, ibid., I:161–62. The Reverend Tucker counters Romans 13 with an argument drawn from Locke, whom he cites; Simeon Howard, "A Sermon Preached to the Ancient and Honorable Artillery Company," Boston, 1773, in ibid., 204ff; Gad Hitchcock, "An Election Sermon," Boston, 1774, in ibid., 285, 302–4; Elisha Williams, "The Essential Rights and Liberties of Protestants," Boston, 1744, in *Political Sermons of the American Founding*, Sandoz, I:79ff. Reverend Williams, after quoting Romans 13, comments,

Whenever the power that is put in any hands for the government of any people is applied to any other end than the preservation of their persons and properties, the securing and promoting of their civil interests (the end for which power was put into their hands), I say when it is applied to any other end, then (according to the great Mr. Lock) it becomes tyranny. . . . How long people are to bear with such tyranny, or what they may do to free themselves from it (I should refer you to that author in his *Treatise of Government*).

See Samuel Sherwood, "Scriptural Instructions to Civil Rulers," in *American Political Writings*, Hyneman and Lutz, 396–99; and Samuel McClintock, "A Sermon on the Commencement of the New Hampshire Constitution," Portsmouth, 1784, ibid., 811.

People, who are more disposed to suffer, than right themselves by Resistance, are not apt to stir." But the people are not obliged always to remain quiescent: "The examples of particular Injustice, or Oppression of here and there an unfortunate Man, moves them not. But if they universally have a perswasion, grounded upon manifest evidence, that designs are carrying on against their Liberties, and the general course and tendency of things cannot but give them strong suspicions of the evil intention of their Governors, who is to be blamed for it?" (II.230). Thus the people do not have to wait until the designs of rulers have manifested themselves to such a degree that it is too late to resist. The people can anticipate future danger to their property and liberty and take preemptive action while there is a chance that resistance will be effective. If they wait until the government's plan of disfranchisement is well advanced, then it is almost always too late for the people to defend themselves.

Madison, in his "Memorial and Remonstrance," written in 1785, remarked that "it is proper to take alarm at the first experiment on our liberties. We hold this prudent jealousy to be the first duty of Citizens, and one of the noblest characteristics of the late Revolution. The free men of America did not wait till usurped power had strengthened itself by exercise, and entangled the question in precedents. They saw all the consequences in the principle, and they avoided the consequences by denying the principle."[25] Madison was referring to the "Declaration of the Causes and Necessity for Taking Up Arms" of 1775, which anticipated the necessity for revolution in Parliament's declaration that it had the "right [to] make laws to bind" the colonies "in all cases whatsoever." America did not have to wait for this assertion of absolute power to manifest itself before taking up arms in defense of its freedom. The statement of the principle that Parliament had the right to bind the colonies was sufficient as a matter of prudence to anticipate the result that the principle would be acted upon. If the "free men of America" had waited for the principle to be put into action, it probably would have been too late to mount an effective resistance. As a matter of prudence, it is best to act when resistance can be effective—that is, when the principle is announced, and not when forces have been marshaled to enforce the principle.

As a general matter, experiments on liberty first appear as innovations on the rights of property. While these innovations might appear slight at first, they should raise alarms because assaults on property rights almost always mean that assaults on liberty will follow. In chapter 4, we will see the sense in which the framers saw an intimate connection between the right to property and all other rights. The right to property was said to be the guardian of every other right so that any innovation on property rights—whether taxation without representation or confiscation without compensation—was at one and the same time an innovation upon the free exercise of religion or freedom of speech. It is prudent therefore to take alarm at the slightest

---

25. Robert A. Rutland et al., eds., *The Papers of James Madison* (Chicago: University of Chicago Press, 1962–), 8:300.

innovations on the right to property in anticipation that innovations on other rights will soon follow.

The entire passage of the Declaration adumbrating the right of revolution deserves quotation here:

> That whenever any Form of Government becomes destructive of these ends, it is the Right of the People to alter or to abolish it, and to institute new Government, laying its foundation on such principles and organizing its powers in such form, as to them shall seem most likely to effect their Safety and Happiness. Prudence, indeed, will dictate that Governments long established should not be changed for light and transient causes; and accordingly all experience hath shewn, that mankind are more disposed to suffer, while evils are sufferable, than to right themselves by abolishing the forms to which they are accustomed. But when a long train of abuses and usurpations, pursuing invariably the same Object evinces a design to reduce them under absolute Despotism, it is their right, it is their duty, to throw off such Government, and to provide new Guards for their future security.

This passage closely reflects Locke's analysis, but Locke never mentions "prudence," nor does he say that the people have a "duty" to resist oppressive rulers. Prudence, or practical wisdom, governs the exercise of the right of revolution in the Declaration. Governments "long established" should not be casually "altered or abolished," and evils should be suffered as long as there is hope that remedies for the evils may be available under existing forms, especially if those forms have been long established. Yet when there is no prospect of relief, when a settled design is evident to reduce the people to absolute despotism, the people have a duty to "alter or abolish" the government. (The phrase in Locke is "remove or alter" [II.149].) The alteration or abolition of government is a fearful and uncertain affair that may or may not succeed in reestablishing just government. In the Declaration, natural law or natural right is governed by the dictates of prudence, the practical principle that governs the sphere of politics. The Declaration, I say, puts this Aristotelian understanding of prudence at the center of its understanding of natural right or natural law. Whether this represents an innovation upon Locke is an inquiry for another occasion.

Prudence dictates that when evils are no longer sufferable, or when the prospects of equitable relief cannot be expected from the forms of government to which the people have been long accustomed, the people have a duty to defend themselves against tyranny. This is a duty that derives directly from the "Laws of Nature and of Nature's God." The same dictates of prudence, however, counsel that whoever acts—whether government or people—in a manner to overturn just government is guilty of a crime against mankind and, as Locke aptly puts it, "is justly to be esteemed the common Enemy and Pest of Mankind; and is to be treated accordingly" (II.230). As we previously emphasized, only the just powers of government are derived from the consent of the governed. These are the only powers that the people are capable of authorizing because they are the only powers authorized by the laws of nature and reason. At the same time, it is the people who reserve judgment about whether the government has exercised its delegated powers for the "Safety and Happiness" of the people.

MADISON ON SOCIAL COMPACT

Gary Rosen rightly commented that "for Madison, the social compact . . . was always the source of his first principles."[26] "To go to the bottom of the subject," Madison wrote in his essay "Sovereignty,"

> let us consult the Theory which contemplates a certain number of individuals as meeting and agreeing to form one political society, in order that the rights the safety & the interest of each may be under the safeguard of the whole. The first supposition is, that each individual being previously independent of the others, the compact which is to make them one society must result from the free consent of *every* individual.[27]

Thus political society or civil society results from the unanimous consent of individuals who were previously independent of one another in the state of nature. Madison doesn't use the term "state of nature," but he clearly alludes to the equal and independent condition of men who existed in that state and who agreed to civil society for the safety of their rights and interests. Madison also wrote on another occasion that just and free governments were actually grounded on two compacts, one to form a people (or society) and another to form government. In a letter to Nicholas Trist, written in 1830, Madison repeated his view that "the idea of compact . . . is a fundamental principle of free Government" and explained,

> The original compact is the one implied or presumed, but nowhere reduced to writing, by which a people agree to form one society. The next is a compact, by which the people in their social state agree to a Government over them. These two compacts may be considered as blended in the Constitution of the U.S.[28]

The idea of two compacts is indeed reflected in the Constitution: the Preamble reads that "We the people of the United States . . . do ordain and establish this Constitution for the United States of America." Thus the people created the Constitution, the Constitution did not create the people. When, then, did Americans become a "people"? Article VII specifies that the Constitution was "Done in Convention by the Unanimous Consent of the States present the Seventeenth Day of September in the Year of our Lord one thousand seven hundred and Eighty seven and the In-

---

26. Gary Rosen, *American Compact: James Madison and the Problem of Founding* (Lawrence: University Press of Kansas, 1999), 109.

27. Hunt, *Writings of James Madison*, 9:569–70; see Madison, Letter to Daniel Webster, March 15, 1833, ibid., 9:605.

28. Madison, Letter to N. P. Trist, February 15, 1830, ibid., 9:355.

dependence of the United States of America the Twelfth." Thus the independence of the United States is fixed on the date of the Declaration. The Declaration refers to Americans as "one people" and as "the good People," and it denominates "the people" as the ultimate authority for independence. Thus, it is clear that the people who established and ordained the Constitution were the same people who dissolved "all Allegiance to the British Crown." And since the Declaration specifies that the only legitimate basis for citizenship is "the consent of the governed," the doctrine of social compact, as we have already argued, is thus clearly intrinsic to the principles of the Declaration.

Madison continues his argument in "Sovereignty" by addressing the question of how the just powers of government should be administered. Unanimity is required to establish civil society, but majority rule must be the practical substitute for unanimity in the operation of government. Once the ends of government have been established by unanimous consent, it is scarcely to be expected that there will be unanimous agreement with respect to the best means to accomplish those ends: "as the objects in view could not be attained, if every measure conducive to them required the consent of every member of the society, the theory further supposes, either that it was the part of the original compact, that the will of the majority was to be deemed the will of the whole, or that this was a law of nature, resulting from the nature of political society itself." Madison, however, is not overly concerned with resolving this particular issue. "Whatever be the hypothesis of the origin of the *lex majoris partis*," he continues,

> it is evident that it operates as a plenary substitute of the will of the majority of the society for the will of the whole society; and that the sovereignty of the society as vested in & exercisable by the majority, may do anything that could be *rightfully* done by the unanimous concurrence of the members; the reserved rights of individuals (of conscience for example) in becoming parties to the original compact being beyond the legitimate reach of sovereignty, wherever vested or however viewed.[29]

Majority rule serves as a complete and "plenary substitute" for the will of society as a whole, but it can only do what can be "*rightfully* done by . . . unanimous concurrence." Thus majority rule is limited—it can only authorize what can be rightfully (or justly) done by unanimous consent. We note here that even unanimous consent is limited by the fact that it too must be rightful and just.

What forms the limit to unanimous consent? The idea that unanimous consent is the rightful origin of civil society is a precept of the law of nature and reason. "The only way," Locke says,

> whereby any one devests himself of his Natural Liberty, and *puts on the bonds of Civil Society* is by agreeing with other Men to joyn and unite into a Community, for their comfortable, safe, and peaceable living one amongst another, in a secure Enjoyment of

---

29. James Madison, "On Sovereignty," in *Writings of James Madison*, 9:570–71.

their Properties, and a greater Security against any that are not of it. This any number of Men may do, because it injures not the Freedom of the rest; they are left as they were in the Liberty of the State of Nature. When any number of Men have so *consented to make one Community* or Government, they are thereby presently incorporated, and make *one Body Politick*, wherein the *Majority* have a Right to act and conclude the rest (II.95).

We remember that the state of nature was a "*State of perfect Equality*, where naturally there is no superiority or jurisdiction of one, over another." The inescapable conclusion was that every individual therefore had the right by nature to enforce the law of nature. This multiplicity of individual wills in the execution of the law of nature inevitably resulted in many "inconveniences"—indeed a state of war—that eventuated in the use of force without right. In consenting to form civil society, each individual agrees not indeed to give up the natural rights he possessed in the state of nature but "to quit every one his Executive Power of the Law of Nature, and to resign it to the publick." "There and there only," Locke concluded, "is a *Political, or Civil Society*." Thus the multiplicity of individual wills that was the manifold cause of the many inconveniences that drove men into civil society is now exercised by the single will of the newly formed community, and that single will acts for the common good. The law of nature required unanimous consent to form civil society, but another requirement of the law of nature was that rule must be for the benefit of the ruled. The law of nature, as we have already learned, is both an injunction of reason (II.6) and "the Will of God" (II.135), and its obligations are binding in the state of nature so that "no Humane Sanction can be good or valid against it" (II.135). It would be unreasonable for any individual to forfeit his executive power to enforce the law of nature by consenting to rule if he did not benefit by it, or if there were no prospect of improving his condition. Early in the *Second Treatise*, Locke stated that the purpose or end of the law of nature was "the Peace and *Preservation of all Mankind*" (II.7). Thus unanimous consent to a civil society organized for the purposes of war or imperial aggrandizement would not be authorized by the law of nature. A gang of robbers or of pirates might be formed by unanimous consent, but its purposes would not be just or rightful under the precepts of natural law. Thus it is clear that the law of nature prescribes standards for unanimous consent. This is precisely what Madison had in mind when he said that majority rule can do only what unanimous consent can rightly or justly do. Unanimous consent is the rightful ground of civil society only to the extent that it is authorized by the "Laws of Nature and of Nature's God," and the same holds true of its plenary substitute, majority rule.

For Locke, once civil or political society is formed by unanimous consent, the next step is to choose a form of government that "has no other end but the preservation of Property" (II.94). Locke, of course, understands "property" in a comprehensive sense to include "Lives, Liberties and Estates" (II.123). Once distinct civil societies are established, the focus of the law of nature is no longer on the "preservation of all

mankind" but on the natural rights of individuals in particular civil societies constituted by social compact. As we have seen, the executive power of the law of nature
that was possessed by every individual in the state of nature is resigned to civil society
to be exercised by a single executive will. In the first instance, this executive will is
placed in the legislative, whether it is composed of one, a few, or many and whether
is it permanently in session or only for designated intervals. Establishing a form of
government therefore consists principally in establishing the legislative power: "the
Constitution of the Legislative [is] the original and supream act of the Society, antecedent to all positive Laws . . . and depending wholly on the People" (II.157) and is
accomplished by majority rule, which "passes for the act of the whole, and of course
determines, as having by the Law of Nature and Reason, the power of the whole"
(II.96). Being the constitutive act of government, the legislative is, Locke avers, the
"the Soul that gives Form, Life and Unity to the Commonwealth" (II.212).

There are, of course, natural law restraints on what powers can be vested in the
legislature by the majority. As a general matter Locke notes that "the Obligations of
the Law of Nature, cease not in Society but only in many Cases are drawn closer, and
have by Humane Laws known Penalties annexed to them, to inforce their observation. Thus the Law of Nature stands as an Eternal Rule to all Men, *Legislators* as well
as others" (II.135). Most important, the legislature must, as "Supream Authority,"
operate by "*promulgated standing Laws, and known Authoris'd Judges*." The natural
law must be enforced by positive law because the natural law, being unwritten, can
be misconstrued and misapplied by interested parties when there are no established
judges or promulgated positive laws. Thus the rule of law is the specific remedy
for the "Inconveniencies which disorder Men's Properties in the state of Nature"
(II.136). "Absolute, Arbitrary Power, or Governing without *settled standing Laws*,"
Locke almost needlessly adds,

> can neither of them consist with the ends of Society and Government, which Men
> would not quit the freedom of the state of Nature for, and tie themselves up under,
> were it not to preserve their Lives, Liberties and Fortunes; and by the *stated Rules* of
> Right and Property to secure their Peace and Quiet. It cannot be supposed that they
> should intend, had they a power so to do, to give to any one, or more, an *absolute Ar-
> bitrary Power* over their Persons and Estates, and put a force into the Magistrates hand
> to execute his unlimited Will arbitrarily upon them: This were to put themselves into
> a worse condition than the state of Nature, wherein they had a Liberty to defend their
> Right against the Injuries of others, and were upon equal terms of force to maintain
> it, whether invaded by a single Man, or many in Combination. Whereas by supposing
> they have given up themselves to the *absolute Arbitrary Power* and will of a Legislator,
> they have disarmed themselves, and armed him, to make a prey of them when he
> pleases (II.137).

Arbitrary government is the exercise of force without right that is, of course,
contrary to the law of nature—it is, in fact, the definition of the state of war (II.19;

II.186). Absolute or arbitrary government thus cannot fulfill the first requirement of civil society, which "has no other *end*, but the *Peace, Safety*, and *public good* of the People" (II.131). What immediately strikes our attention here, however, is that Locke asserts, once again, that the state of nature is preferable to absolute government. At least in the state of nature individuals have a chance of defending themselves, whereas under absolute government they have no chance against the combined forces of government arrayed against them. This idea that absolute government is worse than the greatest "inconveniences" of the state of nature is crucial to Locke's theory of civil government, and it is key to understanding the right of revolution in the *Second Treatise* as well as in the Declaration of Independence. It is important to note that both Locke and the Declaration stand in stark contrast to Hobbes on this issue.[30]

From the point of view of the Declaration, natural law limits run to more than just the prohibition of absolute governments but also to all non-republican forms of government. As we saw in chapter 1, the argument of the Declaration contemplates a regime that solicits the active renewal of consent through regularly scheduled elections, where elections serve as a substitute for the right of revolution. These are the kinds of natural law limits that Madison had in mind in his "Sovereignty" essay when he stated that unanimous consent must be "rightful" and that majority rule as a "plenary substitute" for unanimous consent must also be "rightful." Republican government has as its principal end the "safety and happiness" of the people, which includes the protection of the natural rights to life, liberty, and the pursuit of happiness. Neither unanimous consent nor majority rule, both authorized by the law of nature, can justly or rightly abridge those ends for which civil society and republican government are instituted. Madison advances a kind of typology of regimes: the best regime would be one in which there was unanimous consent for what was just and right. But we know from experience that this regime would exist only in the utopian speculations of those "theoretic politicians" he excoriated in the *Federalist* (10:81). Next would be majority rule authorizing what is right and just; this is, of course, the realistic goal of constitutional government where the majority is rendered capable of ruling in the interest of the whole of society. Constitutional government, including the extended republic with a multiplicity of competing interests and separation of powers, is calculated to prevent majority faction, thus making it possible to protect the rights of the minority through the rule of law. Any form of minority rule, even to the extent that it proved just and right and derived from the consent of the governed, would not be properly a "republican form" required by the principles of the Declaration. Minority rule, however just it might appear at first, could not provide adequate safeguards against future corruption without the active participation of the people. Without regularly scheduled elections that would serve as the periodic renewal of the people's consent, the only check on government would be a recourse to first

---

30. See Edward J. Erler, "Aristotle, Locke, and the American Founding," *Interpretation* 40, no. 3 (Winter 2014): 362–63.

principles, the right and the duty to "alter or to abolish" government that becomes destructive of the people's "Safety and Happiness." But the right of revolution is an ineffective weapon against government abuse of power because it will be used reluctantly, as people are "more disposed to suffer" than to alter or abolish government "to which they are accustomed." The people are also acutely aware that the outcome of any attempt to alter or abolish government will always be unpredictable. Republican government, with well-designed constitutional devices to serve the common good and regularly scheduled elections governed by an active politics of public opinion, is the proper substitute for a resort to first principles. In the American scheme, elections must always be viewed as a constitutional substitute for revolution. Elections serve as a constant reminder that the sovereign right of the people to judge remains the epitome of republican government.

THE CRITICISM OF SOCIAL COMPACT

Professor Michael Zuckert is a severe critic of the social compact origins of the American founding. It is, he alleges, a wholly modern doctrine that would have been rejected by Aristotle. Social compact is a product of human art or invention; in fact, it is a depreciation of nature as a standard of politics. "Well before the American founding," he remarks, "Aristotle firmly asserted what the social contract theory appeared to deny—that political life is natural and that human beings are naturally political beings. Even more to the point, he spoke explicitly of a contractually based polity as a grossly deficient political association. Aristotle, then, is an important authority against social contract thinking and thus apparently against the American Founding."[31] And in a slightly different context, he asserts,

> If political society were a natural growth, as Aristotle had it, then the political community itself would have a natural status supervenient over, or at least rival to, the individual and his or her rights; moreover, political life under the Aristotelian conception serves a natural end that comes into sight only in the fully developed polity. Even if government in some sense naturally emerges, according to the doctrine of the Declaration its "just powers" derive only from rational consent of the governed—that is, consent to rule in the service of rights-securing. Only a rational making, not a natural growth, can produce a just or proper government. Government must therefore be a human artifice.[32]

I have already shown in chapter 1 the mistake of identifying the purpose of the Declaration as the mere protection of private rights. But more important for the purpose here is to determine what Aristotle meant when he said that the *polis* exists

---

31. Michael P. Zuckert, *Launching Liberalism: On Lockean Political Philosophy* (Lawrence: University Press of Kansas, 2002), 235–36.

32. Michael P. Zuckert, *Natural Rights and the New Republicanism* (Princeton, NJ: Princeton University Press, 1994), 13, 17, 53, 55.

by nature. It does not result, as our commentator seems to believe, from a "natural growth." Rather, for Aristotle, the *polis* exists by nature because, while it is last in the order of time, it is first in the order of final causality. All associations—male and female, the family, the tribe, the village—are incomplete, and their incompleteness points to the *polis* as a final cause. And the final cause is nature. The *polis* is not the result of a "natural growth";[33] rather, it had to be "constituted" (*sustesas*) by human art, and the one who first "constituted" the *polis*, Aristotle says, is the cause of the "greatest of goods."[34] And of course we also learn from Aristotle that art is always an imitation of nature.[35] For Aristotle, the *polis* exists by nature but it needs human art to come into existence—it does not "grow" spontaneously from nature; it requires a founder.

Aristotle's *polis* thus seems to be no less the result of artifice than social compact. I am aware, of course, that, as ordinarily understood, the idea of social compact treats the individual as prior to civil society and not in need of civil society for his completion or perfection. Human beings are not drawn to civil society by nature but are compelled to form societies by the harshness of nature. Nature—the state of nature—is something to be avoided; it is not a standard for political life because man has no *telos* by nature. From this point of view of social compact, human beings are asocial or apolitical by nature, possessing rights by nature but having no duties or obligations by nature. Obligations are derivative from rights and are merely the means to the security of rights—rights are prior to duties. This view of social compact was given great weight by the interpretation of Leo Strauss. But Strauss also made this remarkable observation about Hobbes's use of social compact: "He uses that a-political view for a political purpose. He gives that a-political view a political meaning."[36]

Hobbes—and this would be true of Locke as well—faced an entirely different theological-political predicament than the one faced by Aristotle or the classical political philosophers. With the advent of Christianity, the question of political obligation and political authority assumed an entirely new dimension—one that could not have been anticipated by classical political philosophers. In the classical world, the laws of particular cities were always supported by their gods. Obedience to the gods and obedience to the laws were one and the same. As soon as there was a universal God for all cities, however, political obligation to particular cities became problematic. In the Christian world, conflicts between obligations to God and obligations to civil authority became inevitable, and in cases of conflict, the first obligation of Christians was to God or ecclesiastical authority. This reveals the apolitical character of Christianity. As the apostle Paul wrote to the Philippians, "our

33. See Leo Strauss, *Natural Right and History* (Chicago: University of Chicago Press, 1953), 132, 314; see also Leo Strauss, Letter to Karl Lowith, August 20, 1946, "Correspondence Concerning Modernity," *Independent Journal of Philosophy* 4 (1983): 112–13.
34. Aristotle, *Politics*, 1253a30–32.
35. Aristotle, *Physics*, 199a8–20.
36. Strauss, *Natural Right and History*, 169.

government [*politeuma*] is in heaven."[37] The universalism of Christianity, of course, makes an appeal to particular gods as the ground or foundation of the laws of a particular regime impossible. Some ground for political obligation independent of Christian theology had to be found if political life was to be free from the political strife engendered by the theological disputes that arose within Christianity. It was in this sense that the doctrine of the state of nature served an essential political purpose in the theological-political predicament that confronted Hobbes and Locke. Strauss wrote that "the modern efforts were partly based on the premise, which would have been acceptable to the classics . . . that natural law or natural right should be kept independent of theology and its controversies."[38]

It was in this spirit that Harry Jaffa wrote about the theological-political problem facing post-Christian political philosophers. In a path-breaking essay that was perhaps more revealing than anything Strauss wrote on the topic, Jaffa argued,

> Christianity had established within the souls of men the idea of a direct, personal, trans-political relationship between the individual and his God. But this relationship did not determine what the laws were to be, or the precise character of the obligation owed to those laws. The idea of the state of nature—the idea of a non-political state governed by moral law—corresponded to the relationship which every Christian had with every other Christian as he considered himself prior to and apart from his membership in a particular civil society. Just as every Christian was under the moral law, without being a member of civil society, so every human being was under the moral law of the state of nature, prior to entering a particular civil society by way of the social contract.[39]

Both Hobbes and Locke maintained that the obligations of the law of nature are binding in the state of nature, if not always *in foro externo*, then at least always *in foro interno*. Jaffa continued,

> Nowhere in the *Politics* does Aristotle confront the question of how the citizens will be persuaded to obey the laws, if there are no gods to whom those laws will be ascribed. Nowhere does he confront the question of how the authority of an unmediated universal nature will replace the authority of the gods. The state of nature and the social contract supply that mediation. Aristotle recognizes that particular polities will require particular institutions—that they will be the work of legislators acting in particular circumstances. But if these legislators can no longer crown their work by appealing to the authority of particular gods as the foundation of their laws, they must appeal directly to nature. They must have some way of translating the authority of a universal nature into the ground of particular laws. . . . The idea of the state of nature modifies and yet preserves the idea of man as by nature a political animal. Moreover the idea of the state of nature, by treating

37. Philippians 3:20.
38. Strauss, *Natural Right and History*, 164.
39. Harry V. Jaffa, "Equality, Liberty, Wisdom, Morality and Consent in the Idea of Political Freedom," in *The Rediscovery of America: Essays by Harry V. Jaffa on the New Birth of Politics*, ed. Edward J. Erler and Ken Masugi (Lanham, MD: Rowman & Littlefield, 2019), 44.

civil society as a voluntary association, lays a firmer foundation for the idea of the rule of law than in Aristotle's *Politics*.[40]

The idea that the state of nature in any way "preserves the idea of man as by nature a political animal" is a seeming paradox (if not heterodox) from a Straussian point of view. But it is almost certainly what Strauss had in mind when he said that Hobbes used the idea of the state of nature for political purposes. As Jaffa deftly points out, in Aristotle man's universal nature finds its perfection only in particular political communities—not in any trans-political world. For Christians, the highest aspirations are in the life to come, and political life in this world is merely a preparation for the next. As Paul admonished the Colossians, "mind the things above, not the things on earth."[41] From this point of view, man is by "nature" apolitical. Social compact reaffirms man's political nature by establishing particular political communities where this-worldly aspirations are the proper objects of political life. At the same time, man's universal nature is affirmed by the law of nature that is the standard and measure by which particular communities are judged. While reasserting man's political nature, social compact at the same time retains its compatibility with the City of God because natural law is understood to be "the Will of God" (II.135; II.142; II.195) or reason which is "the voice of God" (I.86; II.56).

In the beginning of the *Second Treatise*, we learn that the law of nature wills the "Peace and *Preservation of all Mankind*" and that while "every one as he is *bound to preserve himself*, and not to quit his Station willfully; so by the like reason when his own Preservation comes not in competition, ought he, as much as he can, *to preserve the rest of Mankind*" (II.6). Once civil society has been formed, however, this universal obligation to mankind shifts to obligations to preserve and protect fellow citizens who have pledged mutual security to one another (II.88; II.134; II.159).[42] The law of nature in Locke recognizes universal human nature as well as the necessity of politics—that is, the necessity of political community. In this regard, Locke recognizes that human beings are by nature political, that they could not exist or live well or securely without political life.

The Declaration of Independence, of course, rests firmly on Aristotelian grounds, recognizing the universal character of human nature in the principle that "all men are created equal" but also recognizing that human nature flourishes only in particular political communities by asserting that the "Laws of Nature and Nature's God" entitled America to become a "separate and equal" nation. Social compact also provides, as Jaffa notes, a "firmer foundation" for the rule of law because it provides a basis in reason and voluntary consent that it would not otherwise have possessed in Christianity, which could only offer passive obedience as justification for adher-

---

40. Jaffa, "Equality, Liberty, Wisdom, Morality," 45.
41. Colossians 3:2.
42. Ross J. Corbett, *The Lockean Commonwealth* (Albany: State University of New York Press, 2009), 22.

ence to the laws. Furthermore, the direct appeal to nature—now unmediated by theological authority—provides the ground for the separation of church and state that, in the works of Locke and the American founding, supplies the indispensable ground for constitutional government. Had Aristotle been confronted with the same theological-political problem that challenged Locke, it is not impossible to imagine that he might have agreed that social compact was the prudential solution called for by natural right even though he denied in the *Politics* (1280a34–1280b12) that compact was an adequate basis for political life.

NATURAL RIGHT AND EQUALITY

It is true that the central principle of the social compact doctrine—that "all men are created equal"—is not classic natural right. Classic natural right was inegalitarian; wisdom, not consent, was the title to rule. The few wise had by nature the right to rule the many who were not wise. But in light of the theological-political problems that confronted political philosophy in the post-Christian era, it was obvious that equality was the only access to nature or natural right available to political philosophy. Egalitarian natural right, of course, had been recognized as a possible form of natural right by classical philosophers, but it was not the preferred form because it was a form of natural right where consent necessarily took precedence over wisdom. From a certain point of view, the requirement of consent is a fatal compromise with wisdom and establishes, as Strauss terms it, "a right of unwisdom, i.e., an irrational, if inevitable, right."[43] This would be, according to some commentators, a dilution of natural right that is characteristic of modernity, representing a repudiation of classic natural right. But according to Strauss, in Aristotelian natural right "there is no fundamental disproportion between natural right and the requirements of political society." In other words, "there is no essential need for the dilution of natural right." Aristotle, of course, could not deny that

> the tension between the requirements of philosophy and those of the city; he knows that the simply best regime belongs to an entirely different epoch than fully developed philosophy. But he implies that the intermediate stages of the process, while not absolutely consistent, are sufficiently consistent for all practical purposes . . . the justice which may be available in the cities appears to be perfect justice and unquestionably good; there is no need for the dilution of natural right. Aristotle says, then, simply that natural right is a part of political right.[44]

If it is true, as Aristotle remarked in the first book of the *Politics*, that man is by nature a political animal, then natural right—or at least its potential—is intrinsic to all political life. The manner in which it comes to light in any particular regime will

43. Strauss, *Natural Right and History*, 152.
44. Ibid., 156–57; 191.

depend upon actual political circumstances. Aristotle's *Nicomachean Ethics* contains
his only discussion of natural right, and it is brief. Aristotle does say emphatically,
however, that natural right is a part of political right. And while natural right everywhere has the same force or power, it is everywhere changeable; it will manifest itself
differently according to different political circumstances even though its validity does
not depend on opinion or positive law. Natural right does not in any way depend
on the regime, whereas conventional right, the other part of political right, is wholly
dependent upon the regime. Among the gods, Aristotle muses, natural right would
be unchangeable because the gods have no need of conventional right.[45] Political
right, therefore, is a combination of conventional and natural right. Conventional
right in the beginning, Aristotle says, is indifferent. It is necessary to choose one or
the other, but the choice itself is of little or no consequence until it has been established in positive law or custom.[46] Whether cars are driven on the right- or left-hand
side of the road is a matter of little consequence, but once it has been decided, it is,
of course, a matter of great consequence for traffic safety.

We remember that Hamilton in the first number of the *Federalist* remarked that
the unique challenge that faced America was "to decide the important question,
whether societies of men are really capable or not of establishing good government
from reflection and choice, or whether they are forever destined to depend for their
political constitutions on accident and force" (1:33). One might even speculate that
conventional right is the product of "accident and force" as opposed to "deliberation
and choice." Deliberation and choice, of course, brings to mind natural right because
it implies reason. But all deliberations concerning natural right must adapt to already
existing positive law and opinion, including religion. Political right, properly understood in the Aristotelian sense, will thus be a judicious mixture or combination of
natural right and conventional right, and the legislator will move as far in the direction of natural right as is possible under the circumstances. He will reinforce what
is sound in conventional right and move the regime in the direction of natural right
without harming or weakening what is beneficial in conventional right. This is the
essence of prudence or practical wisdom, the virtue that governs the sphere of politics
or the sphere of human things as such. This is surely the reason that Aristotle made
natural right a constituent part of political right.

Strauss disputed modernity's claim to have banished prudence from the sphere of
political life or that Machiavelli and his epigones had succeeded in destroying the
possibility of natural right.

We cannot reasonably expect that a fresh understanding of classical political philosophy
will supply us with recipes for today's use. For the relative success of modern political
philosophy has brought into being a kind of society wholly unknown to the classics, a

---

45. It requires only a slight stretch of imagination to recall here Madison's famous statement in *Federal-ist* 51 that "if men were angels, no government would be necessary" (51:319). What makes government necessary among human beings is the fallibility of reason (10:73).

46. Aristotle, *Nicomachean Ethics*, 1134b17–1135a15.

kind of society to which the classical principles as stated and elaborated by the classics are not immediately applicable. Only we living today can possibly find a solution to the problems of today. But an adequate understanding of the principles as elaborated by the classics may be the indispensable starting point for an adequate analysis, to be achieved by us, of present-day society in its peculiar character, and for the wise application, to be achieved by us, of these principles to our tasks.[47]

An analysis "to be achieved by us" and a "wise application, to be achieved by us" is a description of Aristotelian natural right—classical wisdom applied to different political circumstances, even circumstances that may not have been in the contemplation of the classics. The repetition of the phrase "to be achieved by us" is striking. Classical prudence is available "for us" and is applicable to our situation as it is more or less applicable to all political situations. Modernity has not altered this enduring legacy from classical political philosophy. Given the peculiarity of the theological-political predicament faced by the American founders, I say, equality was the only access to nature or natural right available to them. This meant, of course, that consent was the sole legitimate basis for the "just powers" of government. But, as already discussed, even on the basis of classical political philosophy (at least in its Aristotelian version), this did not entail a fatal "dilution" of natural right, nor did it enshrine a "right of unwisdom" over wisdom.

In regimes derived from the consent of the governed, it is the job of philosophical statesmanship to reconcile the requirements of wisdom and consent as much as possible through a politics of public opinion. This is the first task of constitutional government. No legislator, of course, ever works from a blank slate; he is always confronted by conditions that are difficult to reform and sometimes faces circumstances that are utterly intractable, as the issue of slavery proved to be. The founders of America inherited a world that was not of their own making, but they probably moved further and faster than any founders in history in the direction of reform; they were Aristotle's *phronimoi* (practically wise statesmen), who had learned from "the great and judicious Mr. Locke" that natural right was now to be transmitted to the world as the "Laws of Nature and of Nature's God."

Strauss writes that "according to the classics, the best way of meeting these two entirely different requirements—that for wisdom and that for consent or for freedom—would be that a wise legislator frame a code that the citizen body, duly persuaded, freely adopts. That code, which is, as it were the embodiment of wisdom, must be as little subject to alteration as possible; the rule of law is to take the place of the rule of men, however wise."[48] Strauss was certainly aware that this description of the classical solution is almost a description of the manner in which the American Constitution was framed and adopted, with one important difference: in the place of an "individual citizen of preeminent wisdom and approved integrity," Americans

---

47. Leo Strauss, *The City and Man* (Chicago: Rand McNally, 1964), 11.
48. Strauss, *Natural Right and History*, 141; see Leo Strauss, *What Is Political Philosophy?* (New York: Free Press, 1959), 83.

entrusted the framing of the organic law to a deliberative body, a "select body of citizens, from whose common deliberations more wisdom, as well as more safety," might be expected.[49] This deliberative body produced a Constitution, ratified by the consent of the people, that embodied the rule of law. At the same time, the framers were confident that the Constitution's design would ensure the selection into its constitutional offices of only those "whose patriotism and love of justice will be least likely to sacrifice it to temporary or partial considerations." An extensive republic of the kind contemplated by the new Constitution would be "most favorable to election of proper guardians of the public weal."[50] Yet, as prudent statesmen, the framers knew that experience had demonstrated the utility of "auxiliary precautions" in the event that patriotism and love of justice might waver or fail when it was needed most. These "auxiliary precautions"—the separation of powers—in which "ambition should be made to counteract ambition" could supply "the defect of better motives" when better motives needed support.[51] Thus from the point of view of classical natural right, the American founding reconciled wisdom and consent—natural right and political right—in probably the only way that it ever can be reconciled. Consent more or less sets the bounds to every regime (except for tyranny, of course, which, if we follow Aristotle, is not properly counted as a regime) but is the real sovereign in every free regime. It is the job of philosophical statesmen (*phronimoi*) in an age of equality to reconcile the requirements of wisdom and consent as much as possible through a politics of public opinion. This is the first task of constitutional government and constitutional statesmanship.

It is true that in *Natural Right and History*, Strauss, as we have already seen, portrays Locke as a radically modern thinker:

> Locke's teaching on property, and therewith his whole political philosophy, are revolutionary not only with regard to the biblical tradition but with regard to the philosophic tradition as well. Through the shift of emphasis from natural duties or obligations to natural rights, the individual, the ego, had become the center and origin of the moral world, since man—as distinguished from man's end—had become that center or origin.[52]

The American founders, of course, made Locke's "teaching on property" the foundation of constitutional government. What is more, protection for the natural right to property provided a common ground for rich and poor that was not available in the classical world. The idea of rights or natural rights, understood as claims or reservations against government, was unknown to classical political philosophy. Aristotle's mixed regime, a combination of oligarchy and democracy, was a regime in which the interests of the rich and poor served to check one another. There was no notion, however, that rich and poor would ever share a common interest. But the right to

---

49. *The Federalist*, 38:228, 229.
50. Ibid., 10:76.
51. Ibid., 51:319.
52. Strauss, *Natural Right and History*, 248.

property supplied such a common interest and could be supported equally by rich and poor. Thus the foundations for republican government anchored in the right of property might hold the prospect of avoiding the kinds of class antagonisms that plagued ancient regimes.

Aristotle had argued that a mixed regime with a large middle class would be the most stable because the middle class would be neither rich nor poor and would serve as a kind of buffer between the two antagonistic classes. A large middle class, of course, would have been a rarity in the ancient world simply because of widespread scarcity. The way of the world was a few wealthy and the many poor. But with a system of private property and the "emancipation of acquisition," all justified in the name of the common good (every private acquisition in a scheme of capital accumulation increases the store of goods available for public consumption), wealth could be produced at a rate hitherto unknown. This increase in abundance makes it possible to have large, middle-class democracies in which the protection of the right to property, considered the most comprehensive right, will be "the first object of government." Constitutional government understood as limited government and based on the rule of law all proceed from Locke's "teaching on property."

What is more, in constitutional government of the kind inspired by Locke and fully endorsed by the founders, justice could be more securely grounded in nature! As Strauss writes in *Liberalism Ancient and Modern*,

> It is a demand of justice that there should be a reasonable correspondence between the social hierarchy and the natural hierarchy. The lack of such a correspondence in the old scheme was defended by the fundamental fact of scarcity. With the increasing abundance it became increasingly possible to see and to admit the element of hypocrisy which had entered into the traditional notion of aristocracy; the existing aristocracies proved to be oligarchies, rather than aristocracies. In other words it became increasingly easy to argue from the premise that natural inequality has very little to do with social inequality, that practically or politically speaking one may safely assume that all men are by nature equal, that all men have the same natural rights, provided one uses this rule of thumb as the major premise for reaching the conclusion that everyone should be given the same opportunity as everyone else: natural inequality has its rightful place in the use, nonuse, or abuse of opportunity in the race as distinguished from at the start. Thus it became possible to abolish many injustices or at least many things which had become injustices.[53]

Thus the Lockean system, adopted and adapted by the founders, made it possible to improve on the ancient models from the point of view of distributive justice or natural right. In the world of Aristotle, aristocracies were in fact almost always thinly disguised oligarchies. Pseudo-aristocracy could now be replaced by genuine aristocracy because the increase in abundance that resulted from the "emancipation of acquisition" made possible a system of distributive justice based on "equal opportunity" where natural

---

53. Leo Strauss, *Liberalism Ancient and Modern* (New York: Basic Books, 1968), 21; Strauss, *Natural Right and History*, 148–50.

talents rather than class or caste would be the basis for advancement. Strauss quoted Jefferson's 1813 letter to John Adams with evident approval: "That form of government is the best, which provides the most effectually for a pure selection of [the] natural *aristoi* into offices of the government." Strauss comments that Jefferson's statement reflected classical political philosophy's answer to the best political order, the "claim to rule which is based on merit, on human excellence, on 'virtue.'"[54] The sentence preceding the one quoted by Strauss is no less remarkable: "the natural aristocracy," Jefferson wrote, "I consider as the most precious gift of nature, for the instruction, the trusts, and government of society. And indeed, it would have been inconsistent in creation to have formed man for the social state, and not to have provided virtue and wisdom enough to manage the concerns of the society."[55] The existence of the natural *aristoi* is thus proof for Jefferson that "creation" has designed man for the social or political state! Man is by nature a political animal, and the best regime by nature is aristocracy. And since it is evident that "virtue and talent" have been "by nature . . . scattered with equal hand through all its conditions," a system of equal opportunity allowing virtue and talent to rise from all classes would be most consistent with "natural right."[56]

Scarcity in the ancient world prevented the actualization of the best regime by nature; "emancipation of acquisitiveness" was the necessary precondition of actualizing a regime that could adopt equal opportunity as its principle of distributive justice. Thus the best regime of classical political philosophy became realizable only on the grounds of a radically transformed notion of the right to property and a scheme of constitutional government designed to protect the right to property. Even though the right to private property is wholly modern—and the "emancipation of acquisitiveness" *wholly alien* to classical political philosophy—it is impossible not to see, as Strauss did, the influence of Aristotelian natural right at work in the creation of the American regime, which, for the first time, held out the prospect that genuine aristocracy based on natural talents and abilities could replace the pseudo-aristocracies of birth and class that had dominated the past. Equality of opportunity—not the accident of birth—was to be the principle of distributive justice that would animate the American regime.

NATURAL LAW, THE RIGHTS OF CONSCIENCE, AND CONSTITUTIONAL GOVERNMENT

Leo Strauss commented that "once the idea of natural right has emerged and becomes a matter of course, it can easily be adjusted to the belief in the existence of

54. Leo Strauss, *What Is Political Philosophy? And Other Studies* (Glencoe, IL: Free Press, 1959), 86. Jefferson's sentence in the original letter to Adams is written in the form of a question. The fact that Strauss changed Jefferson's question to a declarative statement indicates that he adopted it as a statement of his own.
55. Thomas Jefferson, Letter to John Adams, October 12, 1813, in *Jefferson: Writings*, 1306.
56. Thomas Jefferson, "Autobiography," ibid., 32; see *Notes on the State of Virginia*, ibid., query xiv (near the end).

divinely revealed law."[57] It is apparent that Locke understood clearly the theological-political problem as it appeared within Christianity. To accommodate Christianity, as previously mentioned, natural right had to appear in the guise of universally valid natural law.[58] Locke also saw that the integrity of political life and constitutional government depended on separation of church and state. The obligations owed to religion should be separate from those owed to the state. This not only protected political life from the distractions of otherworldly concerns but also insulated religion from the corrupting influence of temporal affairs. Thus Locke argued in his *A Letter on Toleration* that

> the commonwealth seems to me to be a society of men constituted only for preserving and advancing their civil goods . . . and all the right and dominion of the civil power is bounded and confined solely to the care and advancement of these goods [viz., "life, liberty, bodily health and freedom from pain (indolency), and the possession of outward things, such as lands, money, furniture, and the like"]; and that it neither can nor ought in any way to be extended to the salvation of souls.[59]

Locke reasons that each individual is responsible to God for his own salvation and should determine for himself which means of achieving salvation is most pleasing to God. "It does not appear," Locke says,

> that God ever gave any such authority to one man over another as to compel other men to embrace his religion. Nor can any such power be vested in the magistrate by men, because no man can so far abandon the care of his own eternal salvation as to embrace under compulsion a worship or faith prescribed by someone else, be he prince or subject. For no man, even if he would, can believe at another's dictation. It is faith that gives force and efficacy to the true religion that brings salvation. For whatever profession you make, to whatever outward worship you conform, if you are not fully persuaded in your own mind that it is both true and well pleasing to God, far from being any furtherance, it is an obstacle to salvation.

The care of souls thus cannot belong to civil authority because its power consists wholly in compulsion, whereas the salvation of souls, the concern of religion,

---

57. Straus, *Natural Right and History*, 85.

58. See John Locke, *Questions Concerning the Law of Nature*, ed. and trans. Robert Horwitz, Jenny Strauss Clay, and Diskin Clay (Ithaca, NY: Cornell University Press, 1990): Question I: "Does there Exist a Rule of Conduct or Law of Nature? There does" (103). Locke translates the famous "natural right" passage from Aristotle's *Nicomachean Ethics* (1134b18) in this way: "this natural law is that law which has everywhere the same force," and he comments, "from which it is rightly inferred that there exists some law of nature, since there exists some law, which obtains everywhere." The translation should read, "Natural [right] has everywhere the same force [power]." The editors suggest that Locke may have misread or misremembered Aristotle's text. I advance it as a suspicion only that Locke neither misremembered nor misread the passage in question.

59. John Locke, *Epistola de Tolerantia*, ed. Raymond Klibansky, trans. J. W. Gough (Oxford: Clarendon Press, 1968), 67. See Thomas Jefferson, "Notes on Religion," in *Works of Thomas Jefferson*, ed. Ford, 2:264.

consists in "inward persuasion."[60] "Even God himself," Locke claims, "will not save men against their wills."[61]

It is obvious that "the toleration of those who hold different opinions on matters of religion is so agreeable to the Gospel and to reason that it seems monstrous for men to be blind in so clear a light."[62] We note here only in passing that the solution to the problem of conflicting obligations that arose in post-Christian times was solved by Locke on the basis of a separation of church and state and religious toleration. Hobbes, however, attempted to solve the same problem on the basis of the unity of church and state, a solution that the young Locke had considered in his unpublished "Two Tracts on Government" but rejected on the basis that it was utterly impracticable. Either solution holds out the prospect of resolving the problem of conflicting obligations, but only Locke's does so on the basis of free government.

Locke's *A Letter on Toleration* had tremendous influence on the American founders, most clearly reflected in Jefferson's "Bill for Establishing Religious Freedom," to say nothing of the American clergy. Jefferson's "Bill for Establishing Religious Freedom" is perhaps the most important document of the founding era next to the Declaration of Independence. Jefferson argued that religious liberty and political liberty shared the same metaphysical ground in the indisputable fact "that Almighty God hath created the mind free, *and manifested his supreme will that free it shall remain by making it altogether insusceptible of restraint.*"[63] Professor Harry Jaffa made the surprising remark that "the most fundamental of the assumptions underlying the American political tradition is not set forth in the Declaration of Independence." Rather, it was to be found in Jefferson's "magisterial exordium" in the Virginia Statute of Religious Liberty.[64]

All attempts to influence the mind by "temporal punishments, or burthens, or by civil incapacitations," Jefferson argues, "tend only to beget habits of hypocrisy and

---

60. Locke, *Epistola de Tolerantia*, 69.
61. Ibid., 91.
62. Ibid., 65.
63. "A Bill for Establishing Religious Freedom," in *Jefferson: Writings*, 346. Peterson reports that Jefferson wrote the first draft of the bill sometime in 1777 but did not submit it to the Virginia House of Delegates until 1779, when it was debated but not adopted. It was again submitted by Madison in 1785 and subsequently adopted in January 1786 with the passages quoted above from the preamble (in italics) deleted. See "A Bill for Establishing Religious Freedom," in *The Portable Thomas Jefferson*, ed. Merrill D. Peterson (New York: Viking Press, 1975), 251, editor's note. Madison's "A Memorial and Remonstrance" was addressed to the Commonwealth of Virginia in support of the bill. In it he wrote that the religion

of every man must be left to the conviction and conscience of every man; and it is the right of every man to exercise it as these may dictate. This right is in its nature an unalienable right. It is unalienable, because the opinions of men, depending only on the evidence contemplated by their own minds cannot follow the dictates of other men: It is unalienable also, because what is here a right towards men, is a duty towards the Creator. It is the duty of every man to render to the Creator such homage and such only as he believes to be acceptable to him (*Papers of James Madison*, 8:299).

64. Harry V. Jaffa, *New Birth of Freedom: Abraham Lincoln and the Coming of the Civil War* (Lanham, MD: Rowman & Littlefield, 2004), 118–19.

meanness and are a departure from the plan of the holy author of our religion." It was certainly within the Almighty's power to propagate true religion by coercion, but he chose "*to extend it by its influence on reason alone.*" Thus it is simply an "impious presumption" for "legislators and rulers, civil as well as ecclesiastical, who, being themselves but fallible and uninspired men" to dictate "the faith of others, setting up their own opinions and modes of thinking as the only true and infallible." By endeavoring to impose such opinions on others they have "established and maintained false religions over the greatest part of the world and through all time."[65] True religion is thus, as Locke held, the religion of the Gospels, the religion in which individuals are free to exercise the rights of conscience in determining the manner in which the duty to God is fulfilled.

It is evident that God has also not used his omnipotence to impose government or political rule on human beings as those who advocated divine right monarchy and passive obedience claimed. Rather, the evidence for natural equality seems to indicate that human beings were left free by the Almighty to choose their form of government by "deliberation and choice," whereas all other social species seem to have had their government or rule imposed on them by instinct. Thus political liberty also resides in the fact that the human mind has been created free and "insusceptible of restraint." Any attempt to coerce the mind, by either religious authority or civil authority, is tyranny and contrary to the will of God. The proper mode of civil society is, therefore, "free argument and debate." Freedom of conscience and freedom of speech are the two essential pillars of constitutional government and require the constitutional separation of church and state, a separation that is essential for the protection of the integrity of both church and state.

Much has been made of Jefferson's argument that the truth will always prevail when there is free argument and debate. There is no question that free argument and debate is necessary for the production of truth for this is the ground of the Socratic dialectic without which there can be no ascent from opinion to truth. Jefferson was surely aware, however, that the truth would prevail only when there were competent judges to evaluate the results of the debate. The only truly competent judges, of course, would be philosophers, but, as Madison helpfully informed us, "a nation of philosophers is as little to be expected as the philosophical race of kings wished for by Plato" (*Federalist* 49:312). Politics exists in the world of opinion, and opinion is a kind of reflected truth. If political opinion cannot be sufficiently enlightened to support a robust self-interest tempered by considerations of the common good, then an experiment in self-government cannot succeed. The moderation informing opinions can only be the product of free political debate of a kind that will never reach dialectical perfection and that will never produce the unadorned truth pursued by philosophers, though it can be a kind of political truth that is sufficient for political life when it is based on a "philosophic cause," the self-evident truths of the Declaration of Independence. Jefferson knew as well as anyone that political life

---

65. Thomas Jefferson, "A Bill for Establishing Religious Freedom," in *Jefferson: Writings*, 346.

was bounded by opinion and limited what statesmen could accomplish, however enlightened they might happen to be and however much they indulged the rhetoric of the progress of enlightenment.

One curious feature of Jefferson's handiwork was contained in the last section of the Virginia bill. Acknowledging that the bill was merely a statutory act that could be repealed by "succeeding Assemblies, constituted with powers equal to our own, and that therefore to declare this act irrevocable would be of no effect in law," its drafters nevertheless asserted their freedom to declare "that the rights hereby asserted are of the natural rights of mankind, and that if any act shall be hereafter passed to repeal the present or to narrow its operation, such act will be an infringement of natural right."[66] Thus the statute recognizes the rights of conscience and free exercise as natural rights, the violation of which is a trespass against *natural right*. Both free exercise and the rights of conscience are intrinsic to social compact. Most important, however, we see that the metaphysical freedom of the human mind is the source of both religious liberty and political liberty as well as the ground of the separation of church and state.

Locke argued in *A Letter on Toleration* that civil society was not obliged to tolerate atheists or Catholics. Modern-day commentators excoriate Locke for giving way to a seventeenth-century prejudice against Catholics while he was willing to extend tolerance to all sects within Christianity and "to speak the truth, and as becomes one man to another, neither Pagan nor Mahometan nor Jew should be excluded from the commonwealth because of his religion."[67] Those who believe that Locke was merely indulging a prejudice, of course, are woefully ignorant of the political situation that Locke faced and the theological-political problem presented by Catholicism. "What is the effect," Locke asks, "of asserting that kings excommunicated forfeit their kingdoms, if not that they arrogate to themselves the power of exposing kings, since they claim the exclusive right of excommunication for their hierarchy?"[68] Thus, Locke concludes, "that church can have no right to be tolerated by the magistrate which is so constituted that all who enter it *ipso facto* pass into the allegiance and service of another prince. For on these terms the magistrate would make room for a foreign jurisdiction in his own territory and cities, and allow his own people to be enlisted as soldiers against his own government."[69] Excommunication was considered a license for regicide among Catholics and was used as a powerful weapon in the

---

66. Ibid., 348.

67. Locke, *Epistola de Tolerantia*, 145.

68. Ibid., 133.

69. Ibid. Klibansky rightly cites Aquinas, *Summa Theologica*, IIa IIae, question 12 "Of Apostasy," article 2 "Whether a Prince Forfeits His Dominion over His Subjects, on Account of Apostasy from the Faith, So That They No Longer Owe Him Allegiance?" "Consequently, as soon as sentence of excommunication is passed on a man on account of apostasy from the faith, his subjects are *ipso facto* absolved from his authority and from the oath of allegiance whereby they were bound to him." See Edward Erler, "From Subjects to Citizens: The Social Compact Origins of American Citizenship," in *The American Founding and the Social Compact*, ed. Ronald J. Pestritto and Thomas G. West (Lanham, MD: Lexington Books, 2003), 171.

battle between church and crown. Locke's objection was political; the doctrine of the Catholic Church would not allow it to refrain from secular affairs.

A most illuminating commentary of sorts on Locke's *Letter* was promulgated in 1772 by the Freeholders and Inhabitants of the Town of Boston. It was published as a pamphlet and became known as the Boston Pamphlet. It was written by a committee but has been ascribed largely to the pen of Samuel Adams, and it mainly follows the arguments of Locke, both on religious liberty and on the origins of government (citing the *Letter* as well as the *Second Treatise*). The pamphlet begins with a statement that the rightful origin of society is "voluntary Consent" that forms "an equitable *original compact*."[70] After noting that all positive and civil laws should conform as nearly as possible to the law of natural reason and equity, the pamphlet proclaims that "neither Reason requires, nor Religion permits the contrary, every Man living in or out of a State of civil Society, has a Right peaceably and quietly to worship God, according to the Dictates of his Conscience." The pamphlet affirms that "Mr. Lock has asserted, and proved beyond the Possibility of Contradiction on any solid Ground" that the "Spirit of Toleration, in the fullest Extent consistent with the Being of Civil Society, 'is the chief characteristical Mark of the true Church.'" But that toleration extends only to sects "whose Doctrines are not subversive of the civil Government under which they live." And here the pamphlet addresses the issue of the tolerance of Catholics, agreeing with Locke that "the only Sects which . . . ought to be . . . excluded from such Toleration, are those who teach Doctrines subversive of the civil Government under which they live." The assertion of the power of excommunication against apostates creates "that Solecism in Politicks, *Imperium in Imperio*, leading directly to the worst Anarchy and Confusion, civil Discord, War and Bloodshed."[71] Catholic doctrine thus claims a theological ground for asserting secular political power. For the committee of Boston, this was an admixture of church and state that not only endangered religious liberty but also made limited government impossible. Limited government, as all seem to admit, is predicated on the separation of church and state.

But the Catholic issue, if it can be called that, although very much alive in Locke's time, was receding in America, although that was hardly in evidence in the Boston Pamphlet. But even then, however much the Anglican establishment might have threatened Massachusetts liberties, there was no prospect that the pope would place a crown on the head of an American monarch or ever have occasion to declare an American executive apostate. Once the Whig doctrine of *Vox Populi Vox Dei* had replaced divine right, the mediation of the pope was replaced by the "consent of the governed," which was now considered the authentic voice of God. This was undoubtedly the reason that both Jefferson and Madison in their important works on religion did not exclude Catholics from the umbrella of religious tolerance. Politically, the Church was no longer a danger.

---

70. *The Votes and Proceedings of the Freeholders and Other Inhabitants of the Town of Boston, in Town Meeting Assembled, According to Law*, in *The American Revolution: Writings from the Pamphlet Debate*, ed. Gordon S. Wood (New York: Library of America, 2015), 1:764.

71. Wood, *The American Revolution*, 765. The argument "imperium in imperio" is used by Hamilton against the Articles of Confederation in the *Federalist* (15:103). For the use of "solecism," see 20:134.

Christianity, and Catholicism in particular, had been tamed and civilized; the wars of religion waged within Christianity, while still a present memory, might now for the first time begin to recede into the past, but only because they remained a present memory.

Jefferson in his first inaugural spoke of America

> enlightened by a benign religion, professed, indeed, and practiced in various forms, yet all of them inculcating honesty, truth, temperance, gratitude, and the love of man, acknowledging and adoring an overruling Providence, which by all its dispensations proves that it delights in the happiness of man here and his greater happiness hereafter—with all these blessings, what more is necessary to make us a happy and a prosperous people?[72]

This is the "true" religion of Locke's *Letter on Toleration* and Jefferson's "Statute on Religious Liberty," to say almost nothing of Madison's "Memorial and Remonstrance." The "safety and happiness" that formed the ends of the American regime depended upon the extent to which religion had become or had been rendered "benign." But Jefferson reminded the nation that the benign religion that graced America's fortunes would retain its vigor only as long as it retained in its present consciousness the memory of "that religious intolerance under which mankind so long bled and suffered."[73] The American Revolution succeeded because it was presented, as if by some providential fate, with the most favorable circumstances for the resolution of the theological-political problem. The fate of constitutional government depends upon the preservation of that resolution.

The Boston Pamphlet doesn't advocate the proscription of atheists, a prominent feature of Locke's *Letter*: "Those who deny the existence of the Deity are not to be tolerated at all," Locke says, because "promises, covenants, and oaths, which are the bonds of human society, can have no hold upon or sanctity of an atheist; for the taking away of God, even only in thought, dissolves all." An atheist who "undermines and destroys all religion cannot in the name of religion claim the privilege of toleration for himself."[74] It is interesting to note that all of Locke's reasons for not tolerating atheism are political. The contracts, promises, and oaths that are "the bonds of human society" hold no "sanctity" in civil society. The atheist, therefore, cannot be a good citizen because he cannot fulfill his civic engagements in a manner that satisfies his fellow citizens.[75] Contract is the basis of society—it is sacred. But the word of an atheist is not his bond; it inspires no trust. Perhaps most important, the atheist cannot claim "the privilege of toleration." Thus he cannot, as a good citizen, carry a privilege that all citizens must have and that is essential to limited government: the assertion of religious liberty against the overreach of government.

---

72. *Jefferson: Writings*, 494.
73. Ibid., 493.
74. Locke, *Epistola de Tolerantia*, 135.
75. See Christopher Nadon, "Absolutism and the Separation of Church and State in Locke's *Letter Concerning Toleration*," *Perspectives on Political Science* 35, no. 2 (Spring 2006): 99.

Jefferson was such an inveterate hater of religious tyranny that he wanted to ensure freedom even for atheists, although he did suggest, in *Notes on the State of Virginia*, that it was the duty of every citizen to bring the atheist or the polytheist[76] to "true religion" by "reason and free inquiry." The reason, again, was that "our rulers can have authority over such natural rights only as we have submitted to them. The rights of conscience we never submitted, we could not submit. We are answerable for them to our God."[77] The duty of the citizen to persuade atheists was an important one because only a few pages later, in reference to slavery, Jefferson poses this poignant question: "And can the liberties of a nation be thought secure when we have removed their only firm basis, a conviction in the minds of the people that these liberties are of the gift of God? That they are not to be violated but with his wrath? Indeed I tremble for my country when I reflect that God is just: that his justice cannot sleep for ever."[78] These lines, which serve as both a prediction of civil war and inspiration for Lincoln's second inaugural, remind us that atheists cannot believe that liberties come from the hand of God. Atheists must be persuaded to "true religion" if they are to be authentic citizens of a republic, but the only means compatible with free society is "free argument and debate."[79] The atheist can be persuaded that "these liberties" are the gift of "the Laws of Nature and of Nature's God," that the doctrine of natural rights is supported by both reason and revelation. Jefferson doesn't advocate exclusion of atheists; if their word is not bond, if they refuse to solemnize their pledges with an oath to God, or if their testimony cannot be trusted because they will not swear, then the obloquy rests on them, and their pledges and testimony will be rejected. Atheists are not to be excluded, and government cannot force them or instruct them. That is the job of private citizens and churches acting as private associations.[80]

The framers were acutely aware that constitutional government would be impossible without free exercise of religion and the separation of church and state. Sectarian disputes are politically irresolvable and thus must be excluded from politics insofar as possible. Constitutional government requires majority rule and minority acquiescence in the decisions of the majority. At the same time, the majority must rule in a manner consistent with the rights of the minority. If religious questions are a part of ordinary politics, the minority will never be able to acquiesce in the decisions of the majority, for no religious minority could, in good faith, ever abandon or compromise the rights of conscience that it did not and could not submit to majority rule. The imposition of religious decisions on the minority by force under the guise of majority rule would be tyranny. The rights of conscience reserve questions of salvation—or more generally the question of what perfects and completes human life—to the individual, not

---

76. The polytheist because only the monotheist is ultimately capable of theological reason. See the remark below on Plato's *Euthyphro*.

77. *Jefferson: Writings*, 285–87, query xvii. See *Works of Thomas Jefferson*, ed. Ford, "Notes on Religion," 267–68.

78. Ibid., 289, query xviii.

79. See Thomas Jefferson, Letter to Thomas Law, June 13, 1814, in *The Portable Jefferson*, 540–41, for a defense of the morality of atheists.

80. See appendix.

to the political community or to majority rule. Separation of church and state—the reservation of the rights of conscience from government—is "modernity's" solution to the theological-political problem posed by Christianity.

It cannot be surprising that Locke treats almost exclusively of rights in *Two Treatises of Government*, in contrast to *An Essay Concerning Human Understanding*, where he gives a comprehensive account of morality based on law and duty.[81] It is true, as Professor Pangle points out, that "we do not find the words 'moral,' 'morality,' 'moral virtue,' or 'ethics' ever mentioned in *Two Treatises of Government*."[82] We have been prepared for this observation by Locke's argument for the separation of church and state. Matters of moral virtue, those goods of the soul, belong to the church; matters of the body belong to the civil authority. It has been pointed out often enough that Locke's political philosophy makes a "radical separation of private and public" and mounts a thoroughgoing "defense of private from public."[83] This is widely understood to be an essential departure from classical political philosophy where the public sphere was elevated over the private, and where duties or obligations, not rights, took precedence. But, of course, free exercise of religion requires something like the right to privacy. The "rights of conscience," as Locke, Jefferson, Madison, the American clergy, and the founding generation agreed, cannot be submitted to government. In fact, Madison argued, as if encapsulating the Lockean theme of property, "Conscience is the most sacred of all property; other property depending in part on positive law, the exercise of that, being a natural and unalienable right."[84] The theological-political problem was obviously different in the classical world where the issue of free exercise could never arise, nor were there incompatible obligations arising from a conflict between the laws and obedience to the gods. Obedience to the gods was a matter of law, never one of conscience. The theological-political problem of Locke's time was obviously different from the one that confronted Plato or Aristotle. In the second book of Plato's *Republic*, the "theology" of Plato's Socrates transformed the Homeric gods into the Ideas, and on the day he answered the indictment brought against him by Meletus, Socrates made the claim in his dialogue with Euthyphro that the ineluctable choice was between fighting gods and the Ideas. Both Plato and Locke, under entirely different circumstances, endeavored to bring reason to the theological-political calculus.[85] Would it be entirely farfetched to suggest that if Plato had found himself in Locke's circumstances, he might have written, perhaps not *A Letter on Toleration*, but *Reasonableness of Christianity*—or something resembling it—or that Aristotle might have written a *Second Treatise* as a prudential application of natural right to the political circumstances of the late seventeenth century?

---

81. Steven Forde, *Locke, Science, and Politics* (Cambridge: Cambridge University Press, 2013), 126.

82. Thomas L. Pangle, *The Spirit of Modern Republicanism* (Chicago: University of Chicago Press, 1988), 204.

83. Nathan Tarcov, *Locke's Education for Liberty* (Chicago: University of Chicago Press, 1983), 3.

84. *Papers of James Madison*, 14:266; Hunt, ed., *Writings of James Madison*, 9:571. Madison made the same point in his essay on sovereignty.

85. See John Locke, *The Reasonableness of Christianity*, ed. John C. Higgins-Biddle (Oxford: Clarendon Press, 1999), 144.

3

Property and the
Pursuit of Happiness

"The union that has accompanied the declaration will gladden the heart of every true friend to human liberty, and when we have secured this, by a wise and just confederation, the happiness of America will be secured, at least so long as it continues virtuous, and when we cease to be virtuous we shall not deserve to be happy."

—Richard Henry Lee, July 29, 1776[1]

The fact that the Declaration uses the phrase "pursuit of happiness" where "right to property" might have been expected has generated much commentary. Pauline Maier reports, however, that "references to happiness as a political goal are everywhere in American political writings" during the Revolutionary era.[2] No doubt the immediate source of the phrase was George Mason's draft of Virginia's Declaration of Rights, which was adopted in June of 1776. The Virginia document included both property and the pursuit of happiness when it proclaimed,

That all men are by nature equally free and independent, and have certain inherent rights of which, when they enter into a state of society, they cannot by any compact deprive or divest their posterity; namely, the enjoyment of life and liberty, with the means of acquiring and possessing property, and pursuing and obtaining happiness and safety.

Jefferson shortened the phrase "pursuing and obtaining happiness and safety" to the more euphonious "pursuit of happiness," thus discarding the awkward "the means

---

1. Richard Henry Lee, Letter to Sam Adams, July 29, 1776, in *The Letters of Richard Henry Lee*, ed. James C. Ballagh (New York: Macmillan, 1911), I:211. Lee introduced the Declaration of Independence in the Continental Congress.

2. Pauline Maier, *American Scripture: Making the Declaration of Independence* (New York: Alfred A. Knopf, 1997), 134.

of acquiring and possessing property." Did this mean that he did not consider property a natural right? Or did he simply judge the right to property to be included in the more expansive natural right to the pursuit of happiness? Maier concluded that "Jefferson perhaps sacrificed clarity of meaning for grace of language. In general, however, his rewriting of Mason produced a more memorable statement of the same content. Less was more."[3]

Other commentators, however, saw crucial differences. Vernon L. Parrington, the Progressive historian writing in the 1920s, argued that Jefferson's change represented a significant break with Locke's doctrine of property:

> Samuel Adams and other followers of Locke had been content with the classical enumeration of life, liberty, and property, but in Jefferson's hands the English doctrine was given a revolutionary shift. The substitution of "pursuit of happiness" for "property" marks a complete break with the Whiggish doctrine of property rights that Locke had bequeathed to the English middle class and the substitution of a broader sociological conception. It was this substitution that gave to the document the note of idealism that was to make its appeal so perennially human and vital. The words were far more than a political gesture to draw popular support; they were an embodiment of Jefferson's deepest convictions, and his life thenceforward was given over to the work of providing for the enjoyment of those inalienable rights. If the fact that he set the pursuit of happiness above abstract property rights is to be taken as proof that Jefferson was an impractical French theorist, the critic may take what comfort he can from his deduction.[4]

Parrington concluded that Jefferson's revolutionary departure from Locke was "singularly fortunate for America" because "there was need of idealism to leaven the materialistic realism of the times."[5] Idealism as a leaven for materialism was a favorite theme of Progressive ideology, and Parrington was such a devotee of the Progressive cause that he did not deem it necessary to present the slightest scintilla of evidence to support his contention that "the note of idealism" that the rejection of the Lockean right to property injected into the Declaration was "an embodiment of Jefferson's deepest convictions."

A more recent critique of Jefferson's political philosophy by an accomplished scholar, Jean M. Yarbrough, maintains that Jefferson's use of the phrase "pursuit of happiness" was prompted by his belief that "property rights are not strictly speaking natural rights." Unlike Parrington, Yarbrough's account is not driven by an unreflective ideology, and it therefore deserves serious consideration. The bulk of the evidence she puts forward is derived from a letter written by Jefferson in 1813 in which, Yarbrough claims, Jefferson "delivered his most complete thoughts on the nature and origin of property."[6] Isaac McPherson had written to Jefferson asking

---

3. Ibid.

4. Vernon L. Parrington, *Main Currents in American Thought: The Colonial Mind, 1620–1800* (New York: Harcourt, Brace & World, 1927), 350.

5. Ibid.

6. Jean M. Yarbrough, *American Virtues: Thomas Jefferson on the Character of a Free People* (Lawrence: University Press of Kansas, 1998), 88.

him whether he believed there was a natural right to the "exclusive property" in ideas and inventions. Yarbrough notes that Jefferson "made short shrift of McPherson's question: there is no natural right to inventions or ideas." As to property in ideas, Jefferson gives a perfectly classic answer. No one can own an idea; ideas are the only things that are perfectly communizable. The "peculiar character" of an idea, Jefferson noted, "is that no one possesses the less, because every other possesses the whole of it." An idea, therefore, is "incapable of confinement or exclusive appropriation." The same might almost be said of inventions: "Inventions then cannot, in nature, be a subject of property." Inventions, like ideas, are not a subject of "exclusive appropriation" and therefore cannot be a natural right; inventions exist solely for the common good and "benefit of society." Nevertheless, patents or monopolies may be granted for a limited time to encourage innovation and industry, but this would be a matter of conventional, not natural, right.[7]

What Yarborough sees as most important in the letter is Jefferson's more general discussion of the right to property, which she claims is derived from his early interest in Lord Henry Home Kames's writings. Jefferson had extracted some passages from Kames's *History of Property* in his commonplace book some fifty years earlier, and if we are to credit Yarbrough, Kames continued to dominate Jefferson's thinking about property rights. Some ten months after his reply to McPherson, Jefferson wrote to Thomas Law that "Lord Kames, one of the ablest of our advocates, who goes so far as to say, in his Principles of Natural Religion, that a man owes no duty to which he is not urged by some impulsive feeling. This is correct, if referred to the standard of general feeling in the given case, and not to the feeling of a single individual. Perhaps I may misquote him, it being fifty years since I read his book."[8] Indeed, Yarbrough uses references to Kames to argue throughout her book that Jefferson transforms Locke's view of human nature by putting a greater emphasis on virtues that "are more generous and benevolent."[9] Thus

> Jefferson's assertion that human beings are social points to a less egocentric view of human nature than that suggested by Locke. Jefferson's political psychology seeks to combine the realism of an expanded self-interest with the moral dignity of benevolence and, in so doing subtly transforms Locke's understanding of the liberal virtues. Where Locke emphasizes those virtues that promote peaceful acquisition and the accumulation of wealth, Jefferson's understanding of rights and his treatment of virtue tend to be more spirited and more philanthropic.[10]

It is Locke's emphasis on individual natural rights in the *Second Treatise*, particularly the comprehensive natural right to property—that egocentric right to acquisition that might blunt the spirit of philanthropy—that Yarbrough wishes to

---

7. Thomas Jefferson, Letter to Isaac McPherson, August 18, 1813, in *Jefferson: Writings*, ed. Merrill Peterson (New York: Library of America, 1984), 1291–92.

8. Ibid., 1338–39.

9. Yarbrough, *American Virtues*, 4.

10. Ibid., 6.

deemphasize in Jefferson's thought. Yet nothing in the McPherson letter provides any justification for doing so: Jefferson displays no arguments that contradict in any way Locke's exposition of the natural right to property in chapter 5 of the *Second Treatise*.[11] Jefferson writes,

> But while it is a moot question whether the origin of any kind of property is derived from nature at all, it would be singular to admit a natural and even an hereditary right to inventors. It is agreed by those who have seriously considered the subject, that no individual has, of natural right, a separate property in an acre of land, for instance. By an universal law, indeed, whatever, whether fixed or movable, belongs to all men equally and in common, is the property for the moment of him who occupies it; but when he relinquishes the occupation, the property goes with it. Stable ownership is the gift of social law, and is given late in the progress of society.[12]

The word "moot," in this context, means "unsettled" or "disputable," and certainly no one can gainsay Jefferson on this point. What is settled, however, is that Jefferson follows Locke's contention that the earth belongs in common to all men when he states that everything by "natural and universal law . . . whether fixed or movable, belongs equally to all men."

Nature or natural law, of course, does not grant an acre to anyone—if it is to become property, it has to be acquired, and the only ground in nature for acquisition is labor. As Locke argues, "*As much Land* as a Man Tills, Plants, Improves, Cultivates, and can use the Product of, so much is his *Property*. He by his Labour does, as it were, inclose it from the Common."[13] Thus occupation and improvement creates the right to property, and Jefferson mentions that an acre of land becomes the temporary property of the one who occupies it, and that the right to property in that acre ceases when occupation terminates. The reason that the occupier acquires a right to the acre of land is that he has taken it out of the common stock of mankind by adding to it something exclusively his own—his labor. This, in the Lockean understanding, is the origin of the natural right to property. It stems from the exclusive property one has in his own person that he extends to the external world by his labor and thereby acquires whatever he creates by his labor for his exclusive use. Jefferson's truncated statement doesn't give details, but this is the only reason that occupation could con-

---

11. For anyone making even the most casual perusal of Kames's writings on property, it would be difficult to disagree with the editor of *Jefferson's Commonplace Book*, Gilbert Chinard, who wrote, "I am perfectly aware of the undeniable influence of Locke upon the theory of Kames; and it would be unlikely that Jefferson had not read Locke's *Treatise on Civil Government* at that date. Jefferson could have endorsed without any change the whole *Tract on Property*, from beginning to the conclusion—which he echoed in his *Bill to Abolish Entails* and in his proposal to abolish primogeniture. In Kames, at any rate, he found a complete exposition of the theory of natural rights" (Gilbert Chinard, ed., *The Commonplace Book of Thomas Jefferson: A Repertory of His Ideas on Government* [Baltimore, MD: Johns Hopkins University Press, 1926], 19).

12. Thomas Jefferson, Letter to Isaac McPherson, in *Jefferson: Writings*, 1291.

13. John Locke, *Two Treatises of Government*, ed. Peter Laslett (New York: New American Library, 1965), II.32 (further references in the text by treatise and paragraph number).

fer ownership—improvement of that acre by labor is what takes the land out of the common grant to all mankind. Once the occupation and the labor ceases, ownership reverts to the common.

The improvement of one acre of land by labor and industry, Locke calculates, adds the equivalent of ten acres of "the provisions serving to the support of humane life" more than "an acre of Land, of an equal richnesse, lyeing wast in common" (II.37). Thus the private appropriation of one acre by labor gives back to mankind tenfold.[14] One might even argue—although Jefferson does not—that this is the most *effectual* kind of philanthropy. Jefferson does say that "the stable ownership of property is the gift of society." Civil society exists, of course, for the primary purpose of protecting and regulating the use of property by positive or civil law. This does not mean that the natural right to property loses its status as a natural right any more than liberty loses its status as a natural right because every individual cedes the executive power he possesses by the law of nature in the state of nature to civil society to be administered by the rule of law.

Yarbrough also argues that the status of the right to property as a natural right is rendered questionable by the fact that it is not an "inalienable right," property being alienable with the consent of the owner. Inalienable rights, Yarbrough avers, derive "their inalienability from man's inherent nature" and "refer to that category of natural rights that we cannot give up or transfer to another either because it is not possible for others to exercise these rights for us (e.g., the right of conscience) or because such a transfer runs contrary to our own good."[15] There is a fundamental distinction that Yarbrough ignores: the natural right to property is inalienable, but property that is acquired in the exercise of that right is freely alienable, and its alienability is protected by the natural right to property itself. If we follow Locke, as I am convinced Jefferson did, the natural right to property is an inalienable right because it is part of "man's inherent nature," the fact that "all men are created equal." Whatever property a man creates is for his use and convenience, and this means that he may extinguish the property by use or exchange, thus alienating the property he has created without alienating the natural right to property itself. Unlike the right of conscience, which can be exercised to its fullest extent by an individual without the assistance of civil society or its laws, the right to property needs civil law for its protection; laws against trespass, laws against breach of contract, laws of inheritance, and a host of other laws for the orderly possession and disposition of property are necessary to protect the natural right to property within civil society.

Yarbrough thus simply misreads Jefferson's abbreviated account of the right to property in the letter to McPherson, believing that since "stable ownership" requires

---

14. Locke revises his estimate a few paragraphs later, reporting that "if we will rightly estimate things as they come to our use, and cast up the several Expenses about them, what in them is purely owing to *Nature*, and what to *labour*, we shall find, that in most of them 99/100 are wholly to be put on the account of *labour*" (ibid., II.40); three paragraphs later (II.42), the value of labor is revised to account for 999/1,000 the value of land. The reason is that "nature and the Earth furnished only the almost worthless Materials, as in themselves" (ibid., II.43).

15. Yarbrough, *American Virtues*, 90.

"social law," the right to property cannot be a natural right. But she does almost immediately qualify her statement, remarking that it "would be a mistake to conclude
that property rights are simply conventional, that they rest on no firmer foundation than the wishes of the majority. Although 'stable ownership' is established by
consent, it does have a certain natural foundation."[16] By way of support for her
qualification, she cites a letter Jefferson wrote to P. S. Dupont de Nemours in 1816,
in which he casually remarks,

> I believe with you that morality, compassion, generosity, are innate elements of the hu-
> man constitution; that there exists a right independent of force; that a right to property
> is founded in our natural wants, in the means with which we are endowed to satisfy these
> wants and the right to what we acquire by those means without violating the similar
> rights of other sensible beings; that no one has a right to obstruct another, exercising his
> faculties innocently for the relief of sensibilities made a part of his nature.[17]

Yarbrough concludes that this passage indicates that "insofar as property arrangements are based on each individual's 'natural wants' and natural talents, they are
not simply conventional." Thus while the right to property is not a natural right, it
has "a certain natural foundation." There is considerable confusion here. We have
already seen that "stable ownership" is in fact a conventional right on Lockean
grounds, while the acquisition of property prior to "stable ownership" is a natural
right and continues to be a natural right even though positive law is necessary for
its protection.

In *A Summary View of the Rights of British America*, Jefferson made this remarkable
statement revealing the Lockean foundations of the American idea of the right to
property. He noted that a "general principle" was gradually introduced into the common law of England that held that "'all lands in England were held either mediately or
immediately of the crown.'"[18] The phrase (actually paraphrase) that Jefferson doesn't
identify is from Blackstone, who observed in his *Commentaries on the Laws of England*
that "it became a fundamental maxim and necessary principle (though in reality a
mere fiction) of our English tenures, 'that the king is the universal lord and original
proprietor of all the lands in his kingdom; and that no man doth or can possess any
part of it, but what had mediately or immediately been derived as a gift from him, to
be held upon feodal services.'"[19] Jefferson comments, "Our ancestors, however, who
migrated hither, were labourers, not lawyers." This is a clear statement that those who
settled America were adherents of Locke, not Blackstone. Or, to say almost the same
thing, "our ancestors" were adherents of natural right—labor was the title to property,
not grants or titles advanced by kings. Self-ownership, a necessary consequence of the

---

16. Ibid., 90.
17. Thomas Jefferson, Letter to P. S. Dupont de Nemours, April 24, 1816, in *Jefferson: Writings*,
1386–87.
18. Ibid., 119.
19. William Blackstone, *Commentaries on the Laws of England* (Oxford: Clarendon Press, 1765–1769;
reprint Chicago: University of Chicago Press, 1979), II:2.

fact that "all men are created equal," is the origin of property rights as expressed by Jefferson in this important public document. As Jefferson remarked many years later, comparing the American Revolution to various English revolutions, "Our Revolution commenced on more favorable ground. It presented us an album on which we were free to write what we pleased. We had no occasion to search into musty records to hunt up royal parchments, or to investigate the laws and institutions of a semi-barbarous ancestry. We appealed to those of nature, and found them engraved on our hearts."[20] Thus the "album" of natural right was the ground and foundation of the American Revolution, not convention, however much convention might have been sanctified by history. It was Locke, not Blackstone, who inspired Jefferson. Jefferson may have from time to time in private letters indulged sentiments deriving from one form or another of the moral sense school, but I believe that, in the main, he adhered to Lockean natural right as it was understood in the tradition of the "elementary books of public right, as Aristotle, Cicero, Locke, Sidney, &c."

There has been much speculation as to the exact origin of the phrase "pursuit of happiness." Conjecture has centered on James Wilson's *Considerations on the Nature and Extent of the Legislative Authority of the British Parliament*, published in 1774, where Wilson declared, in a passage quoted in chapter 1, "The happiness of society is the first law of every government." Since Wilson cites Burlamaqui as his authority, speculation includes Burlamaqui as well.[21] In addition to James Mason's Virginia Declaration of Rights, others have suggested Blackstone's famous passage in his *Commentaries*;[22] still others have proposed John Adams's remark in *Thoughts on Government* (1776) that "the happiness of society is the end of government"[23] as the inspiration for the Declaration, especially since Adams was on the drafting committee of the Declaration. Others have even mentioned Aristotle as a source, presumably for the reasons already intimated.[24] The one candidate who is conspicuous by his absence and who, unlike those just mentioned, frequently used the phrase "pursuit of happiness" is Locke.[25] This is exceedingly curious, but I think easily explained

---

20. Thomas Jefferson, Letter to Major John Cartwright, June 5, 1824, in *Jefferson: Writings*, 1491. The youthful Alexander Hamilton made a similar remark in 1775 when he wrote that "the sacred rights of mankind are not to be rummaged for, among old parchments, or musty records. They are written, as with a sun beam, in the whole *volume* of human nature, by the hand of the divinity itself; and can never be erased or obscured by mortal power" ("The Farmer Refuted," in *The Papers of Alexander Hamilton*, ed. Harold C. Syrett et al. [New York: Columbia University Press, 1961–1978], I:122).

21. Morton White, *The Philosophy of the American Revolution* (New York: Oxford University Press, 1978), 215–21.

22. The Creator "has graciously reduced the rule of obedience to this one paternal precept, 'that man should pursue his own happiness.' This is the foundation of what we call ethics, or natural law" (Blackstone, *Commentaries on the Laws of England*, I:41).

23. Charles Francis Adams, ed., *The Works of John Adams* (Boston: Charles C. Little and James Brown, 1851–56), IV:193.

24. David N. Mayer, *The Constitutional Thought of Thomas Jefferson* (Charlottesville: University Press of Virginia, 1994), 78.

25. See John M. Murrin, "Fundamental Values, the Founding Fathers, and the Constitution," in *To Form a More Perfect Union: The Critical Ideas of the Constitution*, ed. Herman Belz, Ronald Hoffman, and Peter J. Albert (Charlottesville: University Press of Virginia, 1992), 22, n. 29.

because Locke, as previously mentioned, never says that the pursuit of happiness is a natural right and, in fact, never uses the phrase in *Two Treatises of Government.* Rather, he presents the pursuit of happiness in *An Essay Concerning Human Understanding* as a moral duty. The founders were certainly acquainted with Locke's *Essay,* and the decision to present "the pursuit of happiness" in the Declaration as a natural right may indicate that there was a conscious effort on their part to consider this third of the trilogy of specifically named natural rights as both a right and a duty.

Professor Yarbrough's analysis denied that Jefferson believed the right to property was an individual natural right because it would have undermined what she saw as his attachment to social virtues.[26] But I believe a proper analysis will show that Jefferson, who after all said that in the Declaration he was giving expression to "the American mind" rather than his own opinions, transformed Locke's understanding of "the pursuit of happiness" into both a natural right and a moral obligation. We saw in chapter 1 Professor Jaffa's conclusion that in the dialectical argument of the Declaration, "'rights' become 'ends' which are 'Safety and Happiness,' the alpha and omega of political life in Aristotle's *Politics.*" And, Jaffa continued, "in one form or another this metamorphosis of Lockean 'rights' into Aristotelian 'ends' (or vice versa) recurs in many of the documents of the Founding." Some aspects of the Declaration's use of the phrase "pursuit of happiness" can be similarly understood in Aristotelian terms.

ARISTOTLE AND THE PURSUIT OF HAPPINESS

In his *Nicomachean Ethics,* Aristotle contends that human happiness is achieved by living a complete life according to the virtues. One of the virtues necessary to achieve human happiness is liberality—that is, the correct use of property or wealth (*chrēmata*). Liberality is the mean between two extremes, prodigality and stinginess. Liberality is a virtue, and actions that are in pursuit of virtue are intrinsically noble because they exist for the sake of the noble. The liberal person is best known for giving property or wealth correctly, according to his means, and to those whose character makes them deserving recipients. The liberal takes property or wealth correctly and refrains from the incorrect appropriation of property, although the latter is, strictly considered, not a matter of liberality but of justice. In any case, liberality is mostly a virtue of giving to those to whom the liberal person ought to give and when and

---

26. As evidence that Jefferson's use of "pursuit of happiness" was not meant to exclude the right to property as an inalienable right, scarcely three years after the Declaration, he noted in his revisal of the laws of Virginia,

It frequently happens that wicked and dissolute men . . . commit violations on the lives, liberties, and property of others, and the secure enjoyment of these having principally induced men to enter into society, government would be defective in its principal purpose, were it not to restrain such criminal acts by inflicting due punishment on those who perpetrate them (Julian P. Boyd et al., eds., *The Papers of Thomas Jefferson* [Princeton, NJ: Princeton University Press, 1950–], 2:394–95).

It would be difficult to miss the perfectly Lockean character of this passage.

where he ought to do so. Thus the giving of the liberal person is for the sake of the noble and correct giving since it is according to virtue, will be accompanied by pleasure, and is not painful.[27] Virtuous action is always accompanied by pleasure although the object of virtuous action is never simply pleasure. Liberality is both an end in itself and a means; it is an end because it is desirable for its own sake as a virtue that serves the perfection of human nature. But it also serves as a means to a higher end: human happiness; it is one of the virtues necessary to the pursuit of happiness. The liberal person cannot exercise the virtue of liberality without property, or what Aristotle calls in other places, "external goods." Thus it is clear that property or wealth is the necessary but not sufficient condition of human happiness, or the pursuit of happiness, since virtue (including liberality) is an activity that aims at happiness.

It is even plausible to argue that the Declaration's argument also adopts the view that the right to property is a necessary but not sufficient condition for the pursuit of happiness, and that the founders learned this Aristotelian argument at a distance from Locke. Consider this passage from George Washington's first inaugural, delivered in New York on April 30, 1789:

> There is no truth more thoroughly established, than that there exists in the economy and course of nature, an indissoluble union between virtue and happiness; between duty and advantage; between the genuine maxims of an honest and magnanimous policy and the solid rewards of public prosperity and felicity; since we ought to be no less persuaded that the propitious smiles of Heaven can never be expected on a nation that disregards the eternal rules of order and right, which Heaven itself has ordained.[28]

This statement delineating the natural connection between virtue and happiness is, of course, perfectly Aristotelian. Thus Washington (and Madison, who wrote the speech)[29] understood the "pursuit of happiness" to mean the pursuit of virtue. And this surely encapsulates Madison's statement in the Virginia Ratifying Convention, noted in chapter 1, when he argued that "political happiness" is the end of government and should be the architectonic guide for political deliberations.

It is more than probable that the source for this notable statement in Washington's speech was Locke's *An Essay Concerning Human Understanding*: "For God," Locke says,

> having, by an inseparable connection, joined *Virtue* and public Happiness together; and made the Practice thereof, necessary to the preservation of Society, and visibly *beneficial*

---

27. Aristotle, *Nicomachean Ethics*, trans. Robert C. Bartlett and Susan D. Collins (Chicago: University of Chicago Press, 2011), 1119b21–1122a17.

28. George Washington, "First Inaugural," in *The Papers of James Madison*, ed. Robert A. Rutland et al. (Chicago: University of Chicago Press, 1962–), 12:123.

29. The editors of the Madison papers note a singular set of events that transpired after Washington presented his address: "Having composed the inaugural, [Madison] drew up in turn the address of the House of Representatives in reply to the president (5 May 1789), the president's reply to the House address (8 May), and for good measure the president's reply to the Senate address (18 May)." The editors duly note, "Thus in the opening series of formal exchanges between the president and Congress, [Madison] was in a dialogue with himself" (ibid., 12:120–21).

to all, with whom the Virtuous Man has to do; it is no wonder, that everyone should, not only allow, but recommend, and magnifie those Rules to others, from whose observance of them, he is sure to reap Advantage to himself.[30]

Madison, if not Washington, was well acquainted with Locke's Essay, and this passage would have readily sprung to mind as setting an appropriate tone for "the preservation of the sacred fire of liberty, and the destiny of the Republican model of Government, [that] are justly considered as *deeply*, perhaps as *finally* staked, on the experiment entrusted to the hands of the American people."[31] It is easy to see how these two enlightened statesmen, who were concerned with political things as such, were led by the pressure of events to an understanding of Aristotelian natural right through a reading of Locke.[32]

LOCKE IN AMERICA

Locke, of course, did not present the same understanding of virtue and happiness as Aristotle. He accepted the premises of modern political philosophy. For Locke, virtue is not pursued for its intrinsic goodness or nobility but as a calculated advantage to society and the individual: it is "necessary to the preservation of society, and visibly beneficial to all." In addition, Locke states, it will "reap advantage" to the "virtuous man." As we discussed in chapter 1, this is a kind of self-interest rightly understood, a view of one's own advantage as inseparably connected with the common good of society. It is true that sustained devotion to the common good will produce the habits and manners of public virtue, but the pursuit of the noble for the sake of the noble or the pleasures that accompany that pursuit are for the most part abandoned by modernity and by Locke as unrealistic—or virtue unendowed, as we will later see Locke describe it. But we must remind ourselves once again of the theological-political context that confronted modern political philosophy, a post-Christian context that was wholly unknown to Aristotle. Christianity, as we have seen, promised individuals eternal life in a world to come, which necessarily depreciated life in this world as merely a preparation for the next. In an attempt to reestablish the dignity and stability of political life in this world, the promise of security and stability for "Lives, Liberties and Estates" might appear illiberal from the perspective of the classical world, but in a world beset by religious wars and ecclesiastical despotism, to say nothing of rampant poverty and scarcity, it might appear noble and liberal from a proper political perspective. Some have even traced the theological-political problem presented by Christianity to Aristotle, who, after all, distinguished the good citizen

---

30. John Locke, *An Essay Concerning Human Understanding*, ed. Peter H. Nidditch (Oxford: Clarendon Press, 1975), I.iii.6.

31. Washington, "First Inaugural," in *Papers of James* Madison, 12:123.

32. "The classical philosophers realized, and *practically all men realize*, a necessary connection between a kind of prosperity or happiness and a kind or part of virtue" (Leo Strauss, *Natural Right and History* [Chicago: University of Chicago Press, 1953], 213 [emphasis added]).

from the good man, implying that the good man, like the good Christian, was not dependent on any particular political regime but was independent of politics. In any case, Aristotle was the discoverer of moral virtue, and he described moral virtue independently of regime questions. Aristotle wrote separate treatises: his *Politics*, on regime questions, addressed to future legislators, and *Ethics*, a treatise on moral virtue addressed to gentlemen, those who were not philosophers but whose good character rendered them open to philosophy and who could be educated to be future rulers. Locke also wrote separate treatises: the *Second Treatise*, for legislators of future liberal republics—of whom the American founders were prime examples—and *An Essay Concerning Human Understanding*, in which he propounded his understanding of morality that would be appropriate for republican regimes. We have already suggested why the theological-political problem faced by Locke made it necessary for him to treat regime questions and moral questions in separate works: it was part of the framework he had constructed for the separation of church and state.

Leo Strauss remarked that Locke was "the most famous and the most influential of all modern natural right teachers," one who "wielded an extraordinarily great influence on men of affairs and on a large body of opinion." This resulted, in part, from the fact that "he was an eminently prudent man, and he reaped the reward of superior prudence," the "essence" of which is to "know when to speak and when to be silent." Because Locke quoted orthodox writers such as Richard Hooker and remained silent on more radical authors, particularly the "justly decried" Hobbes, "we are then apparently confronted with an unbroken tradition of perfect respectability that stretches from Socrates to Locke."[33] But what Strauss discovered buried deep in Locke's writings was a Locke who was radically modern, doing his part to extend the philosophic project initiated by Machiavelli and continued by Hobbes. It was only deep below the surface that Strauss discovered a Lockean natural right that was "fundamentally different from Hooker's." In fact, Locke had "embraced" the modern project in essentially Hobbian terms. Strauss's reading of Locke was itself revolutionary. No one had ever before read Locke with the skill, innovation, and penetration of Strauss, including, as far as we know, the most insightful philosophers. It is impossible to believe that the American founders read Locke the way Strauss did. Surely the founders were philosophic statesmen, open to philosophy and guided by the "elementary books of public right," but it would be difficult to argue that they were philosophers in their own right. In Aristotelian terms, they were *phronimoi* (practically wise statesmen). If we are to understand the founders as they understood themselves, then it is imperative that we understand Locke the way they understood him. As one close observer of Strauss's work commented, "There is no evidence the founding generation understood Locke in anything other than the conventional way, and considerable evidence pointing in the opposite direction."[34]

---

33. Ibid., 165.
34. William A. Galston, "Leo Stauss's Qualified Embrace of Liberal Democracy," in *The Cambridge Companion to Leo Strauss*, ed. Steven B. Smith (Cambridge: Cambridge University Press, 2009), 207.

In fact, there is considerable evidence that in *Natural Right and History*, Strauss exaggerated the radical modernity of Locke for rhetorical purposes. Professor Thomas G. West, an intelligent interpreter of Strauss's thought, has written,

> Strauss's lifelong agenda was to restore philosophy in the modern world. Since recent versions of modern philosophy had led to the reigning positivism and historicism, both of which deny the possibility of philosophy . . . Strauss seems to have decided that the philosophers most likely to appeal to modern readers were the Greek classics. . . . Strauss therefore wanted to instill in his readers, as their first reaction to his work, a moral revulsion against modernity, so that they would be more open to the attractions of classical political philosophy.
>
> By exaggerating Locke's hostility to nature, it was rhetorically easier for Strauss to situate him on the slippery slope leading from Machiavelli, who abandoned virtue as the end of politics, to Heidegger, who embraced radical historicism and Hitler. In order to give his readers an incentive to return to the classics, Strauss had to exaggerate the continuity within the history of modern philosophy in order to show, or rather to suggest, how the entire modern philosophic enterprise led to historicism and political irresponsibility.[35]

I believe that Professor West is eminently correct in his observation, although, as he readily admits, it would be difficult to provide definitive proof. In any case, once Strauss's Locke is read in this light—in the light of Strauss's over-all rhetorical purposes—then it is utterly impossible to maintain that the founders read Locke with the same purpose that Strauss did.

Professor Steven B. Smith writes that in *Natural Right and History*, "Strauss accepted the view, less popular today than it once was, that Lockean ideas formed the theoretical foundation of the new American republic. It is not an exaggeration to say that Strauss's judgment on Locke *is* his judgment on America." But what Strauss reveals—in "an irony" that could not have escaped his "attentive readers"—is that "Hobbes, not Locke, was the true founder of America."[36] In Strauss's interpretation, Locke presents merely a "sugar-coating" for "the harsh, even unpalatable teachings of Hobbes. . . . It was Locke's genius to have . . . disguised an otherwise bitter pill."[37] Professor Smith does intimate, however, that Strauss may have exhibited some reservations about the radical character of the American founding, suggesting that the founders might have been saved from "the theoretical radicalism of Lockean principles [by] Locke's own prudence [which] to some degree successfully disguised the nature of [his] radicalism by emphasizing his links with the past. America thus remained something of a theoretical anomaly protected by its Lockean origins from the gusts of later modernity."[38] Smith's suggestion is that the exoteric Locke might

---

35. Thomas G. West, "The Ground of Locke's Law of Nature," *Social Philosophy and Policy* 29, no. 2 (Summer 2012): 24.

36. Steven B. Smith, *Reading Leo Strauss: Politics, Philosophy, Judaism* (Chicago: University of Chicago Press, 2006), 170.

37. Ibid.

38. Ibid., 172–73.

have saved the American founders from the radical modernity of the esoteric Locke. Smith even indicates that Strauss's citation of the Declaration of Independence at the beginning of *Natural Right and History* may have been an "overt teaching" suggesting "a recovery of the possibility of natural right. . . . The book sets out a kind of irredentist strategy for reappropriating an earlier phase of modernity as a prophylactic against the corrosive effects of Rousseau, Marx, and Nietzsche. "Indeed," Smith continues, "*Natural Right and History* is nothing if not an invitation to American readers to take seriously their political founding and the philosophic ideas that gave rise to it. The American founding represented the first wave of modernity in the fullness of its theoretical vigor and self-confidence. It is necessary to recover some of that confidence today through the critique of historicism."[39]

Smith concludes, however, that Strauss's "irredentist strategy" was undermined by his own "deeper teaching," which demonstrates that "such efforts at reappropriation either are doomed to failure or result in fateful concessions to modernity regarding the role of rights, commerce, and technology."[40] The recovery of natural right in modernity thus seems to be impossible. The critique of historicism cannot succeed. For Smith, the headlong slide into radical modernity seems fated by events beyond the control of any practically wise statesmen. Such analysis, however, deftly ignores Strauss's own insistence that a theoretical crisis does not necessarily lead to a practical crisis.[41]

Strauss rarely mentioned the Declaration of Independence; his most extensive discussion, although brief, occurs quite unexpectedly in the "Plato" chapter of *The City and Man*, published ten years after *Natural Right and History*:

> When the signers of the Declaration of Independence say: "we mutually pledge to each other our Lives, our Fortunes, and our sacred Honor," they mean that they are resolved to forsake their lives and fortunes, but to maintain their honor: honor shines most clearly when everything else is sacrificed for its sake, including life, the matter of the first natural right mentioned in the Declaration of Independence. While honor or justice presupposes life and both are meant to serve life, they are nevertheless higher in rank than life.[42]

---

39. Ibid., 173.
40. Ibid.
41. See Galston, "Leo Strauss's Qualified Embrace of Liberal Democracy," 195.
42. Leo Strauss, *City and Man* (Chicago: Rand McNally, 1964), 89. Besides the opening paragraph of *Natural Right and History*, I know of only two other references to the Declaration in the Strauss corpus: one in his review of John Dewey's *German Philosophy and Politics*, originally published in 1943 and reprinted in *What Is Political Philosophy?* (New York: Free Press, 1959), which contains a favorable reference to the phraseology of the Declaration as providing a counterweight to modern "absolutism" (281); and the second in "Progress or Return," originally delivered as a lecture in 1952, first published in 1981 in *Modern Judaism*, and reprinted in Thomas Pangle, ed., *The Rebirth of Classical Political Rationalism: Essays and Lectures by Leo Strauss* (Chicago: University of Chicago Press, 1989), 233. Strauss quotes the words of Lincoln's Gettysburg Address without attribution (using the same words that later became part of the introduction to *Natural Right and History*):

> It is very far from me to minimize the difference between a nation conceived in liberty and dedicated to the proposition that all men are created equal, and the nations of the old world, which certainly were not conceived in liberty. I share the hope in America and the faith in America, but I am

Here Strauss clearly indicates that the authors of the Declaration ranked the goods of the soul higher than the goods of the body by their willingness to sacrifice their natural right to life and property to "honor or justice." For Hobbes, of course, courage is not a virtue, nor is honor any part of the human good. It is utterly impossible to imagine Hobbes ever pledging his "sacred honor" to any cause. This surely means that in Strauss's final estimation, the framers were not Hobbians! And if Smith is correct—as he surely is—in saying that Strauss's interpretation in *Natural Right and History* shows Locke to be essentially (if secretly) a Hobbian, then, by parity of reasoning, the Locke of *Natural Right and History* cannot be the Locke of the American founding. I think it is also safe to conclude that in the light of this passage from *The City and Man*, it is impossible to conclude that Strauss ultimately thought Hobbes "was the true founder of America," nor, we presume, did he believe that a Hobbianized Locke was the true founder of America.

LOCKE ON THE PURSUIT OF HAPPINESS

In *An Essay Concerning Human Understanding*, Locke maintains that happiness is the end to which "we all aim at in all our actions," and that what moves us to action is "uneasiness":

> Pain and *uneasiness* being, by everyone, concluded, and felt, to be inconsistent with happiness; spoiling the relish, even of those good things which we have: a little pain serving to marr all the pleasure we rejoyced in. And therefore that, which of course determines the choice of our *will* to the next action, will always be the removing of pain, as long as we have any left, as the first and necessary step towards happiness (II.xxi.36).

Uneasiness is provoked by the avoidance of pain and the pursuit of pleasure. Thus, according to Locke,

> *Happiness* then in its full extent is the utmost Pleasure we are capable of, and *Misery* the utmost pain . . . therefore what has an aptness to produce Pleasure in us, is what we call *Good* and what is apt to produce Pain in us, we call *Evil*, and for no other reason, but for its aptness to produce Pleasure and Pain in us, wherein consists our *Happiness* and *Misery* (II.xxi.42).

It is little wonder that Locke is sometimes called a rank hedonist. Strauss says in *Natural Right and History*, however, that Locke is a hedonist of a peculiar kind; it is not so much enjoying the greatest pleasures but possessing the means—the power—that produce the greatest pleasures that is the foundation for happiness. In

---

compelled to add that that faith and that hope cannot be of the same character as that faith and that hope which a Jew has in regard to Judaism and which the Christian has in regard to Christianity. No one claims that the faith in America and the hope for America are based on explicit divine promises.

See also *Persecution and the Art of Writing* (Glencoe, IL: Free Press, 1952), 30.

this, according to Strauss, Locke follows Hobbes, who argued that "the power of a man . . . is his present means, to obtain some future apparent good."[43] It was Hobbes, after all, who also famously stated, "I put for a general inclination of all mankind, a perpetuall and restless desire of Power after power, that ceaseth onely in Death."[44] Strauss concludes that for Locke this means that in effect "the greatest happiness consists in the greatest power. Since there are no knowable natures, there is no nature of man with reference to which we could distinguish between pleasures which are according to nature and pleasures which are against nature."[45] In support of this state- ment, Strauss cites the famous passage in *An Essay Concerning Human Understanding* (II.xxi.55) where Locke asserts that "the philosophers of old did in vain inquire, whether *summum bonum* consisted in riches, or bodily delights, or virtue or contem- plation." Strauss comments that "in the absence of a *summum bonum*, man would lack completely a star and compass for his life if there were no *summum malum*" to serve as the effectual substitute for a *summum bonum*. The effectual substitute is "the strongest desire [which] is the desire for self-preservation. The evil from which the strongest desire recoils is death. Death must then be the greatest evil."[46] The *summum bonum* is thus replaced by a *summum malum*, a more reliable ground for human behavior, generated by the most powerful human passion, not "vain" or idle inquiries. This passage in Locke is a reprise of one found in chapter 11 of Hobbes's *Leviathan*: "the Felicity of this life, consisteth not in the repose of a mind satisfied. For there is no such *Finis ultimus*, (utmost ayme,) nor *Summum Bonum*, (greatest Good,) as is spoken of in the Books of the old Morall Philosophers."[47] Thus it seems as if Locke is simply a less boisterous and more prudent version of Hobbes. This is apparently confirmed by the fact that the discussions of happiness being the pursuit of the greatest pleasures in the *An Essay Concerning Human Understanding* occur in a chapter titled "Power," a chapter that also happens to be the longest chapter of the entire book.

Strauss's conclusion here was certainly exaggerated. In the sections immediately preceding the passage cited by Strauss, Locke discusses the "pursuit of happiness" as "our greatest good" and even argues "the necessity of preferring and pursuing true happiness as our greatest good." Human liberty, Locke says, resides in "constant en- deavours after, and a steady prosecution of true felicity." It is liberty that allows the suspension of desire until reason can determine

> whether that particular thing, which is then proposed or desired, lie in the way to their main end, and make a real part of that which is their greatest good. For the inclination, and tendency of their nature to happiness is an obligation, and motive to them, to take care not to mistake, or miss it; and so necessarily puts them upon caution, deliberation,

---

43. See Thomas Hobbes, *Leviathan*, ed. C. B. McPherson (New York: Penguin Books, 1968), ch. 10, 150.
44. Ibid., ch. 11, 161.
45. Strauss, *Natural Right and History*, 249.
46. Ibid., 250.
47. Hobbes, *Leviathan*, ch. 11, 160.

and wariness, in the direction of their particular actions, which are the means to obtain it (II.xxi.52).

Happiness is an inclination and tendency of human nature, and the rule of reason over desire is an "obligation" directed toward the "greatest good." One might even conclude that the rule of reason over desire is a moral obligation proceeding from human nature.

The liberty that makes it possible to suspend the desires and subject them to deliberation and scrutiny is "the great privilege of finite intellectual Beings." This liberty allows men to

> *suspend* their desires, and stop them from determining their *wills* to any action, till they have duly and fairly *examin'd* the good and evil of it, as far forth as the weight of the thing requires. This we are able to do; and when we have done it, we have done our duty, and all that is in our power, and indeed all that needs. For, since the *will* supposes knowledge to guide its choice, and all we can do, is to hold our *wills* undetermined, till we have *examin'd* the good and evil of what we desire (II.xxi.52).

For Locke, then, the use of reason in the pursuit of happiness is a moral obligation, and at one point he avers that it is "a perfection of our nature" (II.xxi.47). Locke does not present the pursuit of happiness as something idiosyncratic or subjective; it rests on a reasoned view of what constitutes "good and evil."

The "*liberty* of intellectual Beings," Locke maintains, creates an obligation to endeavor to secure true happiness, man's "main end." Thus "intellectual beings," those capable of forming abstract ideas, have an obligation to pursue "true felicity" by using informed judgment in the "prosecution" of particular actions. Human liberty resides in this capacity to suspend desires in the light of larger purposes. It is when desires are put to the service of reason and the ends or purposes discerned by reason that human happiness or the pursuit of happiness becomes "our greatest good." Human happiness thus depends upon the distinction between liberty and license. License destroys genuine liberty because the one who indiscriminately indulges his passions is eventually ruled by his passions and becomes enslaved by them, whereas the one who rules his passions through reason enjoys the freedom that accompanies rule. Locke's reasoning here stands in stark contrast to that of Hobbes, who famously insisted that reason was always subordinate to passion: "For the Thoughts, are to the Desires, as Scouts, and Spies, to range abroad, and find the way to the things Desired: All Stedinesse of the minds motion, and all quicknesse of the same, proceeding from thence."[48] For Locke, in contrast, reason properly disciplined and directed controls passion and desire and directs the will to "our greatest good." It is active reason that forms the core of moral virtue for Locke. Moral virtue consists in the choice of those things that promote durable pleasures in preference to those transient and destructive pleasures that result from the exercise of irrational

48. Ibid., ch. 8, 139.

will. The reasoned suspension of will allows individuals to be self-governing and consequently to become members of a self-governing people. Republican government requires a people capable of self-government. But a self-governing people must be composed of individuals who can rule themselves. Self-government must be understood in this twofold sense of ruling and being ruled in turn; this is the indispensable condition for the rule of law. Locke's view of the "pursuit of happiness" in *An Essay Concerning Human Understanding* resembles the description of "self-interest rightly understood" discussed in chapter 1 of this volume, where we argued that self-interest rightly understood was the basis for public happiness in the founders' view of American politics. Self-interest rightly understood entails a prudent regard for the public good as a necessary ingredient of the public happiness of every individual. It is an overtly political concept since it identifies the interest of the individual with the interest of the public; it supposes the happiness of the individual to be intimately connected to the public good or to public happiness. This is what was meant earlier when it was suggested that in the American version, the pursuit of happiness was a right as well as a moral obligation. Because in *An Essay Concerning Human Understanding* the "pursuit of happiness" is considered apart from any political context, it is considered a moral obligation but not a right. In the American context, self-interest rightly understood is a political concept; it therefore transforms the "pursuit of happiness" into a right as well as preserving its status as a moral obligation.

In the sections immediately following the passage quoted by Strauss, Locke remarks that "the eternal Law and Nature of things" is the measure of what "really and truly" constitutes "Happiness" (*An Essay Concerning Human Understanding*, II.xxi.56). It is past doubt, Locke repeats, that "All Men desire Happiness" (II. xxi.68), and it is certain "that every intelligent being really seeks happiness." This being the case, it is "impossible anyone should willingly put into his own draught any bitter ingredient, or leave out any thing in his power, that would tend to his satisfaction, and the completing his Happiness, but only by a *wrong Judgment*" (II. xxi.62). Locke reiterates that the "great use of Liberty" and the "principal exercise of Freedom" is to dispose the passions so as to render them capable of avoiding "*wrong Judgements*" (II.xxi.67). "Men may and should," Locke insists, "correct their palates" and "give a relish" to proper objects of choice. Men have the power to alter both the relish of the mind and body by "practice, application, and custom." It is "reason and consideration" that "at first recommends" a course of action "and begins their trial, and use finds, or custom makes them pleasant. That this is so in Virtue too, is very certain. Actions are pleasing or displeasing, either in themselves, or considered as a means to a greater and more desirable end" (II.xxi.69). The "greater and more desirable end," of course, is happiness. Without too much hyperbole or exaggeration, this passage could be mistaken for an extract from Aristotle's *Ethics*. Unlike Hobbes and others, Locke does not seem content here to take his bearing from how men live but rather from how they ought to live.

IS THERE A *SUMMUM BONUM* IN LOCKE?

Strauss was well aware that Locke, some three hundred pages after the passage at II.xxi.55 he quoted to support his conclusions that Locke had proposed a *summum malum*—the avoidance of death as the greatest evil, as a substitute for the "vain" inquiries of the old moral philosophers for a *summum bonum*—stated that "*Morality is the proper Science, and Business of Mankind in general*" and that individual men who possess the "several Arts, conversant about several parts of Nature" are "fitted to search out their *Summum Bonum*" (IV.xii.11). Locke here is speaking not of a single standard of excellence for all human beings but of a *summum bonum* for each individual that is, according to Professor West, "unique to each person." This view of the *summum bonum*, West argues,

> might be acceptable to an Aristotle or a Plato, if explained in the following way: Each person has his or her own "palate," talents, and disposition, and is therefore fundamentally limited in life choices likely to be beneficial to himself [or herself]. For that reason, the philosophic life cannot be the *summum bonum*, the highest good, for every one. For only by considering a person's nature, the range of passions and tastes, intellectual strengths and weaknesses, can a rational path to happiness for each person be found.[49]

Whether or not Locke's view might have been acceptable to Plato or Aristotle, his view of the *summum bonum* as described by Professor West would have been made necessary, in large measure, by the fact that he faced a political-theological dilemma that was unknown to the classics. The doctrine of individual salvation, the heart of Christian theology, was utterly foreign to the ancient city. Christianity made ultimate perfection available to every believer. The immortality that was reserved in classical philosophy for a few philosophers was available to all believers in Christianity. From the point of view of the classics, non-philosophers—those who fell short of human perfection—were considered defective and even mutilated human beings. This view was, of course, antithetical both to Christian theology and the idea of equality of rights that stood as the dictate of the laws of nature. As Professor West intimates, Locke's idea of the *summum bonum* in this case could easily be understood in terms of Aristotelian natural right.

When Strauss says that without a *summum bonum*, or its effectual substitute, a *summum malum*, "man would lack completely a star and compass," he is undoubtedly aware that he is using a phrase from Locke's *First Treatise* where Locke suggests that reason is man's "only star and compass" and that it is the capacity for reason that distinguishes men from beasts: "The first and strongest desire God Planted in Men, and wrought into the very Principles of their Nature being that of Self-preservation" (I.88). All other animals have similarly been endowed with "a strong desire of Self-

---

49. West, "The Ground of Locke's Law of Nature," 36–37.

preservation," but, Locke avers, "God, I say . . . directed [man] by his Senses and Reason, as he did the inferior Animals by their Sense, and Instinct" (I.86; *An Essay Concerning Human Understanding*, IV.xii.1). Beasts possess instinct but not reason. Men do not always follow reason but hold it as a potential; beasts, we presume, are always impelled to follow instinct. But, Locke almost needlessly adds, man can fall below the level of beasts when separated from reason: "the busie mind of Man" can carry man to great extravagances, including the breeding of children for food and cannibalism. "The imagination is always restless and suggests a variety of thoughts, and the will, reason being laid aside, is ready for every extravagant project," which often carries him "to a Brutality below the level of Beasts, when he quits his reason, which places him almost equal to Angels" (I.58). Man thus exists between the superhuman and the subhuman, possessing imperfect reason but not having the instincts of the beasts. Reason is the divine element in man, given to him as a means to self-preservation. But his "busie mind"—his imagination—can suggest depravities unavailable to animal instinct unmoved by imagination.

Early in the *Second Treatise*, Locke suggests that those who fail to adhere to reason are the enemies of mankind and should be treated as beasts (II.6; see II.172). Everyone in the state of nature—"that *State of perfect Equality*"—possesses by nature the executive power to enforce the law of nature. This, Locke claims, is a necessary consequence of the fact that the law of nature and all other laws would be worthless if they remained unenforced. Thus it is a dictate of the law of nature that "every one has a right to punish the transgressors of that Law to such a Degree, as may hinder its Violation." Since the law of nature is reason, anyone who violates the law

> declares himself to live by another Rule, than that of *reason* and common Equity, which is that measure God has set to the actions of Men, for their mutual security; and so he becomes dangerous to Mankind, the tye, which is to secure them from injury and violence, being slighted and broken by him. Which being a trespass against the whole Species, and the Peace and Safety of it, provided for by the Law of Nature, every man upon this score, by the Right he hath to preserve Mankind in general, may restrain, or where it is necessary, destroy things noxious by them, and so may bring such evil on any one, who hath transgressed that Law, as may make him repent the doing of it, and thereby deter him, and by his Example others, from doing the like mischief. And in this case, and upon this ground, every *Man hath a Right to punish the Offender, and be Executioner of the Law of Nature* (II.7–8).

Those who violate the law of nature abandon the "right Rule of Reason" and "quit the Principles of Human Nature." Whereas beasts cannot abandon their nature, human beings can become "noxious creatures" by abandoning their nature, which is defined by our capacity to reason and follow the moral obligations of the law of nature. Those who have "renounced Reason, the common Rule and Measure, God hath given to Mankind, hath by the unjust Violence and Slaughter he hath committed upon one, declared War against all Mankind, and therefore may be destroyed as a *Lyon or a Tyger*, one of those wild Savage Beasts, with whom Men can have no Society nor Security" (II.11; see II.16). Human nature thus exists between divine nature and beastly nature, capable of exercising reason that draws us closer to the divine but also capable of easily abandoning reason, which places us among the beasts. Humans are in between beings whose security and happiness depends upon adherence to the law of nature.

The distinction between man, beast, and God was also set forth in the first book of Aristotle's *Politics*. Aristotle remarked that those who live apart from the *polis* are either beasts or gods. Man is by nature a political animal, but beasts are below human nature and are therefore incapable of sharing the goods of the *polis*, while gods are above human nature and have no need of the goods of the *polis*. Aristotle also mentions that

> man is the best of animals when completed [*teleōthen*] but when separated from law and adjudication [*dikēs*][50] is the worst of all. For injustice [*adikia*] is harshest when it has arms, and man has arms by nature in prudence [or practical wisdom] and virtue which are very susceptible to being used for their opposites. Hence without virtue he is the most unholy and savage of animals and the worst with respect to sex and food. But justice [*dikaiosunē*] belongs to the *polis*. For adjudication [*dikē*] is an arrangement of the political community and justice is judgment about what is just.[51]

Without law and justice, man exists, even according to Aristotle, in something like a state of nature where virtue is a double-edged sword. Aristotle points to the rule of law and stern justice as the remedy for the tendency of man's natural arms to lead him to become unjust and "the most unholy and savage of animals." Locke is undoubtedly more sanguine in appealing to reason, the divine element in man given to him as a means to self-preservation. Self-preservation guided by reason inevitably points to the rule of law and constitutional government, no less in Locke than Aristotle. They differ, of course, on how government is to be founded and the ends that government is designed to serve. Both of these differences, I say, are due principally to the different political-theological predicaments that confronted the two political philosophers.

Reason, "the Voice of God" in man, eventually impels men into civil society for the protection of their "lives, liberties and estates." The law of nature is the law of reason (I.101), and it is easy to conclude that acting according to the dictates of reason is a moral obligation. How the law of nature is known and promulgated is not easily answered, but in the abstract, the obligations of the law of nature understood as reason should be clear. Properly informed and guided, the desire for self-preservation eventuates in civil society grounded in social compact. This

---

50. I have used Carnes Lord's translation of Aristotle's *Politics*, 2nd ed. (Chicago: University of Chicago Press, 2013), with minor modifications. I follow Lord's translation of the word *dikē* as "adjudication" because the context indicates a judicial or legal proceeding. *Dikē* can also mean "justice," "right," "custom," or "usage." *Dikē* is also the goddess of justice, and this may be the reason that "unholy" and "savage" are both mentioned.

51. Aristotle, *Politics*, 1253a30–35.

is reason's response to the insecurity of property in the state of nature. And, as we have already seen, the "great and *chief end*, therefore, of Men's uniting into Commonwealths, and putting themselves under Government, *is the Preservation of their Property*" (II.123). Reason—the law of nature—dictates the end of government as well as the form of the regime that is most conducive to securing that end. Contrary to the usual interpretation of chapter 10 of the *Second Treatise*, Locke does not argue that any form of government that the people consent to is legitimate. Rather, in reading his account of regime forms we discover that the only legitimate regime based on Lockean principles is a "commonwealth," one in which the legislative predominates and there is a separation between executive and legislative power. As Professor Robert Faulkner concludes, this excludes monarchy and oligarchy as well as hereditary aristocracy.[52] It is true that Locke limits the ends or purposes of government to the security of "lives, liberties and estates"; he reserves the discussion of the goods of the soul, which include morality and human happiness, for *An Essay Concerning Human Understanding*. The separate discussions of the goods of the body and the goods of the soul ultimately provide the foundation for the separation of church and state, the essential ingredient of Locke's entire scheme of constitutional government.

There are thus two elemental desires that animate human beings: self-preservation and happiness. Both, according to Locke, are capable of being ruled by reason, and in fact there is a moral obligation to follow reason in both. "Nature," Locke says, "has put into Man a desire of Happiness, and an aversion to Misery: These indeed are innate practical Principles, which (as practical Principles ought) do continue constantly to operate and influence all our Actions, without ceasing: these may be observ'd in all Persons and all Ages, steady and universal" (*An Essay Concerning Human Understanding*, I.iii.3). These "are Inclinations of the Appetite to good, not Impressions of truth on the Understanding," and therefore they are not practical principles properly so-called—Locke denies that there are any innate practical principles. Professor West argues that this passage shows conclusively that for Locke, "the pursuit of happiness is the fundamental natural inclination—not self preservation, as is often said of Locke." "Happiness," West avers, "is the regulatory principle for preservation, because happiness is the end of human life, and preservation is only part of the means."[53] The surprising—almost shocking—feature of the chapter "Of Power" in *An Essay Concerning Human Understanding* is that its principal object is to elucidate the power of reason to control the appetites and not, as we might otherwise expect, the power of reason to serve the demands of the passions. Professor Steven Forde aptly notes that chapter 21 "evolves into one of the most extended discussions in Locke's entire corpus of the nature of moral action and moral responsibility."[54] And in agreement with West, Forde maintains that "Locke does not in the *Essay*

---

52. See Robert Faulkner, "The First Liberal Democrat: Locke's Popular Government," *Review of Politics* 63, no. 1 (Winter 2001): 26.
53. West, "The Ground of Locke's Law of Nature," 30.
54. Steven Forde, *Locke, Science, and Politics* (New York: Cambridge University Press, 2013), 118.

rest morality on preservation. The specific appetite for preservation plays little or no role in his argument except perhaps insofar as preservation is a precondition of true happiness. Nor is Locke ultimately willing to concede that human happiness is simply relative and idiosyncratic." Locke's argument in *An Essay Concerning Human Understanding*, Forde observes, "is linked not to peace, or indeed to any social or political good, but to the individual comprehensive happiness. This is strikingly different from Hobbes."[55]

THE "VAIN" INQUIRY OF PHILOSOPHERS OF OLD RECONSIDERED

It may be helpful at this juncture to revisit the passage from the chapter "Of Power" that was discussed earlier and where, we recall, Locke boldly remarked,

> The Mind has a different relish, as well as the Palate . . . Hence it was, I think, that the Philosophers of old did in vain inquire, whether *Summum bonum* consists in Riches, or bodily Delights, or Virtue or Contemplation: And they might have as reasonably disputed, whether best Relish were to be found in Apples, Plums, or Nuts; and have divided themselves into Sects upon it. For as pleasant Tastes depend not on the things themselves, but their agreeableness to this or that particular Palate, wherein there is great variety: So the greatest Happiness consists in the having those things which produce the greatest Pleasure; and in the absence of those which cause any disturbance, any pain. Now, these to different Men, are very different things (II.xxi.55).

The implication seems at first glance to be that the "philosophers of old" inquired in vain because the different relishes of the mind were utterly subjective, thereby rendering any search for a *summum bonum* futile. This has led one intelligent observer to conclude that "Locke's 'pursuit of happiness' leads nowhere in particular. In fact, generally, it is a headlong flight from man's most constant companion—the '*uneasiness*' constituted by pain, the anticipation of pain, and the prospect of death."[56] Another insightful author writes that

> while mankind cannot agree on any fixed positive goals of life (any greatest pleasures, or least uneasinesses), our species can agree, especially as it became more reasonable and self-conscious, on what is more important, more gripping: the greatest evil we all seek to avoid or postpone. The most unremitting and powerful uneasiness for human beings is the fear of death and of the physical suffering that attends or intimates death.[57]

---

55. Ibid., 121.
56. Paul A. Rahe, *Republics Ancient and Modern: Classical Republicanism and the American Revolution* (Chapel Hill: University of North Carolina Press, 1992), 294.
57. Thomas Pangle, *The Spirit of Modern Republicanism* (Chicago: University of Chicago Press, 1988), 186.

This was the reasoning that prompted Strauss to conclude, as we saw earlier, that Locke had contrived a *summum malum*, the evil of death, as a more reliable spring to human behavior to replace the disputable claims made on behalf of a *summum bonum*. This reasoning, however, seems to have discounted or ignored some salient features of the passage under consideration.

Our commentators ignore an important qualification in which Locke avers,

> 'Tis not strange, nor unreasonable, that they should seek their Happiness . . . by pursuing all that delight them; wherein it will be no wonder to find variety and difference. For if there be no Prospect beyond the Grave, the inference is certainly right, "*Let us eat and drink,*" let us enjoy what we delight in, "*for tomorrow we shall die.*" This, I think, may serve to show us the Reason, why, though all Men's desires tend to Happiness, yet they are not moved by the same Object (II.xxi.55).

If there were prospects beyond the grave, however, then men's desire for happiness would be moved by the same object—a *summum bonum*. We have already seen Locke describe the pursuit of happiness as man's "greatest good," requiring the rule of reason over will. Most men, of course, when in the presence of uneasiness seek immediate indulgence without calculating the long-term consequences of such instant gratification. Reason and virtue are all too frequently powerless to combat the imprecations of an imperious will because, as we will see Locke argue shortly, virtue was left unadorned by "the heathen philosophers."

But let a man see, Locke says,

> that Virtue and Religion are necessary to his Happiness; let him look into the future State of Bliss or Misery, and see there God, the righteous Judge, ready to "*render to every man according to his deeds; to them who by patient continuance in well-doing, seek for Glory, and Honour, and Immortality, Eternal Life; but unto every Soul that doth Evil, Indignation and Wrath, Tribulation and Anguish*": To him, I say, who hath a prospect of the different State of perfect Happiness or Misery, that attends all Men after this Life, depending on their Behavior here, the measures of Good and Evil, that govern his choice, are mightily changed. For since nothing of Pleasure and Pain in this Life, can bear any proportion to endless Happiness, or exquisite Misery of an immortal Soul hereafter, Actions in his Power will have their preference, not according to the transient Pleasure or Pain that accompanies, or follows them here; but as they serve to secure that perfect durable Happiness hereafter (II.xxi.60).

Locke does not vouchsafe to the readers of *An Essay Concerning Human Understanding* the truth of a future state where a "righteous judge" will mete out justice in the form of infinite happiness or misery for deeds performed in this life, but he does offer his readers a wager of sorts. "The Rewards and Punishments of another life, which the Almighty has established, as the Enforcements of his Law," Locke conjectures, "are of weight enough to determine the Choice, against whatever Pleasure or Pain this Life can show, when the eternal State is considered but in its bare possibility, which no Body can make any doubt of" (II.xxi.70). The man who lives "a

vertuous Life with the certain expectation of everlasting Bliss, which may come" runs
little risk if his expectations are disappointed. The virtuous and pious man may enter
an eternal life of infinite happiness; if not, he will have enjoyed the considerable
benefits of having lived a virtuous and therefore happy life, here reaping its intrinsic
rewards. The vicious man, by contrast, runs considerable risk if his wager that there
is no future judgment loses; he will suffer infinite misery for eternity in addition
to living a present life of unhappiness and misery, regardless of the fact that his life
might have been one of successive, albeit transient, pleasures. Locke acknowledges,

> I have forborne to mention anything of the certainty, or probability of a future State,
> designing here to show the *wrong Judgment*, that anyone must allow, he makes upon
> his own Principles, laid how he pleases, who prefers the short pleasures of a vicious Life
> upon any consideration, whilst he knows, and cannot but be certain, that a future Life
> is at least possible (II.xxi.70).

Happiness, whether considered as a complete life of virtue in this life or as "infinite felicity" in a future state seems to be the "highest good" for human beings. Is it
really so clear cut that Locke has replaced the *summum bonum* of the "old philosophers" with a *summum malum*, or that he argues that since the "old philosophers"
sought in vain for a *summum bonum*, he adopts the position that there is no discov-
erable *summum bonum*? He certainly argues that reason can discover the *summum
bonum* in the case of individuals who are capable of reasoning adequately and can be
supplied by revelation for those who lack such a capacity. It can therefore be supplied
by reason or revelation. In the latter, there is no doubt that Locke argues that the
hope of a future state of eternal happiness serves as the *summum bonum*. Or is it true
that he really maintains that the hope and desire of eternal life is merely a *summum
malum* motivated by the fear of death?

PURSUIT OF HAPPINESS IN THE
REASONABLENESS OF CHRISTIANITY

Locke continued the discussion of the pursuit of happiness in *The Reasonableness
of Christianity*, published anonymously six years after the appearance of *An Essay
Concerning Human Understanding* in 1689. *The Reasonableness of Christianity* might
be characterized as a kind of "original intent" theology, an effort to explicate biblical text by teaching "plainly . . . the Doctrine of our Saviour and his Apostles, as
delivered in the Scriptures, and not as taught by the several Sects of Christians."[58] By
advocating a strict reliance on biblical text, Locke endeavored to diminish the influence of sectarianism and its internecine disputes. Victor Nuovo rightly notes that
The Reasonableness of Christianity "purports to be entirely biblical and exegetical";

---

58. John Locke, *A Second Vindication of the Reasonableness of Christianity*, in *Vindications of the Reasonableness of Christianity*, ed. Victor Nuovo (Oxford: Clarendon Press, 2012), 36.

as such, it "is free of the a priori constraints of orthodoxy, and creedal or confessional standards."[59] Locke relates that he had seen in his own reading of biblical text "what a plain, simple, reasonable thing Christianity was, suited to all Conditions and Capacities."[60] What we seek in Scripture, Locke contends, is not some system of theology or sectarianism but knowledge of "the Will of our Lord." Where that will "is spoken plainly we cannot miss it, and it is evident, he requires our assent." Where, however, there is obscurity or ambiguity, as Locke readily admits there frequently is, there must be a fair effort to understand the text. The effort itself secures the faithful "from guilty Disobedience to his will, or a sinful Error in Faith," however the obscurity or ambiguity is resolved or whether it is left unresolved. If God had required more, he would have declared his will "as clearly, and as uniformly as he did that Fundamental Article, that we were to believe him to be the *Messiah* our King."[61]

Locke was accused of being a Socinian—and, by extension, an atheist[62]—as well as a deist. The charge of Socinianism cannot be taken seriously because, as John C. Higgins-Biddle notes, "some polemicists applied the label to anyone who deviated in any way on matters of the Trinity or atonement, or to those who advocated religious toleration or the use of reason in religion."[63] Locke, of course, denied that he was a Socinian, insisting on the importance and the necessity of revelation. His claim that he had not read Racovian texts, however, should be taken with the same degree of skepticism as his statement that he had never read the "justly decried" works of Hobbes and Spinoza.[64] Locke not only denied being a deist but also claimed, on the contrary, that *The Reasonableness of Christianity* "was chiefly designed" to persuade deists to Christianity.[65] "I was flatter'd to think," Locke wrote,

> it might be of some use in the World; especially to those who thought either that there was no need of Revelation at all, or that the Revelation of our Saviour required the Belief of such Articles for Salvation, which the settled Notions and their way of reasoning in some, and want of Understanding in others, made impossible to them. Upon these two Topicks the Objections seemed to turn, which were with most Assurance, made by *Deists* against Christianity; But against *Christianity misunderstood*. It seem'd to me, that there needed no more to shew them the Weakness of their Exceptions, but to lay plainly before them the Doctrine of our Saviour and his Apostles, as delivered in the Scriptures, and not as taught by the several Sects of Christians.[66]

59. Nuovo, "Introduction," in *Vindications of the Reasonableness of Christianity*, xxix–xxx.
60. Locke, *A Second Vindication of the Reasonableness of Christianity*, 36.
61. Ibid., 70.
62. Locke, *A Vindication of the Reasonableness of Christianity*, in *Vindications of the Reasonableness of Christianity*, 8–9.
63. John C. Higgins-Biddle, ed., "Introduction," in *The Reasonableness of Christianity as Delivered in the Scriptures* (Oxford: Clarendon Press, 1999), lx–lxi.
64. Locke, *A Vindication of the Reasonableness of Christianity*, 18, and editor's note 2; John Locke, *Second Reply to the Bishop of Worcester*, in *The Works of John Locke* (London: R. Johnson, 1801), 4:477. See also Locke, *A Second Vindication of the Reasonableness of Christianity*, 229.
65. Locke, *A Second Vindication of the Reasonableness of Christianity*, 191.
66. Ibid., 36.

Locke himself professed Christianity:

> Truly, I did not think my self so considerable, that the World need be troubled about
> me, whether I were a follower of *Socinus, Arminius, Calvin,* or any other Leader of a Sect
> amongst Christians. A Christian I am sure I am, because I believe *Jesus* to be the *Messiah,*
> the King and Saviour promised, and sent by God: And as a Subject of his Kingdom,
> I take the rule of my Faith, and Life, from the Will declar'd and left upon Record in
> the inspired Writings of the Apostles and Evangelists in the New Testament: Which I
> endeavour to the utmost of my power, as is my Duty, to understand in their true sense
> and meaning. To lead me into their true meaning, I know . . . no infallible Guide, but
> the same Holy Spirit, from whom these Writings at first came.[67]

There is no compelling reason, I believe, not to accept Locke's profession of faith.
It should be already clear, however, that Locke is not an orthodox Christian. He
is heterodox in many respects, but we are surely not surprised to find heterodoxy
among political philosophers. Heterodoxy, however, is not the same as atheism. All
philosophers, in one way or another, ask the question *Quid sit deus?* And all political
philosophers who actively confront the theological-political problem will be subject
to charges of heterodoxy, if not atheism. There is no doubt that Locke sought major
reforms of Christian doctrine that he believed would be politically salutary. Those
reforms were aimed, most immediately, at reducing the corrosive influence of sectarianism on religious tolerance and on preparing the ground for the establishment
of constitutional government.

The *First Treatise* is Locke's most radical exposition of the theological-political
problem. Professor Pangle surely exaggerates, however, when he remarks that
Locke was intent on revealing "what he regards as the absurdity and inhumanity
of the authentic teaching" of the Bible while at the same time preparing a new
teaching "in the service of a new, reasonable conception of *nature's* God."[68] On
this account, the *Second Treatise* would be the "revelation" of "nature's God," adumbrating a reasonable and just account of man's original condition in the state
of nature and his redemption by civil society. Locke's attempt to reconcile reason
and revelation, to the limited extent that it is politically possible to do so, I say,
can hardly be equated with the attempt to replace the biblical God with "nature's
God." We have already seen Locke's statement in the *First Treatise* that "reason" is
our "only Star and compass" (I.58). That statement is qualified, to some extent, by
the fact that reason is said to be "the Voice of God" in man (I.86). God has given
man reason. God has revealed some things plainly and some obscurely and perhaps
has even withheld many things entirely from man. It would be impious to assume
that God did not intend men to use reason in the conduct of their affairs. This
would be to assume that God gave men reason to no purpose or that God worked

67. Ibid., 177, 179.
68. Pangle, *Spirit of Modern Republicanism,* 135.

without a design, even if God's ultimate design remains mysterious. Philosophers press the boundaries of reason without knowing whether God has set limits. There is no doubt that Locke rejects orthodox tenets of biblical theology in those cases where he believes they are so contrary to reason as to be harmful to or destructive of political life. The divine right of kings, which drew support from both Old and New Testament theology, was only the most obvious theological doctrine that Locke opposed. Perhaps just as important for his republican theology was the rejection of Original Sin. Other, far more subtle (and perhaps more far-reaching) theological doctrines also came under his critical scrutiny. Nowhere, as far as I am aware, did Locke ever say that reason was a complete substitute for revelation or that revelation had been rendered superfluous by the advances of modern science. "*Reason*," Locke seemed to maintain, "is natural *Revelation*, whereby the eternal Father of Light, and Fountain of all Knowledge communicates to Mankind that portion of Truth, which he has laid within the reach of their natural Faculties" (*An Essay Concerning Human Understanding*, IV.xix.4). Ultimately, however, Locke does concede that "*Reason* must judge" whether something is in fact a "divine Revelation, or no" (IV.xviii.10). Reason is the only defense against false prophets.

"Mankind, are and must be allowed to pursue their Happiness," Locke proclaims, because "Happiness" is "their chief End."[69] The "philosophers of old" inquired in vain about this *summum bonum* because they were not aware—or only vaguely aware—of the doctrine of a future state of rewards and punishments. And it was the providential combination of reason and revelation represented in the teaching of the Gospels that made it possible for Locke to see clearly "the necessity of preferring and pursuing true happiness as our greatest good" (II.xxi.51).

"The Doctrine of a future State," the promise of "a perfect compleat Life of an Eternal duration," would serve

> as another relish and efficacy, to perswade Men that if they live well here, they shall be happy hereafter. Open their Eyes upon the endless unspeakable joys of another Life; And their Hearts will find something solid and powerful to move them. The view of Heaven and Hell, will cast a light upon the short pleasures and pains of this present state; and give attractions and encouragements to Virtue, which reason, and interest, and the Care of ourselves, cannot but allow and prefer.[70]

The old philosophers had done their utmost, Locke concedes: "they depended on Reason and Her Oracles; which contain nothing but Truth. But yet some parts of that Truth lye too deep for our Natural Powers easily to reach, and make plain and visible to mankind, without some Light from above to direct them."[71] It is "too hard a task," Locke avers,

---

69. Locke, *The Reasonableness of Christianity*, ch. 14, 161.
70. Ibid., ch. 14, 162–63.
71. Ibid., ch. 14, 155.

for unassisted Reason, to establish Morality in all its parts upon its true foundations with a clear and convincing light. And 'tis at least a surer and shorter way, to the Apprehensions of the vulgar, and mass of Mankind, that one manifestly sent from God, and coming with visible Authority from him, should as a King and Law-maker tell them their Duties; and require their Obedience; Than leave it to the long, and sometime intricate deductions of Reason, to be made out to them. Such trains of reasonings the Greatest part of Mankind have neither leisure to weigh; nor, for want of Education and Use, skill to judge of.[72]

In sum, "the greatest part cannot know, and therefore they must believe." Therefore, "the Instruction of the People were best still to be left to the Precepts and principles of the Gospel."[73] "The philosophers," Locke argues, "indeed shewed the beauty of Virtue: They set her off so as drew Men's Eyes and approbation to her: But leaving her unendowed, very few were willing to espouse her." Thus, "'tis not strange that the learned Heathens satisfied not many with such airy commendations."[74] Locke's position is that there can be no effectual truth or morality without the belief in a future state of rewards and punishments. The endowment that the old philosophers could not provide was granted by revelation alone.

Philosophers "before our Saviour's time" had an inkling of "the Doctrine of a future State" but it was "not clearly known in the World." The doctrine of a future state as "a perfect compleat Life of an Eternal duration . . . entered little into their thoughts, and less into their perswasions."[75] Without belief in a future state, there is no solid ground for morality in this world. A useful, universal standard of morality must proceed from either reason or revelation. If from reason, the principles must be "self-evident in themselves" with all its parts capable of being deduced from these first principles "by clear and evident demonstration." If from revelation, there must be evidence of a "Commission from Heaven," coming "with Authority from God, to deliver his Will and Commands to the World."[76] No philosopher has ever succeeded in giving a complete moral code to the world. Although some have succeeded in specifying parts of a code, none have succeeded in composing one in its entirety. None of the philosophers, Locke says,

> before our Saviour's time, ever did, or went about to give us a *Morality*. 'Tis true there is a *Law of Nature*. But who is there that ever did, or undertook to give it us all entire, as a Law; No more, nor no less, what was contained in, and had the obligations of the Law? Who, ever made out all the parts of it; Put them together; And shewed the World their obligation? Where was there any such Code, that Mankind might have recourse to, as their unerring Rule, before our Saviour's time?[77]

---

72. Ibid., ch. 14, 148.
73. Ibid., ch. 14, 157.
74. Ibid., ch. 14, 162, 147.
75. Ibid., ch. 14, 162.
76. Ibid., ch. 14, 152.
77. Ibid., ch. 14, 152–53.

Early in *An Essay Concerning Human Understanding*, Locke posed the question of why "Men should keep their Compacts," a "Rule in Morality" that he said was "great and undeniable." Locke rehearsed three different answers supporting this rule: "A Christian, who has the view of Happiness and Misery in another Life . . . will *give* this as a *Reason*: Because God, who has the power of eternal life and death, requires it of us." A Hobbian, however, would answer, "Because the Publick requires it, and the *Leviathan* will punish you, if you do not." One of the "old *Heathen* philosophers" would answer, "Because it was dishonest, below the Dignity of a Man, and opposite to Vertue, the highest Perfection of humane Nature, to do otherwise" (I.iii.5). Locke concludes, "Hence naturally flows the great variety of Opinions, concerning Moral Rules, which are to be found amongst Men, according to the different sorts of Happiness, they have a Prospect of, or propose to themselves" (I.iii.6). None of the three opinions denies that keeping compacts is a moral rule, but they differ as to *why* it is a moral imperative and the ground of obligation. The two extremes are represented by a Christian and an ancient heathen philosopher. The Christian keeps contracts out of obedience to God's will and the expectation that a life of obedience will be rewarded by "eternal life." The heathen philosopher defends the keeping of contracts because it is intrinsically right to do so; honesty is a virtue and the practice of virtue, in addition to being inherently rewarding, is the perfection of human nature.[78] The Hobbian occupies the middle position: compacts result exclusively from positive law, and the full force and weight of Leviathan offers the most immediate and effective means of holding men to their public obligations.[79]

Locke immediately observes that the differences of opinion about this "great and undeniable rule in morality" are proof that there are no innate practical principles "imprinted in our Minds immediately by the Hand of God" (I.iii.6). Nevertheless, the obedience that is owed to God is "so congruous to the light of reason, that a great part of mankind give testimony to the law of nature," to such an extent "that several moral rules, may receive from mankind, a very general approbation, without knowing, or admitting the true ground of morality; which can only be the will and law of a God, who sees men in the dark, has in his hand reward and punishments and power enough to call to account the proudest offender." So, by this account, the law of nature receives the "general approbation" of mankind—and not just from those who are capable of following complicated chains of reasoning—by a kind of divination that is an integral part of the daily life of

---

78. The only philosopher identified as "heathen" in *An Essay Concerning Human Understanding* is Cicero (II.xxviii.11).

79. Hobbes contends that there are only two "imaginable helps" in "mans nature" to strengthen the performance of covenants. The first is fear of the consequences of breaking one's word; the second is "a Glory, or Pride in appearing not to need to breake it." The second is "a Generosity too rarely found to be presumed on, especially in the pursuers of Wealth, Command, or sensuall Pleasure; which are the greatest part of Mankind." Thus fear is "the Passion to be reckoned upon." And fear has two general objects: the fear of "the Power of Spirits Invisible," and the "Power of those men they shall therein Offend." The former is "the greater Power, yet the feare of the later is commonly the greater Feare" (*Leviathan*, ed. C. B. Macpherson [New York: Penguin, 1968], 200).

every Christian (I.iii.6). It is precisely in this sense, I say, that Aristotle in *Rhetoric* wrote of a common law "according to nature" (*katá phúsin*) that contains the idea of just and unjust by nature and that all men somehow divine even if there is no positive agreement. Neither Aristotle nor Locke believed that the idea of justice and injustice, not to say the law of nature, is innate in human beings. Knowledge of nature and the law of nature begins with experience, the abstraction of the intelligible experience from merely sensible experience. Beyond this, Aristotle and Locke diverge radically in their understanding. Their point of departure, however, is remarkably similar.

Locke suggests another curious example in *The Reasonableness of Christianity* when he poses the question: Was there any morality in existence at the time that could have informed the choice made by Brutus and Cassius to assassinate Caesar? Both were "Men of Parts and Virtue," Locke says, and one even believed in "a future Being." If, to resolve any moral doubts they may have harbored, they had turned to "the sayings of the Wise, and the Declarations of Philosophers," they would have been sent "into a wild Wood of uncertainty, to an endless maze; from which they should never get out." We know, of course, that Brutus was a Stoic and Cassius an Epicurean. Had they adhered to their professed philosophic doctrines, both would have eschewed involvement in politics and accepted the fated course of events. If they had had recourse to "the Religions of the World," Locke continues, it would have been "yet worse," resulting in moral anarchy. And if they had resort "to their own Reason," while there might have been "some light and certainty," there would have been insufficient clarity since reason "had hitherto failed all Mankind in a perfect Rule," nor had doubts that "had arisen amongst the Studious and Thinking Philosophers" been adequately "resolved."[80]

The moral law that might have guided Brutus and Cassius "Jesus Christ hath given us in the New Testament . . . by Revelation. We have from him," Locke insists,

> a full and sufficient Rule for our direction; And conformable to that of Reason. But the truth and obligation of its Precepts have their force, and are put past doubt to us, by the evidence of his Mission. He was sent by God: His Miracles shew it; and the Authority of God in his Precepts cannot be questioned. Here *Morality* has a sure Standard, that Revelation vouches, and Reason cannot gainsay, nor question; but both together witness to come from God the great Law-maker.[81]

Revelation is here characterized as "conformable to reason." Revelation provides the "first knowledge" of morality that is quickly "found to be agreeable to Reason; and such as can by no means be contradicted." These are truths that one "readily assents to, as consonant to reason."[82] Thus, on this account, revelation presents the precepts of morality as self-evident truths, which are difficult for reason to discover but, once

---

80. Locke, *The Reasonableness of Christianity*, ch. 14, 154.
81. Ibid., ch. 14, 152–53.
82. Ibid., ch. 14, 148; see Locke, *An Essay Concerning Human Understanding*, IV.vii.11.

revealed, command reason's assent. All of the parts of a complete moral code can be deduced from the self-evident principles that are revealed. Locke claims that "the Precepts and Principles of the Gospel" contain "All the Duties of Morality" and that those duties "lye there clear, and plain and easy to be understood." This is the reason it is to be accounted "the surest, the safest, and most effectual way of teaching" because it "suits the lowest Capacities of Reasonable Creatures, so it reaches and satisfies, Nay, enlightens the highest."[83]

The morality of the Gospels, had that morality been known to the conspirators, would certainly have counseled them against the attempt on Caesar's life. In political terms, the commands of Gospel morality would have been similar to Epicurianism or Stoicism. We saw St. Paul's admonition in chapter 2 that our government is in heaven, not on earth, and his reproach that our care must be for the things of heaven and not for those of this earth. Similarly, Romans 13 imposes a Christian duty of passive obedience to rulers. But had the morality of the Gospels been followed by those two principal conspirators, the world-historical event that is represented by the assassination of Caesar would not have transpired, nor would Christianity, in all likelihood, have found such propitious conditions for its reception. It was this most un-Christian act that created the universal empire that was the necessary political condition for the establishment of universal religion. On the issue of tyrannicide, Locke's argument in the *Second Treatise* leaves no doubt that the decision of the conspirators to assassinate Caesar was fully justified by reason and natural right. In Shakespeare's *Julius Caesar*, Cassius predicts that the tyrannicide just consummated will be reenacted countless times in the future: "How many ages hence / Shall this our lofty scene be acted over / In states unborn and accents yet unknown!" (III.i). In these prophetic words, one easily recognizes a prefiguration of the American Revolution.

Locke, I say, drew our attention to Caesar because he wanted to emphasize the fact that he understood that the providential history of pagan Rome was the necessary political precondition for the acceptance of Christianity and that the assassination of Caesar was the final act of that pagan drama. Caesar's assassination did not restore the Republic, as the conspirators hoped, but eventuated in the establishment of the Empire. The distinction between Rome and the provinces was abolished, as was the distinction between citizens and non-citizens. Rome became a universal regime—it became the world. As Professor Jaffa remarked,

> If Rome was the world, then political life as heretofore understood—above all, as understood in Aristotle's *Politics*—ceased to exist. The Roman empire became by anticipation, the secular antecedent of the city of God: in which also there are no political identities recognizable as such, and no ruling and being ruled.
>
> Once Roman citizenship became universal citizenship, the separate gods of the separate cities, whose worship Rome had both permitted and protected, lost their reason for being. If everyone was a Roman, then Roman law was everyone's law. The separate gods of the separate cities had been the lawgivers of their cities. If there was but one law

---

83. Locke, *The Reasonableness of Christianity*, ch. 14, 158–59; see ch. 14, 169.

there must be only one God. Some form of monotheism was thus destined to become the Roman religion. The only question was what form. We observe here only that Christianity was able to combine the monotheism of Judaism with the universality of Roman citizenship.[84]

It was thus the apotheosis of the pagan Caesar[85] that made the acceptance of Christianity possible, if not inevitable. In a slightly different context, but one that addresses more directly the point that Locke seems intent on engaging, Jaffa notes,

> The Gospel of man's salvation could not be preached to the world until Caesar had prepared the world for its reception. Christ's kingdom not of this world depended upon Caesar's kingdom in this world. We might say that Jesus' separation of morality from politics, making each man's salvation a personal matter between himself and God, depended upon Caesar's subjection of morality to politics.[86]

The idea of a universal empire supported by a universal monotheistic religion ruled the West for nearly a thousand years. Christianity's morality was universal and therefore apolitical—unconnected to any particular political regime. The attempt to sustain a universal political empire, however, was doomed to failure because it contravened the most powerful instincts of human nature, the desire for attachment, whether to the clan, the tribe, the city, or the nation-state. Human nature rebelled against the universal state. We discussed Aristotle's famous contention that man is by nature a political being. While human beings share a universal nature, the fulfillment of that nature can take place only in particular political communities. The potential of human nature can be actualized only in the presence of political life, and Aristotle maintained that the *polis* was the highest expression of political life. After the Roman Empire dissolved into its constituent parts, Christianity survived as a universal religion. The potential for conflict between obedience to the laws of individual regimes and the laws of the City of God was manifest, especially after sectarianism within Christianity itself not only greatly magnified the potential for conflict but also set the stage for religious warfare.

Sectarian religious warfare was still a present memory when Locke wrote *An Essay Concerning Human Understanding*, *The Reasonableness of Christianity*, and *A Letter on Toleration*. These works were highly controversial when published, and all three in different ways sought to restrain the intolerance and sectarianism that had fueled the wars of religion within Christianity. The City of God and the City of Man, Locke reasoned, could be rendered capable of cooperating for the common good. Mono-

---

84. Harry V. Jaffa, "Equality, Liberty, Wisdom, Morality and Consent," in *The Rediscovery of America: Essays by Harry V. Jaffa on the New Birth of Politics*, ed. Edward J. Erler and Ken Masugi (Lanham, MD: Rowman & Littlefield, 2019), 42–43.

85. In *Julius Caesar*, Octavius proclaims that Caesar suffered "three and thirty wounds" (v.i), whereas Plutarch, Shakespeare's source, reports that Caesar received "three and twenty wounds upon his body."

86. Harry V. Jaffa, *A New Birth of Freedom: Abraham Lincoln and the Coming of the Civil War* (Lanham, MD: Rowman & Littlefield, 2000), 133, 129.

theism is uniquely open to reason, and reason or philosophy must become the hand-maid of theology; in the case of Christianity, this means that reason must become the handmaid of revelation in confronting the theological-political problem.[87] As we have already seen, in the ancient city there was no possibility of a conflict between law and piety because duty to the law and to the gods were one and the same. Each city had its particular gods, and the laws prescribed the obligations of piety. In Juda-ism, there was a universal God but a particular people. Disputes about God's law and secular law therefore did not arise in the way they did within Christianity. Christian-ity was never attached to a particular people or a particular regime, and conflicts be-tween secular law and revealed law or ecclesiastical authority were always close to the surface of political life. It must be acknowledged (and repeated), however, that reason and revelation can never agree on the highest things—what ultimately completes and perfects human life—but there can be agreement on a political and moral level. The articulation of this agreement, I say, was the principal purpose of *The Reasonableness of Christianity* and *An Essay Concerning Human Understanding*.

THE MORAL AND POLITICAL RESOLUTION OF THE THEOLOGICAL-POLITICAL PREDICAMENT

This agreement is perhaps most succinctly expressed by a statement in *An Essay Con-cerning Human Understanding* that we have already had occasion to quote in part: "*Reason* is natural *Revelation*, whereby the eternal Father of Light, and Fountain of all Knowledge communicates to Mankind that portion of Truth, which he has laid within the reach of their natural Faculties." By the same token, Locke says, "*Revela-tion* is natural *Reason* enlarged by a new set of Discoveries communicated by GOD immediately, which *Reason* vouches the Truth of, by the Testimony and Proofs it gives, that they come from GOD. So that he that takes away *Reason*, to make way for *Revelation*, puts out the Light of both" (IV.xix.4). On this account, revelation cannot be known without reason, and reason would not exist without revelation. Revelation is known to reason in the form of self-evident truths, which seems to be the origin of all knowledge. It is reason, not faith or tradition, that judges the truth of revelation, notwithstanding the fact that there are "many Things" "beyond the Discovery of our natural Faculties, and above *Reason*" that are, "when revealed, *the proper matter of Faith*." For example, "that the dead shall rise, and live again" is "be-yond the Discovery of *Reason*" and is purely a matter of faith (IV.xviii.7). But within the proper sphere of reason's domain, accepting something that contradicts reason as God's revelation, Locke avers, would "wholly destroy the most excellent Part of his Workmanship, our Understandings" (IV.xviii.5). "If anything shall be thought *Rev-elation*," Locke assures us, "which is contrary to the plain Principles of Reason, and

---

87. See Thomas Aquinas, *Summa Theologica*, I, qu.1a.5, esp. the reference to Proverbs 4:3 and Jerome's Letter (no. 70).

the evident Knowledge the Mind has of its own clear and distinct *Ideas*, there *Reason* must be hearkened to, as to a Matter within its Province" (IV.xviii.8). Whatever God has revealed is certainly true, since God "cannot err and will not deceive" (IV. xviii.8). No doubt can be made of God's revelations since both knowledge and faith are dependent on his revelations. But the question is whether something is a divine revelation, and here "*Reason* must judge" (IV.xviii.10).

In *The Reasonableness of Christianity*, Locke notes that the heathen philosophers had been unable to articulate from undeniable principles "*Ethics* in a Science like Mathematicks in every part demonstrable." Locke quickly notes that such an ethics would have been ineffective, in any case, since the "greatest part of mankind" lacked the leisure and capacity to follow the required demonstrations.[88] Locke, however, remarks in *An Essay Concerning Human Understanding*, "I am bold to think, that *Morality is capable of Demonstration*, as well as Mathematicks: Since the precise real *Essence* of the Things moral Words stand for, may be perfectly known; and so the Congruity, or incongruity of the Things themselves, be certainly discovered, in which consists perfect Knowledge" (III.xi.165). For Locke, ideas abstracted from sense experience are not intrinsic to the matter and motion experienced by the senses but are purely a creation of the understanding, the "nominal essences" or abstract definitions necessary to organize sense experiences (III.iii.17). The "nominal essences" are not expressions of objective reality but mental constructs—created species, as it were—to facilitate understanding in a universe of matter and motion that would otherwise be incomprehensible. These mental constructs are therefore arbitrary impositions. But once adequate definitions have been settled, the mind can proceed to logical conclusions that yield mathematical certainty. Mathematics is concerned with abstract ideas that are extrapolations from sense perception, and it deals only with relations among ideas wholly independent of reality. Thus mathematics can be a precise discipline yielding precise knowledge. Locke calculates that moral reasoning can produce the same results because it can be made to deal exclusively with relations among abstract ideas divorced from reality in the same way that mathematics does. The nominal essences, as mere mental compositions, can be manipulated as logical constructs as precisely as mathematical proofs.

Morality, of course, belongs to the category that Locke calls "mixed modes." Sense perception yields simple ideas, "those *Ideas*, we have of *Yellow, White, Heat, Cold, Soft, Hard, Bitter, Sweet*, and all those which we call sensible qualities, which . . . the senses convey into the mind . . . from external Objects" (II.i.3). Simple ideas can be combined by active operations of the mind into complex ideas (II.i.4). "As simple ideas are observed to exist in several combinations united together; so the mind has a power to consider several of them united together, as one idea; and that not only as they are united in external objects, but as itself has joined them" (II.xii.1). An illustration of a complex idea "united in external circumstances" might be hard surfaces that are black or malleable surfaces that are yellow. For complex ideas that are purely constructs of the mind, Locke gives these examples: "*Beauty, Gratitude, a Man, An*

88. Locke, *The Reasonableness of Christianity*, ch. 14, 157.

army, the Universe." Each complex idea is "complicated of various simple *Ideas,*" but "when the Mind pleases, considered each by itself, as one entire thing, and signified by one name" (II.xii.1). Complex ideas, "compounded of simple *Ideas* of several kinds, put together to make one complex one, *v.g. Beauty,* consisting of a certain composition of Colour and Figure, causing delight in the Beholder; *Theft,* which being the concealed change of the possession of any thing, without the consent of the Proprietor, contains, as is visible, a combination of several *ideas* of several kinds; and these I call *mixed Modes*" (II.xii.5).

Mixed modes, Locke readily admits, "*are* not only *made* by the Mind, but made *very arbitrarily,* made without Patterns, or reference to any real Existence." To judge the morality of adultery or incest, it is sufficient that one complex idea has been formed into an "*Archetype,* and specific *Idea,* whether ever any such Action were committed *in rerum natura,* or no" (III.v.3). Thus mixed modes—the specific mode of reasoning about morality—is a "voluntary Collection of *Ideas* put together in the Mind, independent from any original Patterns in Nature." Locke reiterates that moral ideas exist and give rise to a train of reasoned conclusions whose truth and knowledge can be certain even if the things to which the moral ideas have reference have no real being or existence. Adultery and incest can be judged morally reprehensible even if those practices had never existed. After adding sacrilege to adultery and incest as an example of the kind of moral reasoning that might proceed under mixed modes, Locke ventures a surprising example: "And, I think, no body can deny, but that the *Resurrection* was a Species of mixed Modes in the Mind, before it really existed" (III.v.5). The mind is dependent upon the real world of experience for simple ideas, but the combination and conjunction of simple ideas that form complex ideas and moral reasoning is the arbitrary creation of the mind without any connection to nature or reality. As Locke concludes, "these Species of mixed Modes, are the workmanship of the Understanding: And there is nothing more evident, than that for the most part, in the framing these *Ideas,* the Mind searches not its Patterns in Nature, nor refers the *Ideas* it makes to the real existence of Things; but puts such together, as may best serve its own Purposes, without tying it self to a precise imitation of any thing that really exists" (III.v.6).

Simple ideas do depend on being and real existence, but according to Locke, science has revealed such a complex world of matter and motion that human sense perception is inadequate for a complete understanding of a universe that seems to be devoid of any real moral structure. Locke does not argue that sense perception is deceptive, only that it is inadequate to detect the bewildering complexities of matter and motion that constitute the universe. Any truly objective account of reality will have to await future scientific progress; it cannot be revealed by unaided sense perception. But crude sense perception and experience—the first step in knowledge—can be relied upon in the formation of simple ideas, and these, in turn, can be aggregated into complex ideas and modes of thinking, the complex mode being the one related specifically to moral reasoning.

We might well be skeptical of Locke's claim that moral reasoning can yield the same precision as mathematical reasoning. Even if we concede that complex moral modes are abstracted from reality in the same way as mathematical concepts, moral reasoning (unlike mathematical demonstration) yields prescriptive or normative results and thus involves something more than mere demonstration; it involves politics and prudence, the practical wisdom that is required to deal with the variable elements of the non-abstract world of political life. Politics and prudence are topics conspicuously missing from *An Essay Concerning Human Understanding*.

The real essence of each species is known through the workmanship of the mind, and such being the case, Locke avers, "*I am bold to think, that Morality is capable of Demonstration*, as well as Mathematicks: Since the precise real Essence of the Things moral Words stand for, may be perfectly known; and so the Congruity, or Incongruity of the Things themselves, be certainly discovered, in which consists perfect Knowledge" (III.xi.16). Thus, once definitions are settled, demonstrative proofs that produce certain knowledge are only a matter of agreement or disagreement among ideas (IV.iv.7).

Locke certainly implies that a complete moral code can be based on this demonstrative method, although he never endeavored to articulate one, even when his friends urged him to do so. It would, of course, have been a task of immense magnitude. Rather, he gives a few examples from which, presumably, the reader can extrapolate the underlying principles. It is striking, however, that Locke does not seem content to let the issue of morality rest with the confident pronouncements he made in *The Reasonableness of Christianity* that the New Testament supplied a complete and adequate code of morality that was confirmed by reason. In detailing how reason reaches mathematical certainty regarding moral issues, Locke is demonstrating how reason confirms revelation. Every self-evident truth and every intuitive knowledge is tantamount to a revelation, and this provides the point of departure in the chain of reasoning that leads to moral truth and moral certainty. We saw earlier that Locke describes the law of nature in *Two Treatises of Government* as both reason and the voice of God (I.101; II.6; II.142; II.195). The voice of God is translated or communicated to reason through demonstration. The laws of nature are the product of this reasoning and provide the metes and bounds of moral truth and can properly be denominated the "Laws of Nature and Nature's God."

Two of the examples that Locke gives demonstrating the mathematical certainty of moral propositions are of particular interest:

> *Where there is no Property there is no Injustice*, is a Proposition as certain as any Demonstration in *Euclid*: For the *Idea of Property*, being a right to any thing; and the *Idea* to which the Name *Injustice* is given, being the Invasion or Violation of that right; it is evident, that these *Ideas* being thus established, and these Names annexed to them, I can as certainly know this Proposition to be true, as that a Triangle has three Angles equal to two right ones.

The second example is, as we recognize from our reading of the *Second Treatise*, closely connected: "*No Government allows absolute Liberty: The Idea* of Government being the establishment of Society upon certain Rules or Laws, which require Conformity to them; and the *Idea* of absolute Liberty being for any one to do whatever he pleases; I am as capable of being certain of the Truth of this Proposition, as of any in Mathematics" (IV.iii:18). It is a simple matter of comparing the congruence or incongruence of two ideas, property and justice. If there is no property, there can be no injustice. Similarly, the two ideas of government and absolute liberty are compared. Government means conformity to rules and law that is clearly incongruent with absolute liberty; thus no government allows absolute liberty. As we expected, these moral proofs are highly abstract, but, as Locke asserts, it is impossible, given the definitions, to deny the train of reasoning that leads to an irrefutable conclusion. The idea of property is clearly inseparable from the idea of justice, a theme that Locke makes central in the *Second Treatise*, as he does the relation of government to a proper understanding of the rule of law and liberty. The rule of law depends on a proper understanding of the distinction between liberty and license.

Locke's examples remind us of the "maxims in ethics and politics" that Hamilton said were of "the same nature" as self-evident truths discussed in chapter 2. Hamilton did not claim mathematical certainty for his maxims, but he did claim that the self-evident character of the maxims he adduced—for example, that the "means ought to be proportioned to the end"—compelled assent. In any case, the right to property and the rule of law, both necessary conclusions from the self-evident truth that all men are created equal, were central principles for the American founders.

4

Locke and Madison on Property

"Man being born [with] all the Rights and Privileges of the Law of Nature, equally with any other Man, or Number of Men in the World, hath by Nature a Power . . . to preserve his Property, that is, his Life, Liberty and Estate, against the Injuries and Attempts of other Men."

—John Locke, *Two Treatises of Government*[1]

"In bestowing the eulogies due to the partitions and internal checks of power, it ought not the less to be remembered, that they are neither the sole nor the chief palladium of constitutional liberty. The people, who are the authors of this blessing, must also be its guardians. Their eyes must be ever ready to mark, their voice to pronounce, and their arm to repel or repair aggressions on the authority of their constitutions; the highest authority next to their own, because the immediate work of their own, and the most sacred part of their property, as recognizing and recording the title to every other."

—James Madison, "Government of the United States," *National Gazette*, 1792[2]

"In a word, as a man is said to have a right to his property, he may be equally said to have a property in his rights."

—James Madison, "Property," *National Gazette*, 1792[3]

---

1. John Locke, *Two Treatises of Government*, ed. Peter Laslett (New York: New American Library, 1965), II.87 (further references in the text by treatise and paragraph number).
2. James Madison, "Government of the United States," in *The Papers of James Madison*, ed. Robert A. Rutland et al. (Charlottesville: University Press of Virginia, 1983), 14:218.
3. Ibid., 14:266.

It has been noted often enough that the right to property is the central theme of Locke's *Second Treatise*. In fact, chapter 5 of the *Second Treatise*, "Of Property," contains the central paragraphs of Locke's *Two Treatises of Government*. This is hardly surprising, since Locke's teaching on property is revolutionary and forms the revolutionary core of his doctrine of republican government. In chapter 5, Locke articulates a private right to property derived from nature or natural right. His success in this endeavor prepared the ground for the eventual demise of monarchy, or at the least the ground for parliamentary supremacy. We had occasion in chapter 3 to quote Blackstone's *Commentaries on the Laws of England* to explain a crucial point made by Jefferson's unattributed paraphrase of Blackstone in *A Summary View of the Rights of British America*. Blackstone's original text bears repeating: "It became a fundamental maxim and necessary principle (though in reality a mere fiction) of our English tenures, 'that the king is the universal lord and original proprietor of all the lands in his kingdom; and that no man doth or can possess any part of it, but what had mediately or immediately been derived as a gift from him, to be held upon feodal services.'"[4] Jefferson's answer to Blackstone, we recall, was perfectly Lockean: "Our ancestors . . . who migrated hither, were labourers, not lawyers." Natural right grounded in labor, not royal prerogatives, was the basis for the right to property adopted in America. The feudal system of property, like the feudal system of birth-right subjectship, could not withstand the scrutiny of "right reason." Right reason is grounded in natural right or the laws of nature. Labor of the individual is the "original Law of Nature for the *beginning of Property*" (II.30), not prescription. Property therefore is a private right—a natural right—not the prerogative of kings or aristocrats.

We saw earlier Jefferson's support for the natural right of expatriation in opposition to the "perpetual allegiance" that was the basis for feudal subjectship. Jefferson similarly expressed pure Lockeanism when, scarcely three months after drafting the Declaration, he proposed a revision of the laws in Virginia to abolish primogeniture and entail, those feudal institutions designed to perpetuate hereditary aristocracy. Holly Brewer, a perceptive commentator, rightly noted that Jefferson's intention was to make Virginia's laws "conform with the principles of the Revolution." Brewer quotes Jefferson who said some years later that his effort was an attempt to destroy "every fibre . . . of ancient or future aristocracy," which he described as necessary to establish a truly republican form of government.[5] The appeal to natural right—"the fundamental principles of the Revolution"—undermined the whole system of feudalism and the structure of hereditary authority upon which monarchy and aristocracy rested.

---

4. Thomas Jefferson, *A Summary View of the Rights of British America*, in *Jefferson: Writings*, ed. Merrill Peterson (New York: Library of America, 1984), 119, paraphrasing William Blackstone, *Commentaries on the Laws of England* (Oxford: Clarendon Press, 1765–1769; reprint Chicago: University of Chicago Press, 1979), II:51. As Jeremy Waldron notes, "As the king was the fount of all law, so also he was the origin of all the property rights that his subjects had; it followed that it was absurd for a subject to assert his own rights of property in the face of the king and his fiscal prerogative" (*The Private Right to Property* [Oxford: Oxford University Press, 1988], 148).

5. Holly Brewer, "Entailing Aristocracy in Colonial Virginia: 'Ancient Feudal Restraints' and Revolutionary Reforms," *William and Mary Quarterly* 56, no. 2 (April 1997): 307.

Once the private right to property grounded in natural right wholly independent of the common law had been established, the end of monarchical authority was foreordained, if not inevitable. Locke's articulation of a natural right to property prepared from afar the ultimate demise of monarchy. The watchword of the American Revolution—no taxation without representation—showed the importance of the right to property for Americans; it was a clear statement of Locke's position that property could never be taken justly without consent.[6] The acceptance of Locke's view by the American founders truly sounded the death knell of monarchy and all non-republican forms of government.

GOD'S WORKMANSHIP

The right to property, however, makes its first appearance, not in chapter 5 of the *Second Treatise*, but in the *First Treatise*, where it is presented as a necessary conclusion from the fact that God planted in man and

> all other Animals, a strong desire of Self-preservation, and furnished the World with things fit for Food and Rayment and other Necessaries of Life, Subservient to his design, that Man should live and abide for some time upon the Face of the Earth, and not that so curious and wonderful a piece of Workmanship by its own Negligence, or want of Necessaries, should perish again, presently after a few moments continuance (I.86).

Locke emphatically vouchsafes God's plan ("I say"), noting, as we have already discussed, that beasts were granted sense and instinct for their preservation, whereas men were accorded sense and reason. Thus the strong desire for self-preservation was "planted" in man in order to preserve God's workmanship. The beasts, of course, were also part of God's workmanship but apparently not "so curious" and not such a "wonderful piece of Workmanship" as man, who alone was granted reason. Since the "strong desire of Preserving his Life and Being" was planted in man

> as a Principle of Action by God himself, Reason, which was the Voice of God in him, could not but teach him and assure him, that pursuing that natural Inclination he had to preserve his Being, he followed the Will of his Maker, and therefore had a right to use of those Creatures, which by his Reason or Senses could discover would be serviceable thereunto. And thus Man's *Property* in the Creatures, was founded upon the right he had, to make use of those things, that were necessary or useful to his Being (I.86; II.26).

Man's property in the creatures was thus, in large measure, a discovery of his reason—"the Voice of God in him." God directs the creatures by sense and instinct

---

6. Locke, *Two Treatises of Government*, II.138.

alone. Animals feel the impulse and obey instinct. Men feel the same impulses but have the power to resist with the use of reason. It is in the capacity to resist impulses that man experiences freedom unavailable to beasts. God's grant of reason was thus also a grant of freedom or liberty—a liberty (or at least a potential liberty) to resist impulses by the use of reason or deliberation. And it is in the exercise of reason to resist impulse that human beings acquire the potential for moral choice, the freedom to choose one course of action over another. Animals don't have moral choice because they don't have reason to resist impulses and therefore have no freedom to choose alternative courses of action. As we will discuss shortly, reason necessarily implies liberty and choice, and it is in choice that morality resides—choice can be praiseworthy or blameworthy. In the less elevated but more immediate sense of choice, men can use their reason to discover how to make necessities of life useful to their preservation and well-being in ways that are beyond the capacity of beasts.

Man's reason places him above the beasts, but having only imperfect reason, men cannot attain the perfection of God. God was nevertheless pleased with his workmanship. After all, he made man in his own image, a clear sign that man was, as it were, the coin of the realm.

A controversy, more imaginary than real, has surrounded the question of God's workmanship and the status of property in *Second Treatise*. In an early passage, Locke argues that everyone in the state of nature is obliged by the law of nature, which Locke says is simply "reason" (II.6, I.101). This paragraph presents the most extensive discussion of the law of nature in the *Second Treatise* and is couched entirely in terms of obligation, a surprising revelation in a book famous for its advocacy of rights. The natural law, Locke assures us, is available to "all Mankind, who will but consult it," and it commands "that being all equal and independent, no one ought to harm another in his Life, Health, Liberty or Possessions." The reason that men are "equal and independent" and obliged to follow reason is because "Men being all the Workmanship of one Omnipotent, and infinitely wise Maker; All the Servants of one Sovereign Master, sent into the World by his order and about his business, they are his Property, whose Workmanship they are, made to last during his, not one anothers Pleasure" (II.6). God's ownership of men thus derives from his "workmanship." God is omnipotent and omniscient and a "Maker"—a workman. What he created, however, remains, like his infinite wisdom, mysterious. We cannot know why he created such a "curious and wonderful" being as man, or why he created man between the beasts and the divine, granting him reason but also troubling him with a "busie mind," imagination, that carries him "to a Brutality below the level of Beasts, when he quits reason, which places him almost equal to Angels" (I.58). While man has reason, he frequently ignores its counsels when his passions command immediate attention. Reason should rule passion, but "the imagination," Locke notes, "is always restless and suggests a variety of thoughts, and the will, reason being laid aside, is ready for every extravagant project" (I.58). It is this interplay between reason and passion that has indeed made for a creation veiled in an almost impenetrable mystery.

We have already seen in *An Essay Concerning Human Understanding* Locke's argument that the pursuit of happiness is the pursuit of our greatest good and that
human liberty is the capacity of "finite intellectual Beings" to suspend desire from
determining will until reasoned deliberation has chosen the right course of action.[7]
Happiness is a tendency and inclination of human nature, and Locke clearly argues
that the rule of reason—deliberation—in pursuit of "true felicity" is a moral obligation that is grounded in human nature.

God obliged men to follow the law of nature; yet God accorded man imperfect
reason "as his only star and compass." What is more, God compounded the difficulty
of fulfilling obligations to the law of nature by burdening man, as we have seen, with
the vexations of a "busie mind."

Deliberation—that is, practical wisdom or prudence—is the kind of reasoning
that deals with moral and political choice. Prudence, however, is always based on
an incomplete understanding of the whole and an imperfect understanding of the
relation of the transitory human sphere to the imperishable divine sphere. Those
choices made by individuals, given the obligation God has placed on them to follow
the law of nature, will be praiseworthy or blameworthy, moral or immoral according
to whether they conform to reason. Man's freedom is thus moral freedom and will
be judged by God in the light of its conformity to the law of nature, which is, we
remember, "the Voice of God" (I.86).

Man always aspires to the divine but too often does not rise above the beast. That
is, it seems, the human condition. God having granted man imperfect reason and
charged him with the obligation of obeying the law of nature at the same time, it is
little wonder that Locke describes God's workmanship as "curious and wonderful."
It is less wonderful, perhaps, that God would want to preserve such workmanship.

In the hierarchy of God, man, beast, man's superiority in reason was his title to
rule the beasts. Man did not create the beasts, therefore his title to rule them did
not derive from his workmanship. Workmanship is therefore not the only rightful
ground of property rights. If man is God's property, of course, no man can be the
property of anyone else. Every man is therefore "equal and independent" with respect
to every other human being. This means that each man, in effect, belongs to himself
and is solely responsible to God for his own actions in fulfilling his obligations to the
law of nature and reason—those obligations that God has imposed for the preservation of his workmanship. But what could it possibly mean to be owned by God? As
a product of God's "workmanship," man was created in the image of God. What is
that image? And what does it mean to own an image?

God is unique, and his "image" is therefore unknowable. Any attempt to portray
it assumes knowledge that we do not—and cannot—possess. God is "invisible"
and cannot be understood to have "any corporeal or visible resemblance."[8] In what

---

7. John Locke, *An Essay Concerning Human Understanding*, ed. Peter H. Nidditch (Oxford: Clarendon
Press, 1975), II.xx.52.

8. John Locke, *The Reasonableness of Christianity as delivered in the Scriptures*, ed. John C. Higgins-
Biddle (Oxford: Clarendon Press, 1999), ch. 11, 114.

sense, then, is man made in the "image" of God? Is he made in the "idea" of God, participating, as it were, in God's essence, but only imperfectly, in the same way that man participates imperfectly in God's reason? God is omniscient, and he is omnipotent because he is omniscient. In the *First Treatise*, Locke notes that when God made man "*in his own Image after his own Likeness,*" he made him "an intellectual Creature, and so capable of *Dominion.*" Whatever else "the *Image of God* consisted [of], the intellectual Nature was certainly a part of it," and it was this intellectual nature that gave man dominion "over the inferiour Creatures" (I.30; I.40). As we have already noted, Locke argues that it is dominion over the inferior creatures that gives rise to the right of property. Thus man's right to the use of inferior beings for survival was an aspect of self-preservation—God's desire to see his curious and wonderful workmanship survive. Yet it is evident that "God cannot have property in an image He has made of Himself"[9] since an image, like an idea, is not subject to ownership of any kind.

The difficulty—or seeming difficulty—arises when Locke, some twenty-one paragraphs later, in the third paragraph of chapter 5, "Of Property," and the twenty-seventh paragraph of the *Second Treatise* writes, "Though the Earth and all inferior Creatures be common to all Men, yet every Man has a *Property* in his own *Person.* That no Body has any Right to but himself" (II.27; II.44; II.173). Many commentators have been quick to point out a contradiction—are men the property of God, or do they have a property in their own persons?[10] In the first case, men are God's property because they are the product of his workmanship, the most valuable part of which we have just learned is their reason (I.30; *An Essay Concerning Human Understanding,* IV.xviii.5, IV.iii.18); how, then, did men acquire a property in their own persons?

God obligated men to follow the law of nature—the commands of reason. Being individually responsible to God and having the freedom and independence to act on the basis of reason, man is, so to speak, an independent actor and free to fulfill his obligations in the manner he reasons best. God has set the individual free and made him "Master of himself, and Proprietor of his own Person" so that he might go about God's business in the manner he determines best (II.44; II.123; II.190). Professor Mansfield aptly comments, "We may conclude that God made men for the sake of their own preservation, and that they follow the will of their Maker when they regard themselves as their own property. Man, then, not being the property of God, has received no property from God."[11] Self-ownership is the basis for individual

---

9. Harvey C. Mansfield Jr., "On the Political Character of Property in Locke," in *Powers, Possessions and Freedom: Essays in Honor of C. B. Macpherson,* ed. Alkis Kontos (Toronto: University of Toronto Press, 1979), 30.

10. Mansfield, "On the Political Character of Property in Locke," 29–30. See A. John Simmons, *The Lockean Theory of Rights* (Princeton, NJ: Princeton University Press, 1992), 256; Paul A. Rahe, "The Political Needs of a Toolmaking Animal: Madison, Hamilton, Locke, and the Question of Property," *Social Philosophy & Policy* 22, no. 1 (January 2005): 23–24, esp. n. 114; John T. Scott, "The Sovereignless State and Locke's Language of Obligation," *American Political Science Review* 94, no. 3 (September 2000), 551.

11. Mansfield, "On the Political Character of Property in Locke," 30–31.

rights, and the idea of individual rights is derived from the fact that in the Christian universe, man's relationship to God is personal; thus the political relationship must correspondingly be grounded in individual rights—including the right that one has in his own person. No one can fail to see that this is good Protestant theology, and we know that Locke always had the theological-political question in the forefront of his political reflections, the question of how to make natural right compatible with revealed law.

It is rather unbelievable nonetheless that some would suggest that God's creation of man represents "the paradigm case . . . of a labor theory of property,"[12] as if God's creation involved an act of labor rather than an act of image-making. This commentator continues, "Human making, not divine making, is the primary moral fact. The chapter on property leads up to the suggestion that human beings are self-owners because they are the makers of their selves and they own what they make."[13] On this account, the self-creating self is the ground of man's self-ownership, which displaces the ownership of God. Locke, of course, does not give any such explanation for self-ownership; it is our author's invention to explain "the most elusive point in all of Locke's political philosophy," a point that despite its elusiveness "represents the core of his philosophy—the notion of human beings as rights bearers by nature because they are self-owners." These private rights derive exclusively from the self-ownership produced by the self-creating self.[14] If the ownership of God had not somehow been transferred, however tendentiously in Locke's thought, into self-ownership, there would be no ground for private rights. How God's ownership became self-ownership is a mystery to our author—or at least a mystery he attributes to Locke. Our commentator does not say, however, whether human beings create themselves in the image of God. This omission, whether deliberate or not, or whether intended as a silent jest, demonstrates an inexcusable lack of awareness of Locke's abiding concern for the theological-political problem.

In any case, Locke made it clear that human creativity is of an entirely different order from God's creation. It is true, Jeremy Waldron writes,

> that Locke regards man as a God-like creature, made in God's image. But when he uses this description, Locke is referring to man's intellectual nature not to man as *homo faber* or *homo laborans*. He never once connects man's God-likeness with his productive capacity. If anything, Locke is at pains to distinguish man and God in this regard. The idea that productive labour involves an act of creation runs into the same sort of difficulty as the idea that the conception of a child is an act of creation by its parents. There Locke's argument was that, since a father does not know how literally to *make* a child, he cannot acquire a creator's rights over it.

---

12. Michael P. Zuckert, *Natural Rights and the New Republicanism* (Princeton, NJ: Princeton University Press, 1994), 217.

13. Ibid., 278.

14. Michael P. Zuckert, *Launching Liberalism: On Lockean Political Philosophy* (Lawrence: University Press of Kansas, 2001), 192–97.

Waldron concludes, "Nowhere does Locke give any indication that he wants to connect this labour theory of use-value with any doctrine of creator's entitlement."[15] Indeed, Locke argues in the *First Treatise* that those who argue that begetting children gives fathers an absolute power over them because giving life bestows ownership upon the father "are so dazled with the thoughts of Monarchy, that they do not, as they ought, remember God, who is the *Author and Giver of Life: 'Tis in him alone we live, move and have our Being*. How can he be thought to give Life to another, that knows not wherein his own Life consists?" (I.52). The most advanced anatomists, Locke insists, are ignorant of the structure and use of many parts of the body and of the operations of which life consists. Philosophers, after the "most diligent enquiries," are still ignorant about the soul and its movements; how, then, can "the Rude Plough-Man, or the more ignorant Voluptuary, frame or fashion such an admirable Engine as this is, and then put Life and Sense into it?" The bare act of procreation cannot therefore give rise to a claim of ownership based on workmanship. What is utterly beyond human workmanship—because it is exclusively the province of "God our Maker"—is the omniscient power to endow "this curious structure" man with a "living and rational Soul." It is beyond doubt that for Locke, the "living and rational soul" is the true image of God in whose likeness man is created (I.53).

Endowing man with a rational soul, God at the same time endowed man with freedom. The rational soul is not determined but possesses metaphysical freedom. This metaphysical freedom of the mind or rational soul is the basis of man's moral— and political—freedom. Man's metaphysical freedom is the essence of human nature; it is the image of God in man. It is because every individual possesses a rational soul that all are men created "equal and independent," incapable of being the property of anyone else; the possession of a rational soul thereby renders each man the owner of himself.

PROPERTY, NATURAL RIGHT, AND NATURAL RIGHTS

Chapter 5 of the *Second Treatise* consists of twenty-seven paragraphs, the first paragraph of which begins with an agreement between "natural *Reason*" and "*Revelation*": God gave the world in common to all mankind. Locke reminds us of his previous argument that the supposition "that God gave the World to *Adam*, and his posterity . . . it is impossible than any Man, but one universal Monarch, should have any *Property*" (II.25). In tracing this argument to its logical conclusion Locke had previously concluded in the *First Treatise* that absolute monarchy or anarchy was the inevitable result. These two extremes of the human condition, tyranny and anarchy, exclude the possibility of any political life. Republican government, which Locke forcefully argues is the only form consistent with natural right, is grounded

---

15. Jeremy Waldron, *The Right to Private Property* (Oxford: Clarendon Press, 1988), 199–200.

in the natural right to property. Locke consequently endeavors to "shew, how Men might come to have a *property* in several parts of that which God gave to Mankind in common, and that without any express Compact of all the Commoners" (II.25). Even the sober Locke cannot resist a (not infrequent) laconic joke: had consent been a requirement of appropriation "Man had starved, notwithstanding the Plenty God had given him" (II.28).

While reason and revelation concur that God gave the world in common to man, it is the "Law of reason" (II.30) alone that establishes the private right to property in what was formerly the common possession of all mankind. Locke's principal purpose in chapter 5 is to articulate a natural right ground for the right to property, thereby also articulating a natural right ground for the right to "life, Liberty and Estate" (II.87).

Natural right provides the greatest challenge to conventional right. As one political philosopher famously remarked, an appeal from convention to nature is "dynamite" for any traditional or prescriptive society.[16] Natural right uncovers and exposes the origins that convention and prescription seek to obscure and obfuscate. It is only on the basis of natural right that governments can be founded on "deliberation and choice." The origins of all prescriptive or conventional forms of government are ultimately traceable to "accident and force." These origins are indefensible when seen in the light of the claims of natural right. Conventional or prescriptive right is most authoritative when it has been established for a long time. When its origins are obscured by the mists of time, it gains even greater authority since the beginnings of government are invariably accompanied by "Force and Violence" (II.1). An appeal to natural right, however, has an incomparable advantage over even the most ancient conventions: nature or natural right is older than all conventions. Natural right appeals to the eternal, what is right or just everywhere and always. If the ground of authority is antiquity, natural right is the oldest authority even though it may not be the oldest recognized authority. Natural right, however, does not seek to rest its authority on antiquity but on "the Law of right Reason" (II.118).

Locke was certain that the natural right to property could be easily deduced from the principles of human nature and natural right. Since equality is the primary fact of human nature, every individual is by nature possessed of the right to life, liberty, and property. This is an irrefragable deduction from the fact that among human beings, there are no rulers by nature. Consent, therefore, is clearly the natural right basis for legitimate rule (II.95). "Consent," Locke avers, "is that, and that only, which did, or could give *beginning* to any *lawful Government* in the World" (II.99). Since the end or purpose of government is the protection of property, taking property without consent would be a violation of the first principles of government. As Locke says, where property can be taken without consent, there is no property (II.139; II.140); conversely, it might be argued that where government can take property without consent, there is no government—or, to use Lockean

---

16. Leo Strauss, *Natural Right and History* (Chicago: University of Chicago Press, 1953), 153.

terms, where government expropriates property without consent, it has effectively dissolved itself.

Natural right also disqualifies all forms of government not animated by the rule of law (II.138). Arbitrary government in all its forms is a violation of natural right because those governments do not have as their end and purpose the protection of the natural rights of those who consent to be governed. "Consent of the governed" and "the rule of law" are thus reciprocal terms in the Lockean political universe. No rational person would leave the "inconveniences of the state of nature" for arbitrary rule because the inconveniences attendant on absolute government are worse than those of the state of nature. Among other things, the defense of life and property is infinitely more difficult against the combined forces of government. As previously mentioned, Locke's natural right arguments are directed not just against absolute monarchy, although that seems to be (rhetorically at least) his principal target, but also against all non-republican forms of government. The idea that Locke might have supported limited or constitutional monarchy, aristocracy, oligarchy, or any form of mixed regime is simply not supported by a fair or close reading of the text. Parliamentary government—derived from the sovereignty of the people—is the heart of Locke's republican revolution, and the natural right to property is the core of his revolutionary politics.

How, then, does Locke argue for a natural right to property? How does God's gift of the earth and all its resources in common to all mankind become the property of individual human beings? Is it as mysterious as some commentators would have us believe?

We have had a preview of Locke's argument in the *First Treatise*. We remember that man, having had the strong desire for self-preservation planted in him by God for the preservation of His workmanship, thereby acquired a right to property in inferior creatures "necessary or useful to his Being" (I.86). No one, of course, has a private right to the spontaneous productions of nature, but since all things given in common by God are for "the best advantage of Life, and Convenience," there "must of necessity be a means *to appropriate* them some way or other before they can be of any use, or at all beneficial to any particular Man." If there were no "means *to appropriate*" the "Earth, and all that is therein"—those things produced by "the spontaneous hand of Nature," the "Fruits it naturally produces, and Beasts it feeds" (II.26)—such a "curious and wonderful a piece of Workmanship" would perish after a very short existence. Appropriation is prior to use and use is necessary to "Life and convenience." Appropriation is therefore essential to fulfill God's plan.

We have already learned how every individual came to have an exclusive property in his own person. This exclusive property includes, of course, his labor, the unique product of his body. When an individual mixes his labor with something that exists in common, the act of labor removes the object from the common state that nature has left it in and makes it his private property, thereby excluding "the common right of other Men." Whatever has been transformed by labor so as to make it useful or convenient to human life becomes "the unquestionable Property of the Labourer, no

Man but he can have a right to what that is once joined to, at least where there is enough, and as good left in common for others" (II.27). That property has its origin in labor is the "Law of reason" and is the "original Law of Nature for the *beginning of Property*" (II.30). The right to property is established by an admixture of labor—the quintessential expression of self-ownership—and the spontaneous products of the earth that belong to the common. This admixture of private and common weighs in favor of private property; it could only do so, of course, if the value of labor outweighed the intrinsic value of the land and the spontaneous products of nature that God gave in common to mankind.

We learn in short order that "'tis *Labour* indeed that *puts the difference of value* on every thing (II.40). In fact, Locke contends, "Nature and the Earth furnished only the almost worthless Materials, as in themselves," and it is labor that "puts the greatest part of value upon Land, without which it would scarcely be worth any thing" (II.43). In the preceding paragraphs, Locke builds slowly to this shocking conclusion: "I think it will be but a very modest Computation to say, that the *Products* of the Earth useful to the Life of Man 9/10 are the *effects of labour*: nay, if we will rightly estimate things as they come to our use, and cast up the several Expenses about them, what in them is purely owing to *Nature*, and what to *labour*, we shall find, that in most of them 99/100 are wholly to be put on the account of *labour*" (II.40). Three paragraphs later, Locke further revises the calculation to account labor as 999/1,000 the value of land. God's grant to mankind, the great common of the world, unimproved nature—nature without the intervention of human art—is "little more than nothing" (II.42) for the preservation and conveniences of life. Locke uses the example of America as proof. America possesses abundant land and rich soil but does not improve it by labor; thus a "King of a large fruitful Territory there feeds, lodges, and is clad worse than a day Labourer in *England*" (II.41). This contrast of land and labor is stark. Uncultivated land is "wast" (II.42). And "in the beginning all the World was *America*, and more so than that is now" (II.49).

Labor increases the productivity of the "almost worthless" land and thereby increases the "Products of the Earth useful to the Life of Man." In cultivating one acre of land, by the most modest calculation, a man gives nine acres back to mankind— that is, he increases the common stock available for life and convenience by nine acres. Thus every act of private appropriation is simultaneously a contribution to the common good. No one acts out of a regard for the common good or from a motive of public spiritedness but from purely private interest. Nevertheless, the return to the common is real and substantial.

THE "FIRST AGES OF THE WORLD": FIRST STAGE

In the "first Ages of the world," which Locke suggests lasted for a long time, men subsisted almost exclusively on the spontaneous products of the earth. They hunted

game, tamed and herded animals, and gathered fruits and berries. Generally, they
lived a nomadic existence without fixed property in land. This was a time when
"Right and conveniency went together" (II.51). In a second example of "the Voice
of Reason confirmed by Inspiration," Locke, in the second of only two citations of
the New Testament in *Second Treatise*, quotes 1 Timothy 6:17: "God has given all
things richly." Locke then asks, "But how far has he given it us?" Answering his own
question, he continues the quotation: "to enjoy" (II.31). This biblical reference is
used to support Locke's natural law contention that

> as much as any one can make use of to any advantage of life before it spoils; so much
> he may by his labour fix a Property in. Whatever is beyond this, is more than his share,
> and belongs to others. Nothing was made by God for Man to spoil or destroy. And thus
> considering the plenty of natural Provisions there was a long time in the World, and the
> few spenders, and to how small a part of that provision the industry of one Man could
> extend it self, and ingross it to the prejudice of others; especially keeping within the
> *bounds*, set by reason of what might serve for his *use*; there could be then little room for
> Quarrels or Contentions about Property so establish'd (II.31).

The natural productions of the earth are of little value without human art and
industry, so the abundance that God gives "richly" may be somewhat misleading
since what he gives is not ready for use or convenience but must be transformed
by labor. Without labor—with only the spontaneous products of nature—men
would be faced with unremitting penury. After all, "God, when he gave the World
in common to all Mankind, commanded Man also to labour, and the penury of his
Condition required it of him. God and his Reason commanded him to subdue the
Earth, *i.e.* improve it for the benefit of Life, and therein lay out something upon it
that was his own, his labour" (II.32). Thus what God gave richly was of virtually
no value without the addition of labor. God placed man in a condition of penury;
Locke, in articulating the basis for the natural right to property, prepared the ground
for plenty.

Locke seems to have engaged in something of a jest when he used the quotation
from Timothy. Saint Paul says that we come into the world with nothing and leave
the world with nothing, and during our sojourn in this world we should be content
with food and clothing only. Those who desire to be rich, Paul warns, fall into temp-
tations that plunge many into destruction. Indeed, the love of money is the root of
all evils and drives men from the faith. The rich, Paul admonishes, should put their
faith in the things that God alone furnishes richly. This is hardly the message that
Locke wishes to convey when he advises individuals to acquire as much as possible
before it can be consumed or exchanged before it spoils. As we will see presently, the
invention of money abrogates the natural law spoilage limits on accumulation and
opens the door to unlimited acquisition. To say nothing of a host of other considerations no less important, Locke hardly considers money the root of all evil; Timothy
may be "the Voice of Reason confirmed by Inspiration," but it is Locke's inspiration,

not biblical inspiration. Money is the means to the emancipation of acquisition, and acquisition is the ground of capital accumulation. This emancipation will liberate men from the greatest of all tyrannies: poverty.

In any case, in "the first Ages" no one would have an incentive to acquire more than he could use because it would simply be an irrational waste of labor power. It is use that entitles individuals to property, and it is the appropriation of more than can be used that is against reason and "the common Law of Nature" (II.37) even if the world did place men in a condition of "plenty." No one would appropriate more than he could use for immediate or future consumption or exchange before what he had accumulated spoiled. Reason and natural law thus sets spoilage as the limit to property, a limit that is easily known and easily obeyed. It appears that in the "first Ages," the "Law of Nature" was "intelligible and plain to a rational Creature" and was not the sole preserve of "a Studier of that Law" (II.12). There was a moral qualification attached to God's gift to man: "He gave it to the use of the Industrious and Rational, (and *Labour* was to be *his Title* to it;) not to the Fancy or Covetousness of the Quarrelsome and Contentious" (II.34). Rationality and Labor were the virtues appropriate to acquisition and the right to property, and these were the virtues that governed "the first Ages."

The "first Ages" of nomadic existence, which we imagine occupied the bulk of this era, were mostly times of peace because there were few opportunities for the "Quarrelsome and Contentious." There were no surplus stocks to invite envy or luxurious living to entice excesses. But still, life was difficult, and despite the fact that God gave "richly," we imagine a relative scarcity and hard labor. In the nomadic stage of the "first Ages," the spontaneous productions of the earth available to men might be affected by seasonal fluctuations, droughts, and other natural disasters. Scarcity and desperate circumstance would not be unknown and might be frequent—indeed, probably the rule. This was a veritable "poor but vertuous Age" (II.110) where rationality and industry were the most important virtues and where life constantly teetered on the edges of extreme poverty.

A second natural law constraint on the accumulation of property in the "first Ages" was the requirement that labor exclude the common right of others only "where there is enough, [and] as good, left in common for others" (II.27). But, as Locke emphasizes, there were few spenders at this time, and even though the age was poor, the greatest scarcity was labor. No one's labor could appreciably diminish "the great Common of the World" to the disadvantage of anyone else. In fact, "the same *measure* may be allowed still, without prejudice to any Body, as full as the World seems." The Earth "is of so little value *without labor*," Locke says,

> This I dare boldly affirm, That the same *Rule of Propriety*, (*viz.*) That every Man should have as much as he could make use of, would hold still in the World, without straitning any body, since there is Land enough in the World to suffice double the Inhabitants had not the *Invention of Money*, and the tacit Agreement of Men to put a value on it, introduced (by Consent) larger Possessions, and a Right to them (II.36).

Thus had the natural law limits on appropriation remained in place and before money altered the intrinsic value of things, the "good and enough" requirement would never have been exhausted. Labor was the measure of wealth, and wealth was limited by use value. Industry and rationality were the mainstays in enforcing the law of nature.

THE "FIRST AGES OF THE WORLD": SECOND STAGE

What we might loosely call the second "stage" of the "first Ages of the world" begins when "the *chief matter of Property* being now not the Fruits of the Earth, and Beasts that subsist on it, but the *Earth it self;* as that which takes in and carries with it all the rest" (II.32). Land is acquired under the same rules of natural law and natural right as the spontaneous products of the earth, and the acquisition of land is subject to the same natural law limits. Thus "*as much Land* as a Man Tills, Plants, Improves, Cultivates, and can use the Product of, so much is his *Property*. He by his Labour does, as it were, inclose it from the Common," creating a right to property "which another had no Title to, nor could without injury take from him" (II.32). Once labor had been invested, a man had a natural right to property in what he enclosed from the common, and he could not be divested of that right without a violation of the law of nature.

The same use limits apply to the acquisition of property in land as apply to the acquisition of the spontaneous products of the earth. A man can enclose, till, plant, reap, raise cattle, and otherwise make use of as much land as he can before the productions of his labor spoil. "But," Locke cautions, "if either the Grass of his Inclosure rotted on the Ground, or the Fruit of his planting perished without gathering, and laying up, this part of the Earth, notwithstanding his Inclosure, was still to be looked on as Waste, and might be the Possession of any other" (II.38). The use limit would have confined each man's property "to a very moderate Proportion," "nor could his Enjoyment consume more than a small part; so that it was impossible for any Man, this way, to intrench upon the right of another, or acquire to himself, a Property, to the Prejudice of his Neighbor" (II.36). The natural law requirement that there be "enough, and as good left in common for others" would be easily satisfied in the "first Ages" because of the abundance of available land.

When the earth itself became the chief object of property, nomadic existence began to decline. As men cleared land and made it ready to be tilled and planted and improved it in a multitude of other ways, they began to realize the value of the labor invested in "almost worthless" land. They also quickly realized the value of the agricultural arts in increasing the productivity of the land thus improved (II.44). In short, those men who invested their rationality and industry in the land become attached to the land by virtue of their investment and the expectation of future rewards from their art and labor. Also "different degrees of Industry were apt to give Men Possessions in different Proportions." Although this was prior to the invention of money, the differences in wealth would be modest because the use limitations would also limit the amount of excess production that could be accumulated. Still, superior fields and habitations might attract the attention and envy of the less industrious and quarrelsome. Instead of investing their labor in making new and unimproved land productive, the lazy and quarrelsome might prefer to turn to darker and more nefarious arts to expropriate already improved land from the rational and industrious. In the nomadic state of the "first Ages" when there were no fixed habitations, such actions would be rare and hardly worth the efforts of the quarrelsome. Once the earth itself became the principal object of property, this calculus undoubtedly changed. Contests and quarrels about property and what constituted the obligations of natural law surely became more frequent, especially in the absence of positive laws and recognized judges to arbitrate disputes. Increased production from labor invested in the earth made the invention of money inevitable, and the convention that created money was responsible for ending what Locke later terms "the *Golden Age*" (II.111).

Money destroyed the "intrinsick value of things"—their use value—and made value depend on appetite. The natural limits on property were overthrown by the "*Invention of Money*," a convention based on "tacit Agreement." Natural law limitations on the accumulation of property were overthrown because gold and silver—useless metals that did not tarnish—could be amassed without depriving anyone of anything useful for life and convenience. The ensuing emancipation of acquisitiveness ended the "Golden Age." But why would mankind voluntarily leave a golden age? After all, the acceptance of money was based on "tacit" consent. Why not heed the biblical injunction that money is the root of all evil?

MONEY AND PROPERTY

Locke begins his account of the "tacit Agreement" whereby men "*agreed, that a little piece of yellow Metal*, which would keep without wasting or decay, should be worth a great piece of Flesh, or a whole heap of Corn" in the central paragraph of the *Two Treatises of Government* (II.37). It was this agreement that introduced "the desire of having more than Men needed" and "altered the intrinsic value of things," which depended solely on their usefulness. The just possession of property was never determined by the amount of property accumulated but by the useless perishing of any property acquired. The invention of money, however, abolished the natural limits on acquisition. We know that "the greatest part of *things really useful* to the Life of Man . . . *are* generally things of *short duration*; such as, if they are not consumed by use, will decay and perish of themselves" (II.46). "Gold, Silver, and Diamonds"—those "things that Fancy or Agreement hath put the Value on" (II.46)—are durable, scarce, portable and of little intrinsic value; they have only a "Phantastical imaginary value" (II.184). Their accumulation would not, therefore, invade the rights of any other individual since their durability means they cannot spoil. Unlimited accumulation of these durable goods is therefore of no prejudice to anyone else, nor does it work any injury or injustice to anyone; in fact, it redounds to the benefit of mankind by encouraging industry that returns surpluses to the common stock of the world.

In the "first Ages," the "Rational and Industrious" manifested the virtues peculiar to that epoch, and we speculated that the laws of nature that established and limited the accumulation of property were easily known and easily obeyed because they depended upon a simple rationality that was easily acted upon because it was enforced by necessity. In the Golden Age, rationality—the law of nature—was the measure of value; in the post–Golden Age era, money becomes the measure of value. But the value of money is not regulated by the law of nature or reason but by a "Phantastical imaginary value." The simple rationality of the law of nature that ruled the "poor but virtuous age" is now complicated by the "Phantastical" imagination. We remember Locke's characterization of the human soul in the *First Treatise*: man was distinguished from the beasts by his reason but was also said to possess a "busie mind" and a restless imagination that was ready, when reason was abandoned, for "every extravagant project" (I.58).

Imagination is engaged by money and is anchored in "Fancy or Agreement." But it is money that gives incentive to rationality and industry. Both were confined and limited by the laws of nature in the ages before money. Now rationality and industry are given leave to direct the emancipation of acquisitiveness that has been made possible by the invention of money. The "busie mind" is a destructive force when reason is "laid aside," but the "busie mind" ruled by reason, steadily improving the productive capacity of the earth through the useful arts, holds out the prospect of alleviating the economic scarcity that prevents the emergence of genuine republics based on the consent of the governed rather than class or caste—generally oligarchies masquerading as aristocracies or oligarchies masquerading as republics.

IS PLENTY A PART OF GOD'S PLAN?

God has given richly the material for plenty, but the production of plenty is left to human innovation: labor and art (II.44). Part of God's design requires human art to complete His intention. Art, as we have mentioned, imitates nature and is required to complete the ends of nature and nature's God. As we learned from Aristotle, although the *polis* exists by nature, it would never come into being without human art. Plenty, which was surely a part of God's plan, similarly would not come into being without human art, and the largest incentive for the progress of the arts of production was supplied by the invention of money. Without money, there would be no incentive to enlarge possessions beyond their use value (II.48). Accumulation of money spurs the desire for having more, and the desire for having more is the spur to the production of plenty.

In a passage that was later echoed by the *Federalist*, Locke remarks that "different degrees of Industry were apt to give Men Possessions in different Proportions" (II.48). Locke here does not mention reason or art but indicates only that unequal property would result from different degrees of industry even when natural use limits were in force. The voluntary agreement to assign value to gold and silver and "tacitly agreeing in the use of Money" was at one and the same time a tacit agreement to accept "disproportionate unequal possessions of the Earth" (II.50). In the "first Ages" there was inequality of property because some men were more industrious than others. But within natural law limits, inequalities of wealth were scarcely noticeable. The use of money, however, introduced a greater degree of inequality and justly authorized "an inequality of private possessions" (II.50). The exchange of surplus for money, of course, increases the stock of goods available to mankind by a thousandfold (to take Locke's last calculation of the advantage of labor). And the greater incentive to produce greater surpluses produces an even greater return to the common. The emancipation of acquisitiveness, which is facilitated by the invention of money, is authorized by mere convention or agreement, but we understand it to be necessary for the production of "plenty," which we assume to be the ultimate intention of God and nature.

God and nature intend plenty but human art is necessary for its actualization. Human art accomplishes what nature intends but does not produce spontaneously. Before human art could accomplish its task in producing plenty, political philosophy had to prepare the natural right ground for private property and the justification for acquisitiveness beyond natural law limits. The production of plenty held the potential of liberating men from the grinding heel of poverty, the most insidious and pervasive of all tyrannies. The right to property, now understood to be an individual natural right, would also serve as the basis for non-tyrannical government. It would serve as a clarion call for revolution against not only tyranny and absolute monarchy but all government not based on the consent of the governed.

MADISON'S ESSAY "PROPERTY"

In March 1792, Madison published an article anonymously in the *National Gazette* titled "Property." It was one of a series of articles he published in 1791–1792, generally referred to as the Party Press Essays, that were intended to generate opposition to the Federalists. These essays, which we have referred to on several occasions, rehearse serious arguments that may have been intended to serve as a platform for the nascent Republican Party. Although the essays cover a broad range of topics, one issue is conspicuous by its absence: slavery. Slavery must have been constantly on Madison's mind when he wrote the "Property" essay, and it is difficult to imagine that he was not tempted to repeat a sentiment he had expressed at the Constitutional Convention where he remarked that he "thought it wrong to admit in the Constitution the idea that there could be property in men."[17] Madison, of course,

---

17. Max Farrand, ed., *The Records of the Federal Convention of 1787* (New Haven, CT: Yale University Press, 1966 [orig. pub. 1911]), II.417.

was obviously aware that the Constitution did in fact recognize "property in men,"[18] and he surely must have agreed with Roger Sherman's accurate observation made earlier in the debate that a tax on the importation of slaves that was permitted in the Constitution until 1808 "implied [that slaves] were *property*."[19] In the Virginia Ratifying Convention, Madison was forced to defend the twenty-year extension of the slave trade and the importation tax on prudential grounds, remarking, "I should conceive this clause to be impolitic, if it were one of those things which could be excluded without encountering greater evils."[20] The greater evil to be avoided by the compromise, according to Madison, was "dismemberment of the Union." If the slave states "should disunite from the other states for not indulging them in the temporary continuance of this traffic, they might solicit and obtain aid from foreign powers" and endanger the attempt to found a new government. The compromise with slavery, while it allowed the foreign slave trade to continue for twenty years, was nevertheless an improvement on current conditions, Madison argued, since there were no limitations on the slave trade under the Articles of Confederation. "There is, therefore," Madison said, "an amelioration of our circumstances" that was purchased at the price of allowing the evil to continue for a specified period with the prospect that it might be eliminated entirely at a later date.[21] This is the statesmanship that exemplified the founding. Disunion, of course, would almost certainly have meant the indefinite perpetuation of slavery in the slave-holding states. Union held out at least the prospect of a future abolition of slavery because the principles of the regime,

---

18. See James Madison, Letter to Robert J. Evans, June 15, 1819, in *The Papers of James Madison: The Retirement Series*, ed. David B. Mattern et al. (Charlottesville: University of Virginia Press, 2009), 1:469.

19. Farrand, *Records of the Federal Convention of 1787*, II.374.

20. Jonathan Elliot, ed., *The Debates in the Several State Conventions on the Adoption of the Federal Constitution* (Washington, DC: United States Congress, 1836), III.453.

21. Madison's defense of the compromises with slavery in the proposed constitution in the *Federalist* is qualified. In fact, he is unwilling to include a defense of the Three-Fifths Clause in his own name, assigning it rather to "one of our Southern brethren" and enclosing it in quotation marks. Even so, the "brethren" under the tutelage of Madison admits that the slaves to be counted as three-fifths of a person for purposes of representation appear to Southerners in a dual capacity: they serve as property, in which they are "degraded from the human rank, and classed with irrational animals," but "the slave is no less evidently regarded by the law as a member of the society, not as a part of the irrational creation; as a moral person, not as a mere article of property" because the law protects the slave in his "life and in his limbs, against the violence of all others, even the master of his labor and his liberty; and in being punishable himself for all violence committed against others" (*Federalist*, 54:334). Madison qualifies his defense of the provision in Article I, Section 9, which prohibits Congress from abolishing the foreign slave trade before 1808 in the same manner that he did in the Virginia Ratifying Convention. He expresses regret that "the unnatural traffic" could not be immediately suppressed but states that "it ought to be considered as a great point gained in favor of humanity that a period of twenty years may terminate forever, within these States, a traffic which has so long and so loudly upbraided the barbarism of modern policy; that within that period it will receive a considerable discouragement from the federal government" and may, in fact, "be totally abolished" by the few states that continue the traffic (*Federalist* 42:262–63). The *Federalist* does not defend at all the Fugitive Slave Clause, which was the most malicious of the three clauses in the Constitution protecting slavery because it made slavery legal in the entire United States. Wherever an escaped slave was, slavery was legal; in a sense, the Fugitive Slave Clause nationalized slavery. It may have been a necessary compromise, but it was difficult to defend. The compromise was necessary, of course, because the mere act of union would otherwise have made every free state a sanctuary for slaves.

enumerated in the Declaration of Independence, placed a moral imperative upon the nation to live up to that "father of all moral principles,"[22] "all men are created equal." Here evil was tolerated only by necessity and only because there was a future prospect of abolition when political circumstances permitted. In the meantime, the principle that must be maintained was that, under the Constitution, freedom was the rule and slavery the exception, and as long as American statesmen understood that the Declaration supplied the architectonic principles of the Constitution, slavery had been put "in the course of ultimate extinction."[23]

In 1792, when the essay "Property" was published, Madison already saw the beginnings of the great political schism that would divide the young nation. He no doubt calculated that the issue of slavery, which would inevitably agitate the very question of whether the Constitution's compromises with slavery were in fact necessary to preserve the Union or whether any compromises with the principles of the Declaration were justified, was a matter that reached to the very core of regime principles and might prove to be too great a test for a nation still struggling to find its political bearings. Madison may simply have thought that it was impolitic to broach the subject of slavery in a series of essays that were meant to serve as the platform of the emerging Republican Party, especially since its principal base of power was to be in Virginia.

Even without the slavery issue, the politics of the 1790s were some of the most divisive in America's political history. It was particularly fortunate that the issues surrounding the French Revolution entered the American political scene late in the decade. Had those issues been present during the drafting and ratification of the Constitution, it is doubtful that the "assembly of demigods," as Jefferson described the members of the Constitutional Convention from his vantage in Paris, would have been able to produce the balanced republican government that it did.

There is no doubt that the framers accepted Locke's idea that the chief end of civil society was the preservation of property and all of the implications that flowed from the idea that the right to property occupied a prominent place in a republican government. Property was an essential part of the moral and political universe that was articulated by Locke, and it played the same role for the American founders. In the essay "Property," however, Madison took a more expansive view of the right to property than was ever expressed by Locke. Locke spoke of property as including "life, Liberty and Estate" (II.87), but Madison expanded the idea of property to include a range of attributes that we might call the goods of the soul. Madison's summary statement in the essay—"In a word, as a man is said to have a right to his property, he may be equally said to have a property in his rights"[24]—expresses his idea that rights are property and the right to property is the comprehensive right.

22. Abraham Lincoln, "Speech at Chicago, Illinois," July 10, 1858, in *The Collected Works of Abraham Lincoln*, ed. Roy P. Basler (New Brunswick, NJ: Rutgers University Press, 1953), II:499.

23. Ibid., II:498.

24. James Madison, "Property," in *Papers of James Madison*, 14:266.

Madison began "Property" by quoting—or rather paraphrasing—William Blackstone on property without attribution: "This term in its particular application means 'that dominion which one man claims and exercises over the external things of the world, in exclusion of every other individual.'"[25] Madison, however, quickly registered his disagreement with Blackstone: "In its larger and juster meaning, it embraces every thing to which a man may attach a value and have a right, and which leaves to every one else the like advantage."[26] Almost everyone would certainly have recognized this last phrase as a clear reference to Locke, who, as we have just seen, asserted as a natural law limit to acquisition that there be "enough, and as good left in common for others" (II.27). Like Jefferson before him, Madison indicated that the Americans rejected the common law basis for property in favor of natural right. Blackstone's definition was neither large enough nor just enough to fulfill the proper understanding of natural right.

In Blackstone's sense of property, Madison notes, "a man's land, or merchandize, or money is called his property." It is hardly a point of contention that land, merchandise, or money is properly part of "the external things of the world" over which individuals can claim exclusive dominion and therefore count as private property. But how does Madison extend property to the internal world—to the goods of the soul? For Madison, the goods of the soul comprise the "larger and juster meaning" of property. It is not surprising that of all the rights Madison assigns to the "larger and juster meaning" of property, the rights of conscience predominate.

"Conscience," Madison avows, "is the most sacred of all property; other property depending in part on positive law, the exercise of that, being a natural and unalienable right."[27] Seven years earlier Madison had written "Memorial and Remonstrance against Religious Assessments" in opposition to a bill that nearly passed the Virginia legislature in November 1784 that would have established a general tax for the support of "teachers of the Christian Religion." Madison saw a grave danger in this seemingly innocuous bill. "Who does not see," Madison asked, "that the same authority which can establish Christianity, in exclusion of all other Religions, may establish with the same ease any particular sect of Christians, in exclusion of all other Sects?"[28]

Madison began "Memorial and Remonstrance against Religious Assessments" by citing Article 16 of the Virginia Declaration of Rights of 1776: "We hold it for a fundamental and undeniable truth, 'that Religion or the duty which we owe to our Creator and the manner of discharging it, can be directed only by reason and conviction, not by force or violence.'" Madison commented,

---

25. Ibid. The unattributed quote of Blackstone is from *Commentaries on the Laws of England* (Oxford: Clarendon Press, 1765–1769; reprint Chicago: University of Chicago Press, 1979), II:2. Blackstone had written, "The right of property; or that sole and despotic dominion which one man claims and exercises over the external things of the world, in total exclusion of the right of any other individual in the universe."

26. Madison, "Property," in *Papers of James Madison*, 14:266.

27. Ibid.

28. Ibid., 8:300.

The Religion then of every man must be left to the conviction and conscience of every man; and it is the right of every man to exercise it as these may dictate. The right is in its nature an unalienable right. It is unalienable, because the opinions of men, depending only on the evidence contemplated by their own minds cannot follow the dictates of other men: It is unalienable also, because what is here a right towards men, is a duty towards the Creator. It is the duty of every man to render to the Creator such homage and such only as he believes to be acceptable to him.[29]

It is a simple but profound truth that the convictions of conscience cannot be coerced. How one decides to pay homage or meet his obligations to his Creator is a matter of individual conscience, and the right to make such decisions unfettered by government is comprehended within the rights of conscience. Madison's comments closely track the arguments that we saw earlier in Jefferson's "A Bill for Establishing Religious Freedom." In Christianity, of course, each individual is responsible for his own salvation, and God does not appear to have authorized any man to compel others to embrace any religion not of their own choosing. Madison rightly notes that "the establishment proposed by the Bill is not requisite for the support of the Christian Religion. To say that it is, is a contradiction to the Christian Religion itself, for every page of it disavows a dependence on the powers of this world."[30] The establishment of religion in the tax to support teachers of Christian religion was surely a small innovation, but Madison knew that even the smallest innovations upon regime principles should be anticipated and prevented in advance, or (if not anticipated) corrected as quickly and unobtrusively as possible. Small innovations, if unnoticed or deemed harmless, tend to loom large in the future and are most destructive when they have become accepted practice.[31] This, I say, accounts for Madison's strident argument against the assessment. By the time he wrote "Property," the Bill of Rights had been ratified with its prohibition against Congress making any law respecting an establishment of religion. This still left the states with the power to continue establishments or to create new ones, although I believe Madison knew that the weight of public opinion would eventually turn against establishment in the states.

Madison continues his argument in "Property" by extending the idea of property rights to "opinions and the free communication of them"; this also includes "a property of peculiar value" an individual has "in his religious opinions, and in the profession and practice dictated by them."[32] The right to property thus includes political opinions

---

29. Ibid.
30. Ibid., 8:301.
31. Two months after writing "Memorial and Remonstrance," Madison wrote to Caleb Wallace, who had solicited advice on drafting a constitution for Kentucky. Madison warned that "temporary deviations from fundamental principles are always more or less dangerous. When the first pretext fails, those who become interested in prolonging the evil will rarely be at a loss for other pretexts. The first precedent too familiarizes the people to the irregularity, lessens their veneration for those fundamental principles, & makes them a more easy prey to Ambition & self Interest. Hence it is that abuses of every kind when once established have been so often found to perpetuate themselves" (Letter to Caleb Wallace, August 23, 1785, ibid., 8:355).
32. Ibid., 14:266.

and religious opinions and embraces the free exercise of religion. Religious opinions are distinguished from other opinions as being "a property of a peculiar value." The latter is related to but distinguishable from the rights of conscience since religious opinions might be those opinions that are shared with others as a matter of religious doctrine. Like the rights of conscience, however, they remain of "peculiar value." Safety and liberty are also mentioned as "very dear" to a person. Blackstone clearly considers safety and liberty as personal rights—even natural rights—but he does not consider life and liberty as aspects of property because they are not "external things of the world."

A man "has an equal property in the free use of his faculties and free choice of the objects on which to employ them." In *Federalist* 10, Madison had made his famous argument that the "the diversity in the faculties of men" is the origin of the "rights of property" (10:73). "Faculties" refers to natural talents and abilities, both intellectual and physical. Individuals have a property in those talents and abilities and the right to exploit them. This would encompass the choice of an occupation suitable to one's talents and abilities free from artificial restraints such as monopolies or guild restrictions. Madison notes, "That is not a just government, nor is property secure under it, where arbitrary restrictions, exceptions, and monopolies deny to part of its citizens that free use of their faculties, and free choice of the occupations, which not only constitute their property in the general sense of the word; but are the means of acquiring property strictly so called."[33]

Madison, of course, argues that "a just security to property is not afforded by that government, under which unequal taxes oppress one species of property and reward another species." In the only other use of the word "sacred" in the essay, Madison argues the injustice of taxing individual industry "in violation of the sacred property, which Heaven, in decreeing man to earn his bread by the sweat of his brow, kindly reserved to him, in the small repose that could be spared from the supply of his necessities."[34] Madison is obviously referring to labor as the title to property, but throughout the essay he seems intent on avoiding any discussion that property originates in labor, preferring, as he had done in the *Federalist*, to ascribe the origin of the right to property to "faculties."

In the peroration to the essay, Madison repeats his central point in abbreviated form: "If the United States mean to obtain or deserve the full praise due to wise and just governments, they will equally respect the rights of property, and the property in rights." Those today who insist that the framers stressed the importance of property rights as opposed to the rights of persons (or human rights) profoundly misunderstand Madison and the founders. For them, the right to property was the comprehensive human right. Rights of conscience, free exercise of religion, freedom of speech, the right to employ one's faculties freely were all integral parts of the right to property. The right to property was a seamless whole; it was the sum total of human rights—it expressed the metaphysical freedom of the human mind.

33. Ibid., 14:266–67.
34. Ibid., 14:267.

FEDERALIST 10

In the *Federalist*, Madison employed a familiar form of regime analysis. Every regime has its peculiar disease or inherent defect that, if not checked, will eventually lead either to its destruction or to its transformation into another kind of regime. The disease that is most frequently found in popular governments is faction. And, as Madison noted, it was the "factious spirit" that was chiefly responsible for the "unsteadinese and injustice" that made reform of the Articles of Confederation imperative. Factions are minorities or majorities "combined and actuated by some common impulse of passion, of interest, adverse to the rights of other citizens, or the permanent and aggregate interest of the community" (10:72). In popular government, majority faction is the principal danger since minority faction will be defeated by the form of the government itself, which dictates majority rule. In dealing with majority faction, a system of rule that renders the majority capable of ruling in the interest of the whole—the common good—rather than in the interest of the part that constitutes the majority must be discovered. The extended republic with a multiplicity of competing interests makes it unlikely that a majority will ever combine to express one interest or a narrow range of interests. Indeed, the majorities that form will be coalitions of minority interests that change from one election to the next so that it is unlikely there will ever be permanent majorities and permanent minorities. The majority rules in every case, and it is never the same majority expressing the same interest but a new coalition expressing different interests in response to changing political and economic conditions. This is how majority rule is made compatible with the protection of minority rights. Majority rule must be rendered compatible with minority rights because the social compact demands the equal protection of the equal rights of every individual who consents to be governed. Rights belong to individuals and are not conditioned by one's status as a member of the majority or minority. Majority tyranny, no less than minority tyranny, would be a violation of the very natural law principles that authorize majority rule itself.

In *Federalist* 10, Madison argues that there are two methods of removing the causes of faction—both incompatible with republican government. The first is to destroy the liberty "which is essential to its existence." Faction could indeed be prevented by the destruction of liberty, but since liberty is "essential to political life," this would be a "remedy . . . worse than the disease" (10:73). The second method of removing the causes of faction is to give "to every citizen the same opinions, the same passions, and the same interests" (10:73). Whereas the first method is "unwise," the second is deemed by Madison to be "impracticable." The reason is human nature: "the latent causes of faction . . . are sown in the nature of man" (10:73). The latent causes of faction are a permanent feature of human nature; what translates the potential for faction into actual faction will depend upon particular political circumstances. Any attempt, therefore, to create a uniformity of opinions, passions, and interests—a situation in which the common good would no longer be problematic—was thus bound to fail because it would require violence to human nature, and only a thoroughgoing tyranny could contemplate such violence. "Theoretic politicians," Madison writes, "have erroneously supposed that by reducing mankind to a perfect equality in their political rights, they would at the same time be perfectly equalized and assimilated in their possessions, their opinions, and their passions" (10:76).

Thus powerful attributes of human nature conspire against the practicability of assimilating opinions, passions, and interests. The first is the fallibility of human reason: "As long as the reason of man continues fallible, and he is at liberty to exercise it, different opinions will be formed" (10:73). Reason is defective because of the connection that subsists between reason and self-love. This will ensure that opinions and passions "will have a reciprocal influence on each other; and the former will be objects to which the latter will attach themselves" (10:73). If human reason were infallible—that is, if reason could be exercised apart from the influence of passion and self-love—the common good would never be in dispute. This would be the enviable situation of a community of gods or a "nation of philosophers."

No less of an "insuperable obstacle to a uniformity of interests" resides in "the diversity in the faculties of men, from which the rights of property originate" (10:73). Madison continues,

> The protection of these faculties is the first object of government. From the protection of different and unequal faculties of acquiring property, the possession of different degrees and kinds of property immediately results; and from the influence of these on the sentiments and views of the respective proprietors ensues a division of the society into different interests and parties (10:73).

As we saw Madison argue in "Property," a man has a right to the free use of his faculties and to the choice of the objects on which to employ them. Faculties are the peculiar possession of individuals; they are unique talents and abilities, both physical and mental. Each individual possesses "different and unequal faculties of acquiring property," and the result is "the possession of different degrees and kinds of property." If human beings by nature possessed the same and equal faculties for acquiring or producing property, the natural form of human community would be communism. It is only *because* individuals possess "different and unequal faculties" that the private right to property exists. The source of private property derives from these diverse faculties, the unique creative capacities possessed by individuals not only to produce and acquire different goods but also to produce and acquire at unequal rates. It is the display of the private and unique capacity to produce—the different and unequal faculties—that is the very ground of private property. Thus the "first object of government" is to protect the source of property, as opposed to property itself, because protecting the source is a more powerful and substantial means of protecting the private right to property.

Locke, of course, had written that the "great and *chief end* . . . of Mens uniting into Commonwealths, and putting themselves under Government, is the *Preservation of their Property*" (II.124; II.94; II.95; II.134; II.137–39). Making the protection of "different and unequal faculties" the "first object of government," however, seems to be considerably more expansive. Locke always thought of the origin of property in terms of labor, "the *Labour* of [the] Body, and the *Work* of [the] Hands" (II.27), although it is also possible to acquire property by hiring servants to perform labor (II.28). It was the protection of the results of labor, the property itself, that was most important to Locke and consequently the chief end of government. In Madison's adaptation, what was most important was to protect the ability to acquire property, the faculties that made acquisition possible. The emphasis was on acquiring property not the possession of property. In other words, the "first object" of government was to protect the origin or source of the right to property. Property would be more effectually secured by protecting its origin. Removing the causes of faction was either unwise or impracticable and, in any case, utterly incompatible with free government. Thus the solution to the problem of faction must reside not in removing the causes of faction but in controlling the effects of faction. The most powerful way of doing this was by protecting the different and unequal faculties for acquiring property, which would in turn produce the requisite diversity of interests and political opinions necessary to obviate majority faction.

In Madison's account, faculties are associated with interests. "Those who hold and those who are without property," Madison notes,

> have ever formed distinct interest in society. Those who are creditors, and those who are debtors, fall under a like discrimination. A landed interest, a manufacturing interest, a mercantile interest, a moneyed interest, with many lesser interests grow up of necessity in civilized nations, and divide them into different classes, actuated by different sentiments and views (10:74).

"Civilized nations" are thus commercial or capitalist nations, nations with a diversity of interests. The protection of "different and unequal faculties of acquiring property" naturally results in the "possession of different degrees and kinds of property." This, in turn, influences "the sentiments and views of the respective proprietors" and divides "the society into different interests and parties" (10:73). The result will be a diverse society divided into a multiplicity of different interests expressing a variety of different opinions on matters of public interest. The principal division in society will not be between rich and poor but between the various interests that make up the diverse economy. The clash of interests will replace the divisions and contests between classes. There will still be rich and poor, but the dynamic economy that will be created by unleashing the vast human productive capacity will almost certainly create a large middle class the likes of which the world has never known. A large middle class will in all likelihood mitigate the distinction between rich and poor, and class mobility will become common. In any case, everyone—rich and poor—will have an interest in the protections afforded by the right to property: the rich in maintaining their property and the poor in the prospect of acquiring property through the application of their "different and unequal abilities." The extended commercial republic will produce a great variety of interests that will, in turn, engender a multitude of political opinions and parties. The result will be that the majorities that do form, being coalitions of various interests, will almost certainly be consistent with the common good of society and the rights of minorities. Thus it could hardly ever be in the interest of such a majority simply to invade the rights of the minority. The majority would be too diverse and diffusive for such a coalition to have such a single-minded and narrow interest.

THE RIGHT TO PROPERTY AND DISTRIBUTIVE JUSTICE

Let us remind ourselves of Madison's statement about "faculties" in *Federalist* 10: "the protection of [the] different and unequal faculties of acquiring property . . . is the first object of government. From the protection of different and unequal faculties of acquiring property, the possession of different degrees and kinds of property immediately results" (10:73). The question of distributive justice is naturally invoked by this statement. The "faculties of acquiring property" exist by nature; they are the natural endowments of the individual, but they need the protection of civil society for their exercise. We have seen throughout that the central principle of natural right that animates the American regime is that "all men are created equal." This means that all human beings have equal rights and that individuals consent to be governed for the equal protection of their equal rights. We have noted that "all men are created equal" does not mean that all men are created equal in all respects. What, then, would be the principle of distributive justice that takes into account the natural equality of all men combined with the natural inequality of all men?

The principle of distributive justice that prevailed in the United States until relatively recent times was equal opportunity. This principle recognizes equality by eliminating class and caste barriers to opportunity: everyone has an equal opportunity to display natural talents and abilities. But it also recognizes unequal natural talents and abilities by recognizing the justice of inequality of results. This was precisely the principle of distributive justice Madison had in mind in *Federalist* 10 because it was derived from the principles of natural right and human nature. Equal opportunity with unequal results based on natural talents and abilities was the system of distributive justice that ruled America for most of its history until the proper understanding of the meaning of equality was forgotten. Somehow the nation has become convinced by its leading intellectuals and constitutional scholars, including the Supreme Court, that equal results is the true test of equal opportunity, that to reward natural talents and abilities is itself an act of social injustice. Natural right is no longer the standard of distributive justice.

Professor Harvey Mansfield, a follower of Leo Strauss who has created something of a republic of letters among Strauss's followers, has argued that "a regime based on the self-evident half-truth that all men are created equal will eventually founder because of its disregard of the many ways in which men are created unequal. Even if such a regime seems powerful at the moment, it will be subject to revolution by the partisans, in this case of the few, whom it ignores." This analysis is said to be derived from the Aristotelian point of view that regimes are always vulnerable and subject to revolution because they are "partial and partisan. Although they claim to advance the common good, in fact they represent the good of a party, typically the party of the few or the many."[35] Mansfield makes obvious reference here to a short dialogue that Aristotle included in chapter 10 of book 3 of the *Politics*. The many poor make a democratic claim, arguing that free birth or equality is the superior claim to rule. The few wealthy make an oligarchic claim, justifying their argument on the inequality of wealth. Aristotle remarks that both claims hit on a part of justice but not the whole of justice. Both claims are only partial and therefore partisan. The *polis* needs free and equal citizens no less than it needs wealth. Both claims to rule are valid, but both are incomplete. Aristotle suggests that a mixed regime that he calls a polity, or *politieia*, could combine the two claims to rule. In the polity, the interests of the two antagonistic classes would balance one another. The particular configuration of the regime would depend on many circumstances, including the size and relative wealth of the oligarchic class and the size and relative poverty of the democrats along with a host of other considerations. What Aristotle makes clear, however, is that the oligarchs and democrats will not share a common good. Mansfield seems to agree wholeheartedly with Aristotle's assessment: the equal and the unequal can never coexist in a regime animated by the principle that "all men are created equal." Although there may be pious talk of a common good, each side will remain fiercely partisan.

Today, the democrats, of course, are able to display their partisanship openly while the oligarchs must disguise their partisanship as enthusiasm for the welfare of the democrats, or the "least advantaged." This concealed partisanship, Mansfield calculates, cannot last forever, especially when the headlong slide into "permissive egalitarianism" makes it impossible for the oligarchs to continue dissembling their contempt for democracy and egalitarian natural right.

Thus, according to Mansfield, the founders' idea that the principle of equality, properly understood as the equal protection of equal rights, could provide the common ground for the few and the many was merely an illusion. The unequal can never seek common ground with the equal because both seek incommensurable goods that have no common denominator. There can be no common good; the world of politics is always (and only) partisan. But, as we have argued, the right to property—an idea unknown to Aristotle—provides common ground or a common good for the few and the many. Both have a common interest in supporting the right to property. The few do not want to be dispossessed by the many, and the many want to keep what they possess in security, knowing that if they prosper in the future, their property will be secure. It bears repeating that "the first object of government" is "the protection of [the] different and unequal faculties of acquiring property, [from which] the possession of different degrees and kinds of property immediately results" (*Federalist*, 10:73). The natural right principle of distributive justice inherent in the principle of

---

35. Harvey C. Mansfield Jr., "Returning to the Founders: The Debate on the Constitution," *New Criterion* 12, no. 1 (September 1993): 50–51.

equality reconciles both the claims of equality and the claims of inequality—equality of opportunity and the justice of the inequality of results.

This view of the founders' principle of distributive justice was adopted in full by Abraham Lincoln. Lincoln expressed a Lockean view of the right to property when he noted in his first State of the Union Address, "Labor is prior to, and independent of, capital. Capital is only the fruit of labor, and could never have existed if labor had not first existed."[36] Thus Lincoln repeats the understanding of Locke and the founding generation that labor is the origin of the right to property. "Labor is the superior of capital" because it is the foundation of the right to property, although it is undoubtedly true that "capital has its rights, which are as worthy of protection as any other rights." "The prudent, penniless beginner in the world," Lincoln continued, "labors for wages awhile, saves a surplus with which to buy tools or land for himself, then labors on his own account another while, and at length hires another new beginner to help him. This is the just, and generous, and prosperous system, which opens the way to all—gives hope to all, and consequent energy, and progress, and improvement of condition to all."[37] The "prudent" laborer is, of course, Locke's rational and industrious man, who fits seamlessly into the scheme of distributive justice that is based on equal opportunity envisioned by the founders. A few years later Lincoln wrote,

> Property is the fruit of labor—property is desirable—is a positive good in the world. That some should be rich, shows that others may become rich, and hence is just encouragement to industry and enterprize. Let not him who is houseless pull down the house of another; but let him labor diligently and build one for himself, thus by example assuring that his own shall be safe from violence when built.[38]

Here Lincoln clearly recognizes the common interest that rich and poor have in supporting the right to property, something not contemplated by Aristotle—or by Professor Mansfield. But would not Aristotle—and should not Mansfield—see the potential for a natural right solution to the primary political question of distributive justice in equal opportunity that recognizes unequal talents and abilities and rewards them in proportion? And would not this natural right solution be clearly consistent with Aristotelian principles?

In book 5 of *Nicomachean Ethics*, Aristotle describes two different kinds of justice: justice in exchanges and justice in distribution. Justice in exchanges is governed by a numerical equality that must be present at the beginning and end of every transaction. The parties to the exchange are equal and the justice of the exchange is intrinsic to the exchange itself and does not depend on the character of the parties—that is,

---

36. Abraham Lincoln, "State of the Union Address," December 3, 1861, in *Collected Works of Abraham Lincoln*, V:52.

37. Ibid.

38. Ibid., VII:259; see also II:364 and III:478.

on their differing talents and abilities, to say nothing of their moral or political virtue. Justice in exchanges is equality of result.

Justice in distributions—distributive justice—is an entirely different matter. Here justice requires inequality of result. Distributive justice is governed by proportional equality—that is, equality properly understood. This means that just distributions should be determined by unequal shares to unequals and equal shares to equals because giving unequal shares to equals and equal shares to unequals would be unjust. The winner of the race should be awarded first place and the second-place finisher should be awarded second place. The same holds for the distribution of honors, offices, and economic rewards. Any other scheme of rewards not based on equality rightly understood—that is, recognizing the justice of inequality of results—would be unjust from an Aristotelian point of view. Is this not precisely the system of distributive justice envisioned by the founders that came to be known as "equal opportunity," a system that eliminated artificial barriers to the development of natural talents and abilities and at the same time authorized a system of rewards based on the unequal expression of those talents and abilities? It is only with the slightest hyperbole that we might call this "the truest and best equality," which is "the natural equality given to unequals on each occasion [*to katá phúsin íson anísois ekástote dothén*]."[39]

---

39. Plato, *Laws*, 757b5–d5.

5

From the Founding to *Kelo v. City of New London, Connecticut*: The Decline and Fall of the Right to Property

"It is certain that there are many ways in which the property of individual owners can be better employed or occupied when the general public is considered than it actually is by the owners themselves."

Thomas M. Cooley, *A Treatise on Constitutional Limitations*[1]

"Any property may now be taken for the benefit of another private party. . . . The beneficiaries are likely to be those citizens with disproportionate influence and power in the political process, including large corporations and development firms. As for the victims, the government now has license to transfer property from those with fewer resources to those with more. The Founders cannot have intended this perverse result."

Justice Sandra Day O'Connor, in *Kelo v. City of New London, Connecticut*.[2]

Madison wrote his seminal essay "Property" less than three years after he introduced the amendments that became the Bill of Rights in the House of Representatives on June 8, 1789, and a little more than three months after the amendments were ratified. The Fifth Amendment contains what is today widely referred to as the Takings Clause. The original language introduced by Madison stated, "No person shall . . . be obliged to relinquish his property, where it may be necessary for public use, without a just compensation." The House Committee of Eleven Report of July 28, 1789, modified the language to read "nor shall private property be taken for public use without just compensation." There was apparently never any debate

---

1. Thomas M. Cooley, *A Treatise on Constitutional Limitations* (Boston: Little, Brown, and Company, 1868), 532.
2. *Kelo v. City of New London*, 545 U.S. 469, 505 (2005) (O'Connor, J., dissenting).

about the substance of the amendment; its importance, however, should not be underestimated. Given what we have learned about the centrality of property and social compact to Madison's thought and the thought of the founding generation, one perceptive legal scholar perfectly captured the spirit of the founding when he noted that the Takings Clause "represents a twelve-word distillation of social contract political theory."[3]

Eminent domain, the power of the government to take private property for public use, is inherent in the idea of sovereignty. It is necessary to meet the exigencies of war and other emergencies, both foreign and domestic, because in emergencies the government can't wait for judicial or legislative determinations. Being inherent in sovereignty, the power of eminent domain is also in its nature an unlimited power: it doesn't require the consent of the property owner. Such irresistible power is always liable to abuse whether the dangers are real or only a pretext. Constitutional government, however, requires that the use of such power be limited in the sense that it must be made compatible with the principles and purposes of republican government. There can be no doubt that the Takings Clause was meant to be a crucial feature of limited constitutional government.

EARLY CASES AND SOCIAL COMPACT

Some early Supreme Court cases recognized the importance of social compact and the natural right to property in the American founding. Justice William Patterson's opinion in *Vanhorne's Lessee v. Dorrance* (1795),[4] written as a charge to the jury while serving on circuit in the District of Pennsylvania, has been frequently cited. Having quoted several provisions of the Pennsylvania Constitution relating to property rights, Justice Patterson remarked,

> From these passages it is evident; that the right of acquiring and possessing property and having it protected, is one of the natural inherent and unalienable rights of man . . . its security was one of the objects, that induced them to unite in society. No man would become a member of a community, in which he could not enjoy the fruits of his honest labor and industry. The preservation of property then is a primary object of the social compact, and, by the late constitution of Pennsylvania, was made a fundamental law. Every person ought to contribute his proportion for public purposes and public exigencies; but no one can be called upon to surrender or sacrifice his whole property, real and personal, for the good of the community, without receiving a recompence in value. This would be laying a burden upon an individual, which ought to be sustained by the society at large.[5]

---

3. Richard A. Epstein, *Supreme Neglect: How to Revive Constitutional Protection for Private Property* (New York: Oxford University Press, 2008), 34.
4. *Vanhorne's Lessee v. Dorrance*, 2 U.S. (2 Dall.) 304 (C.C. Pa. 1795 [Patterson, J.]).
5. Ibid. at 310.

The argument here is familiar social compact reasoning. The right to property is an "unalienable," natural right, and men unite for the principal purpose of securing their property.

Patterson, of course, recognizes that the power of eminent domain is inherent in sovereignty and that "public exigencies" often require that private property be sacrificed for the public good. This "despotic power," as Patterson calls it, must be checked by the requirement that the property taken can be confiscated only for "public use" and that there must be recompense to the owner. Without recompense, it would be "an exercise of power and not of right." Recompense is a matter of simple justice; no individual should be made to bear a public burden that ought in justice to be borne by the community as a whole. As Patterson phrased it, "this would be laying a burden upon an individual which ought to be sustained by the society at large."[6] Right or justice requires a common sharing of the burden when the common good is served. This idea of justice, of course, is inherent in social compact.

The act in question in *Vanhorn's Lessee v. Dorrance* was one in which the Pennsylvania legislature attempted to divest one set of citizens of their landed property "for the purpose of vesting the same property in another set of citizens."[7] The constitution of Pennsylvania expressly declared that "the right of acquiring, possessing, and protecting property is natural, inherent, and unalienable." This is not a right granted by the legislature, Patterson avowed, but from the constitution. "It is," he argued, therefore "sacred; for it is further declared, that the legislature shall have no power to add to, alter, abolish, or infringe on any part of the constitution."[8] The constitution is the measure of legislative authority, and any law that violates the constitution is therefore ipso facto null and void. Even if it were conceded that the legislature was competent to determine that "the public exigencies, or necessities of the state" required the transfer of the vested private property of A to private party B, then

> the dictates of reason and the eternal principles of justice, as well as the sacred principles of the social contract, and the constitution, direct, and they accordingly declare and ordain that A shall receive compensation for the land. But here the legislature must stop; they have run the full length of their authority, and can go no further; they cannot constitutionally determine upon the amount of the compensation, or value of the land. Public exigencies do not require, necessity does not demand, that the legislature should, of themselves, without the participation of the proprietor, or intervention of a jury, assess the value of the thing, or ascertain the amount of the compensation to be paid for it.[9]

---

6. Ibid. This idea has been repeated several times in Supreme Court decisions. See inter alia *Armstrong v. U.S.* 364 U.S. 40, 49 (1960) (Black, J.): "The Fifth Amendment's guarantee that private property shall not be taken for a public use without just compensation was designed to bar Government from forcing some people alone to bear public burdens which, in all fairness and justice, should be borne by the public as a whole." *Dolan v. City of Tigard*, 512 U.S. 374, 384 (1994) (Rehnquist, C. J.).

7. Ibid. at 311.

8. Ibid.

9. Ibid. at 312–13.

Pennsylvania law had established a board to determine the amount of the compensation for the confiscated land. The law did not require notice to the landowner or a hearing, nor did it allow for determinations by juries. In addition, the compensation was limited to an exchange of land. But as Patterson noted, just compensation could only be by payment in money because money is the universal measure of value, and compensation in equivalent land can never be a measure of equity without the consent of the aggrieved landowner. Thus the legislature exercised unlimited power of eminent domain under its own legislative act. "Omnipotence in Legislation," Patterson declared, "is despotism. According to this doctrine, we have nothing that we can call our own, or are sure of for a moment; we are all tenants at will, and hold our landed property at the mere pleasure of the Legislature." In short, the law invoking the eminent domain power of the State of Pennsylvania had been exercised despotically by the legislature. Patterson concluded that the "act is void; it never had constitutional existence; it is a dead letter, and of no more virtue or avail, than if it never had been made."[10]

Justice Patterson may have been the first to advocate the use of strict scrutiny to protect a fundamental right: "Every statute, derogatory to the rights of property, or that takes away the estate of a citizen ought to be construed strictly."[11] The reason he singled out the right to property for such strict examination was that the preservation of property was the primary object of social compact that, we remember, Madison said was the ground of all just and free government. This fundamental right bears such a close relationship to the foundation of just government that the slightest encroachment, however insignificant it may appear at first glance, must be examined with the greatest care and treated as if it were the first sign of a full-scale assault on all liberties.

Patterson's opinion in *Vanhorne's Lessee v. Dorrance* has come to stand for the idea that the minimum or irreducible requirement of the Takings Clause is that private property cannot be taken from private person A and transferred to private person B without a compelling reason. Otherwise, the right to property as a private right would cease to exist.

> When the legislature . . . attempt[s] to take the property of one man . . . in order to transfer it to another, even upon complete indemnification, it will naturally be considered as an extraordinary act of legislation, which ought to be viewed with jealous eyes, examined with critical exactness, and scrutinized with all the severity of legal exposition. An act of this sort deserves no favor; to construe it liberally would be sinning against the rights of private property.[12]

Current takings jurisprudence, of course, no longer considers the right to property as a fundamental right that demands strict scrutiny or regards the greatest danger to the rights of property as emanating from the legislative branch. The right to property

---

10. Ibid. at 316.
11. Ibid.
12. Ibid. at 318.

is the only fundamental right in the Bill of Rights that does not automatically trigger strict scrutiny review by the Supreme Court. Legislatures are given deference to determine when a "public purpose" is served by eminent domain. The Fifth Amendment has been amended by construction of the court from "public use" to "public purpose." This was accomplished under the tutelage of Progressivism's "indifference to individual rights and support for deference to legislative majorities."[13] Solicitude for individual rights—particularly the right to property—would have made it difficult for the government to regulate social institutions. From the time of the founding, rights were always viewed as a limit on government power. Progressivism was undoubtedly the prime mover in the Supreme Court's decision to expel the right to property from the pantheon of fundamental rights that make up the Bill of Rights. Any law implicating freedom of speech or free exercise of religion, for example, would today be subjected to the strictest scrutiny by the Supreme Court, but if it were merely a matter of property rights, the legislature would only have to advance the thinnest pretext for invading what was once regarded as the most fundamental comprehensive right. The decline of the right to property, culminating in its near extinction in the *Kelo* decision, was due, in large measure, to Progressivism, a subject we will address *in extenso* in due course.

Three years later in the case of *Calder v. Bull* (1798),[14] Justice Samuel Chase also made liberal use of social compact theory in an oft-cited opinion. The question before the court was not about property rights but whether a legislative act that ordered a probate court to conduct a new trial over the disposition of a will amounted to an ex post facto law. The unanimous opinion of the court was that the ex post facto prohibition applied only to criminal laws; therefore, the Article I, Section 10 provision of the U.S. Constitution barring the states from passing such laws didn't apply in this civil case. The court further held that state courts had final authority to determine the constitutionality of laws under state constitutions, and the federal courts thus had no jurisdiction where no federal issue was presented.

Justice Chase, however, took the occasion to expound the social compact basis of constitutional government, much as Justice Patterson had done in *Vanhorn's Lessee v. Dorrance.* As to legislative power, Justice Chase reasoned,

> the purposes for which men enter into society will determine the nature and terms of the social compact; and as they are the foundation of the legislative power, they will decide what are the proper objects of it: The nature, and ends of legislative power will limit the exercise of it. This fundamental principle flows from the very nature of our free Republican governments, that no man should be compelled to do what the laws do not require; nor to refrain from acts which the laws permit. . . . An act of the Legislature (for I cannot call it a law) contrary to the great first principles of the social compact, cannot be considered a rightful exercise of legislative authority. The obligation of a law

---

13. David E. Bernstein, *Rehabilitating Lochner: Defending Individual Rights Against Progressive Reform* (Chicago: University of Chicago Press, 2011), 46.
14. *Calder v. Bull,* 3 U.S. (3 Dall.) 386 (1798).

in governments established on express compact, and on republican principles, must be determined by the nature of power, on which it is founded.[15]

It scarcely needs to be pointed out that when Justice Chase refers to "social compact" and "express compact," he refers, no less than Justice Patterson in *Vanhorne's Lessee v. Dorrance*, to the Declaration of Independence, the principled basis and foundation for governments in America, both state and federal. Justice Chase gives some examples of the obligation of the laws in governments based on republican principles and express compact: ex post facto laws are prohibited not because they violate positive law or constitutions but because they are "contrary to the great first principles of the social compact."[16] In other words, ex post facto laws are a violation of natural law and natural right. Laws that impair the obligations of contract would fall under a like consideration, while a law that makes a man a judge in his own case or a law that takes property from A and gives it to B would be a similar violation of natural right. These laws are against reason and justice—they are violations of the first principles of the social compact and thereby contravene the principles of natural law and natural right. No legislature—or constitution—can authorize what violates the first principles of the social compact.[17]

Justice James Iredell, in his separate opinion, was less troubled by the claims that the legislature may have invaded the judiciary's prerogatives because it had no bearing on the question of whether the act under consideration was ex post facto. He did, however, have an answer of sorts to Justice Chase's foray into the realm of natural right and natural law. "It is true," Justice Iredell remarked, "that some speculative jurists have held, that a legislative act against natural justice must, in itself, be void," but he expressed severe reservations about whether constitutional courts could declare laws invalid on that basis. Both the federal Constitution and state constitutions since the Revolution, he added, have specified with great precision the powers that legislatures possess, and these constitutions, not natural justice, are meant to be the measure of legislative power. "If any act of Congress, or of the legislatures of a state, violates those constitutional provisions, it is unquestionably void; though, I admit, that as the authority to declare it void is of a delicate and awful nature, the court will never resort to that authority, but in a clear and urgent case."[18] Where the legislature, whether of the Union or a member state, passes a law within its general authority,

---

15. Ibid. at 388.
16. Ibid. at 388. In *Federalist* 44, Madison wrote, "Bills of attainder, *ex post facto* laws, and laws impairing the obligations of contracts are contrary to the first principles of the social compact and to every principle of sound legislation. . . . Very properly, therefore, have the convention added this constitutional bulwark in favor of personal security and private rights. . . . The sober people of America are weary of the fluctuating policy which has directed the public councils. They have seen with regret and indignation that sudden changes and legislative interferences, in cases affecting personal rights, become jobs in the hands of enterprising and influential speculators, and snares to the more industrious and less informed part of the community. They have seen, too, that one legislative interference is but the first link of a long chain of repetitions, every subsequent interference being naturally produced by the effects of the preceding" (278–79).
17. Ibid.
18. Ibid. at 398–99.

the court cannot pronounce it to be void, merely because it is, in their judgment, contrary to the principles of natural justice. The ideas of natural justice are regulated by no fixed standard; the ablest and the purest men have differed upon the subject; and all that the court could properly say, in such an event would be that the legislature (possessed of an equal right of opinion) had passed an act which, in the opinion of the judges, was inconsistent with the abstract principles of natural justice.[19]

Justice Iredell says that the "ablest and the purest men" have differed on what constitutes "natural justice." This statement is certainly true, but it is hardly to the point. The framers did not disagree with respect to natural justice. Natural law and natural right as understood by the founders traced its pedigree in an unbroken line through Locke to Aristotle. There have been many disputes among philosophers about the status and content of natural law, but the founders were statesmen who mined the "elementary books of public right" for practical wisdom. There was virtually no disagreement about the social compact principles expressed in the Declaration of Independence or about the central "abstract" idea that animated those principles, the "self-evident truth" that "all men are created equal." As to how the principles of the Declaration would be implemented and what precise form the government under those principles would take, there was inevitable disagreement. But the disagreement over how to implement the principles did not imply disagreement about the principles themselves. The Federalists and anti-Federalists believed they were guided by the same principles, and neither side believed that their arguments were merely irresolvable disputes about "natural justice" or "abstract ideas." There was agreement on the first principles: free and just government derived from social compact, and just powers of government derived from the consent of the governed. Under social compact, governments exist to protect natural rights that they don't create. In explaining why the Constitution forbids the legislature from taking property from private person A and giving it to private person B, reference to the natural right to property and social compact is perfectly appropriate and hardly a reference to a vague or abstract idea of "natural justice." It is a reminder that the principles of the Declaration are embodied within the Constitution and also a reminder that recourse to first principles should be frequent in republican government.

Marbury v. Madison is another seminal case that relies heavily on social compact theory, which Chief Justice Marshall regarded as embodying "principles . . . long and well established."[20] The chief justice noted "that the people have an original right to establish, for their future government, such principles, as, in their opinion, shall most conduce to their own happiness."[21] This, Marshall concluded, "is the basis on which the whole American fabric has been erected" and "the principles

---

19. Ibid. at 399.
20. *Marbury v. Madison*, 5 U.S. (1 Cranch.) 137, 176 (1803) (Marshall, C. J.). See Edward Erler, "*Marbury v. Madison* and the Progressive Transformation of Judicial Power," in *The Progressive Revolution in Politics and Political Science*, ed. John Marini and Ken Masugi (Lanham, MD: Rowman & Littlefield, 2005), 163–218.
21. *Marbury v. Madison* at 176.

. . . so established, are deemed fundamental. . . . This original and supreme will organizes the government, and assigns to different departments their respective powers. It may either stop here, or establish certain limits not to be transcended by those departments."[22]

Marshall never uses the terms "social compact" or "natural rights" in his opinion, but he employs language redolent of both concepts throughout. The foundation of the "just powers" of government, we learned from the Declaration of Independence, was the "consent of the governed." Marshall explains this as the "original and supreme will" of the people to establish a government that they calculate will secure their "safety and happiness." The principles that result from the exercise of this will must, of course, be deemed "fundamental" and "permanent." The Constitution, as a result, is "paramount law" and controls ordinary laws passed by the legislature—those acts passed only by the authority of the Constitution. Social compact, as we have seen, contemplates limited government of delegated powers. So "that those limits may not be not mistaken, or forgotten," Marshall says, the American founders devised a written constitution.[23] And in context, Marshall clearly means that the limitations on the powers of government are principally directed against the legislative branch. If the Constitution is to be considered "fundamental and paramount law," as it surely must be as the product of the "original and supreme will" of the people, then "the theory of every such government must be that an act of the legislature, repugnant to the constitution, is void." This theory, Marshall continues, "is essentially attached to a written constitution, and is, consequently, to be considered, by this court, as one of the fundamental principles of our society."[24] The very essence of the judicial duty is to decide conflicts between ordinary acts of legislation and the Constitution. Any ordinary act of legislation passed under the Constitution's authority that conflicts with any of its provisions is null and void. Judicial review is inherent in the very idea of a written constitution and is part of the idea of limited government, which is, in turn, intrinsic to social compact. Social compact, in its turn, is intrinsic to the Constitution because it embodies the principles of the Declaration of Independence.

THE DECLARATION OF INDEPENDENCE AND THE RECONSTRUCTION AMENDMENTS

The Declaration of Independence played a crucial role in the adoption of the Reconstruction Amendments. There is no doubt that the omnipresent spirit of Abraham Lincoln presided over the Reconstruction Amendment debates. Lincoln had always viewed the American founding as incomplete. The Revolution had vindicated the principle of consent for most, but insofar as the Constitution allowed the continued

22. Ibid.
23. Ibid.
24. Ibid. at 177.

existence of slavery, it did not extend that principle to all. The Civil War, he thought, was the second battle in the Revolutionary War, fought this time to vindicate the principle of consent for all men. It was the adoption of the Reconstruction Amendments that brought the Constitution into formal harmony with the principles of the Declaration. The idea that the Thirty-Ninth Congress was engaged in completing the founding was expressed so frequently during debates that it is difficult to doubt that it was this idée fixe that inspired its actions.

In December 1865, Schuyler Colfax was elected Speaker of the House of Representatives for the Thirty-Ninth Congress. A few weeks before the first session began, Colfax remarked in a speech delivered on November 18, 1865, in Washington, DC, that terms for restoration must be accepted by the rebellious states. In addition to repudiating the various ordinances of secession and ratifying the Thirteenth Amendment—"extinguishing slavery, that the cause of dissension and rebellion might be utterly extirpated"—the states formerly in rebellion must agree to "other terms upon which I think there is no division among the loyal men of the Union, to wit: That the Declaration of Independence must be recognized as the law of the land, and every man, alien and native, white and black, protected in the inalienable and God-given rights of life, liberty, and the pursuit of happiness."[25] And in his acceptance speech as speaker, Colfax said it was the responsibility of Congress to "afford what our Magna Charta, the Declaration of Independence, proclaims is the chief object of government, protection to all men in their inalienable rights."[26] This was Colfax's attempt to set the terms for the coming debate in the House. The Republican Party can be fairly said to have taken this suggestion as their architectonic guide for Reconstruction.

On May 8, 1866, Representative Thaddeus Stevens, House chairman of the powerful Joint Committee on Reconstruction, rehearsed a theme that was frequently heard in both chambers of the Thirty-Ninth Congress:

> I beg gentlemen to consider the magnitude of the task which was imposed upon the committee. They were expected to suggest a plan for rebuilding a shattered nation—a nation which though not dissevered was yet shaken and riven. . . . It cannot be denied that this terrible struggle sprang from the vicious principles incorporated into the institutions of our country. Our fathers had been compelled to postpone the principles of their great Declaration, and wait for their full establishment till a more propitious time. That time ought to be present now.[27]

The first section of the proposed Fourteenth Amendment, Stevens explained, prohibits the states from abridging the privileges or immunities of citizens of the United States and from denying to any person life, liberty, or property without due process of law and of depriving any person within their jurisdiction equal protection of the

25. O. J. Hollister, *Life of Schuyler Colfax*, 2nd ed. (New York: Funk and Wagnalls, 1886), 270–71.
26. *Congressional Globe*, 39th Cong., 1st Sess., 5 (1865) (Rep. Colfax).
27. *Congressional Globe*, 39th Cong., 1st Sess., 2459 (1866) (Rep. Stevens).

laws. "I can hardly believe," Stevens declaimed, "that any person can be found who will not admit that every one of these provisions is just. They are all asserted in some form or other, in our DECLARATION or organic law."[28]

A few months earlier, Representative William A. Newell, Republican of New Jersey, had made similar comments on the relation of the Declaration and the Constitution, noting,

> The framers of the Constitution did what they considered best under the circumstances. They made freedom the rule and slavery the exception in the organization of the Government. They declared in favor of the former in language the most emphatic and sublime in history, while they placed the latter, as they fondly hoped, in a position favorable for ultimate extinction.[29]

No one on the floor of the House would have missed the references to Lincoln. On February 19, 1866, Senator Richard Yates, Republican of Illinois, delivered an impassioned speech agreeing that the framers of the Constitution had to depart from the principles of the Declaration of Independence "for the sake of concord among the States and to secure the adoption of the Constitution." Yates shared Lincoln's view that the Constitution had put slavery "in the course of ultimate extinction" and that it was the departure from those principles that ultimately thrust the nation into civil war. He quoted Lincoln's "great proposition that this nation could not remain half slave and half free," although he did not allude to the fact that Lincoln's proposition probably did more to make war inevitable than anything else that was said by any politician. "There is," he insisted, "only one basis upon which [the] difficulties [facing the nation] can be settled, and that is to return to the fundamental principles which were aimed to be established by our fathers . . . the principles laid down in the Declaration of Independence."[30]

Senator Luke Poland, Republican of Vermont, spoke in favor of the due process and equal protection provisions of the first proposed Fourteenth Amendment on January 5, 1866. These provisions, Senator Poland proclaimed, that would control the states, represented "the very spirit and inspiration of our system of government, the absolute foundation upon which it was established. It is essentially declared in the Declaration of Independence and in all the provisions of the Constitution."[31] It would be difficult to argue that the protection of "life, liberty and property" was not part of the Declaration's understanding of the purpose of government, nor that "equal protection" was not intrinsic to the theory of social compact.

It would be possible to multiply the quotations many times over from the Reconstruction debates illustrating reliance on the principles of the Declaration. There can

---

28. Ibid. Stevens was speaking in support of the final version of section 1 of the Fourteenth Amendment (but before the Citizenship Clause was introduced in the Senate on May 30, 1866).

29. *Congressional Globe*, 39th Cong., 1st Sess., 866 (1866) (Rep. Newell).

30. *Congressional Globe*, 39th Cong., 1st Sess., 866 (1866) (Sen. Yates).

31. *Congressional Globe*, 39th Cong., 1st Sess., 866 (1866) (Sen. Poland).

be little doubt that the goal of Congress was to complete the regime of the founding by bringing the Constitution into harmony with the principles of the Declaration of Independence.

THE CIVIL RIGHTS ACT OF 1866

The first attempt at Reconstruction by the Thirty-Ninth Congress was the Civil Rights Act of 1866. Its principal author was Senator Lyman Trumbull of Illinois, who introduced the bill in the Senate on January 5, 1866. Trumbull had been coauthor of the Thirteenth Amendment and was convinced that the amendment provided authority for the sweeping provisions of the act. The pressing issue was to settle the citizenship of the newly freed slaves. *Dred Scott* had held that blacks of African descent, whether slave or free, were no part of the people who framed and ratified the Constitution and therefore could never be citizens of the United States. Many thought that the Thirteenth Amendment, by abolishing slavery, had secured the citizenship of blacks of African descent by its declaration of universal freedom. Others wanted to make the grant of citizenship explicit. The first version of Section 1 of the Civil Rights Act, which contained the Citizenship Clause, read,

> That all persons of African descent born in the United States are hereby declared to be citizens of the United States, and there shall be no discrimination in civil rights or immunities among the inhabitants of any state or territory of the United States on account of race, color, or previous condition of slavery.[32]

This bill, Trumbull remarked, was intended to give effect to the principles of the Thirteenth Amendment, which were grounded in the Declaration of Independence:

> Of what avail was the immortal declaration "that all men are created equal; that they are endowed by their Creator with certain inalienable rights; that among these are life, liberty, and the pursuit of happiness," and "that to secure these rights Governments are instituted among men," to the millions of the African race in this country who were ground down and degraded and subjected to a slavery more intolerable and cruel than the world ever before knew?[33]

Presumably the grant of U.S. citizenship carried with it automatic citizenship in the state where the newly enfranchised citizens resided. This would be made explicit later in the Fourteenth Amendment, but it was clearly assumed in the Civil Rights Act, otherwise the states could prevent federal protection of civil rights and immunities of state citizenship by withholding state citizenship. I believe that there is little doubt that the framers of the Civil Rights Act and the Fourteenth Amendment intended

---

32. *Congressional Globe*, 39th Cong., 1st Sess., 866 (1866) (Sen. Trumbull).
33. Ibid.

the federal government to have the power to enforce the rights and privileges and immunities that attached to both U.S. citizenship *and* state citizenship.

Trumbull argued that the "civil rights or immunities" protected by the bill were those of Article 4, Section 2 of the Constitution: "the citizens of each State shall be entitled to all privileges and immunities of citizens in the several States." Trumbull then proceeded to quote Story's *Commentaries* to the effect that Article 4 created a "general citizenship" that "transcended state citizenship." Trumbull referred at length to Justice Bushrod Washington's opinion in *Corfield v. Coryell* (1823), which defined the extensive privileges and immunities "of citizens in the several states" and which Trumbull said were "the very rights belonging to *a citizen of the United States* which are set forth in the first section of this bill."[34] Justice Washington's opinion, from a case in the Circuit Court for the District of Pennsylvania, was cited frequently during debates over the Civil Rights Act and the Fourteenth Amendment as an exemplar of the meaning of privileges and immunities. "We feel no hesitation," Justice Washington said,

> in confining these expressions to those privileges and immunities which are in their nature fundamental; which belong of right to the citizens of all free Governments; and which have at all times been enjoyed by the citizens of the several States which compose this Union, from the time of their becoming free, independent and sovereign. What these fundamental principles are it would perhaps be more tedious than difficult to enumerate.[35]

Justice Washington proceeded to give an extensive (if partial) list of those privileges and immunities:

> The right of a citizen of one state to pass through, or to reside in any other state, for purposes of trade, agriculture, professional pursuits, or otherwise; to claim the benefit of the writ of habeas corpus; to institute and maintain actions of any kind in the courts of the state; to take, hold and dispose of property, either real or personal; and an exemption from higher taxes or impositions than are paid by the other citizens of the state . . . to which may be added, the elective franchise, as regulated and established by the laws or constitution of the state in which it is to be exercised. These, and many others which might be mentioned, are strictly speaking, privileges and immunities [of the citizens of the several states].[36]

Trumbull commented, however, that Justice Washington had overextended himself when he added the elective franchise to the list, even though he had qualified it by saying "as regulated and established by the laws or constitution of the state in which it is to be exercised."[37] Trumbull and other supporters of the Civil Rights Act

34. Ibid. at 474–75 (emphasis added).
35. Ibid. at 475. The case is *Corfield v. Coryell*, 6 F. Cas. 546 (1823).
36. Ibid.
37. Ibid. *Corfield v. Coryell*, 6 F. Cas. 546, 552.

denied that voting was protected, rightly estimating that the issue of black voting was too volatile to be considered so early in the debates.

Trumbull concluded that "persons of African descent, born in the United States, are as much citizens as white persons who are born in the country," and they are entitled to "the great fundamental rights set forth in this bill: the right to acquire property, the right to go and come at pleasure, the right to enforce rights in the courts, to make contracts, and to inherit and dispose of property. These are the very rights that are set forth in this bill as appertaining to every freeman."[38] Trumbull seems clearly to be arguing that those privileges and immunities that previously were thought to attach to the citizens of the several states were now to be regarded as the privileges and immunities that belonged to citizens of the United States, and those privileges and immunities that were formerly guaranteed to citizens who migrated from one state to another were now conferred on residents of the several states as citizens of the United States and enforceable against the states. These were the "fundamental rights" that were guaranteed by the Civil Rights Act.[39]

Raoul Berger points out that Senator Garrett Davis, Democrat of Kentucky, recognized Trumbull's legerdemain. "There are, let me say for argument's sake," Wade retorted, "two hundred thousand free negroes in the State of Kentucky that were born there, that have never been residents of any other State." Senator Trumbull "proposes to make these two hundred thousand negroes and every free negro in America, whether he has ever been out of the State in which he was born and in which he resides, or not, the subject of this bill." Senator Benjamin Wade, Republican of Ohio, alleged that there was no constitutional authority to extend federal protection to "such classes of our people." Rather, he explained, "only when a citizen of one State goes into another State, either to change his residence to that other State, or to acquire property there, or to exercise some other right or privilege which a citizen of that other State is entitled to in that State" do the "privileges and immunities" of United States citizens come into play.[40] After quoting *Corfield*, Davis rightly concludes, "All these rights and privileges are attributed by the decision of the court to the citizens of one State going into another State." There was no support whatsoever, Wade claimed, for the "idea that a citizen, black or white, of a State, born in that State, having no business, no transactions in another State, not having gone into another State to change his place of residence, but still living and residing in the State where he was born, is or can become the subject of congressional legislation under this provision [viz. Art. IV, Sec. 2] of the Constitution."[41]

Congressman James Wilson, Republican of Iowa, and chairman of the Judiciary Committee, had introduced the Civil Rights Bill in the House on March 1, 1866.

---

38. Ibid.

39. Raoul Berger, *Government by Judiciary: The Transformation of the Fourteenth Amendment* (Cambridge, MA: Harvard University Press, 1977), 42.

40. *Congressional Globe*, 39th Cong., 1st Sess., 595 (1866) (Sen. Wade); see Berger, *Government by Judiciary*, 41.

41. *Congressional Globe*, 39th Cong., 1st Sess., 597 (1866) (Sen. Wade).

His argument was similar to Trumbull's. He did not speak in terms of federal and state citizenship but of arming the federal government with the means to protect "the great fundamental civil rights" of "each and every citizen . . . of the great national family."[42] A week later, Representative Michael Kerr, Democrat of Indiana, rose to oppose the bill, arguing that the provision in Section 1 proclaiming the grant of citizenship to the newly freed slaves was merely cover for the fact that Congress' attempt to protect the rights of these newly created citizens in the states was not authorized by the Privileges and Immunities Clause of the Constitution. If the former slaves acquired citizenship by birth, Kerr argued, no legislation was necessary. The only way Congress could confer citizenship was by naturalization, and Section 1 did not purport to be a naturalization bill. Kerr concluded that there was something transparently fraudulent about the Citizenship Clause, and he pointed to the same sleight of hand that had been earlier identified by Senator Wade. Article 4, Section 2 "only requires the citizens of *each State* shall enjoy certain privileges in the other States to which they may temporarily or permanently remove; but not that citizens of the United States shall enjoy such privileges in the *States*."[43] Both Kerr and Davis had accurately discerned the intent of the framers of the Civil Rights Act, an intent that, while they did not attempt to conceal it, they certainly did not broadcast it. What is not in doubt is that the Civil Rights Act was meant to revolutionize the federal relation by using the power of the federal government to protect the fundamental rights and privileges and immunities of U.S. citizens in the several states. Those privileges and immunities that were once thought to belong to the citizens of the states would now be attached to federal citizenship and be given priority by virtue of the fact that federal citizenship would take precedence over state citizenship. Thus it is clear that the Civil Rights Act was intended to work a significant change (if not a revolution) in the federal relation—if, that is, such a revolution could be accomplished by legislation rather than by a constitutional amendment.

The Civil Rights Act passed the Senate on February 2, 1866, and the House on March 13. In its final version, Section 1 had been amended to read,

> That all persons born in the United States and not subject to any foreign power, excluding Indians not taxed, are hereby declared to be citizens of the United States; and such citizens, of every race and color, without regard to any previous condition of slavery or involuntary servitude, except as a punishment for crime whereof the party shall have been duly convicted, shall have the same right, in every State and Territory in the United States, to make and enforce contracts, to sue, be parties, and give evidence, inherit, purchase, lease, sell, hold, and convey real and personal property, and to full and equal benefit of all laws and proceedings for the security of person and property, as is enjoyed by white citizens, and shall be subject to like punishment, pains, and penalties, and to none other, any law, statute, ordinance, regulation, or custom, to the contrary notwithstanding.

---

42. Ibid. at 1117.
43. Ibid. at 1268.

Notably absent from the final version was any language about privileges and immunities, although the rights adumbrated were universally understood to be the privileges and immunities of U.S. citizens. The bill was vetoed by President Andrew Johnson on March 27, 1866. In his message to the Senate, the president said that his primary objection was that Section 1's protection of the rights of federal citizens intruded on the police powers of the states in "matters exclusively affecting the people of each State," including the expediency of discriminating "between the two races."[44] In an impressive display of unity, Congress passed the Civil Rights Bill over the president's veto and it became law on April 9, 1866.

Well before the bill's final passage, however, many members of Congress had second thoughts about whether the Thirteenth Amendment provided adequate constitutional grounds for such sweeping legislation and whether a simple legislative act could overturn the *Dred Scott* decision. In addition, there was the stark realization that future congresses could repeal the act by simple majorities. These considerations provided the impetus for the Fourteenth Amendment.[45] Raoul Berger remarks that "the Amendment was designed to '*constitutionalize*' the [Civil Rights] Act, that is, to 'embody' it in the Constitution so as to remove doubt as to its constitutionality and to place it beyond the power of a later Congress to repeal."[46] Berger cites a statement by Representative George Latham of West Virginia that "the civil rights bill which is now a law . . . covers exactly the same ground as this amendment."[47] Senator Jacob Howard made a similar remark when he said that the Fourteenth Amendment enacted the substance of the Civil Rights Act: "the celebrated civil rights bill which has been passed during the present Congress, which was the forerunner of the constitutional amendment, and to give validity to which this constitutional amendment is brought forward, and which without this constitutional amendment to enforce it has no validity."[48] This was certainly the view of Congressman Bingham, who originally supported the Civil Rights Act but came to doubt its constitutional validity. On March 9, he rose in the House to argue that the act was an unconstitutional encroachment on the "reserved powers of the States."[49] Bingham subsequently withheld his vote on the bill, although he expressed "an earnest desire to have the bill of rights in your Constitution enforced everywhere. But I ask that it be enforced in

---

44. President Andrew Jackson, March, 27, 1866, in *A Compilation of the Messages and Papers of the Presidents*, ed. James D. Richardson (Washington, DC: Bureau of National Literature and Art, 1905), VI:407.

45. See inter alia, *Congressional Globe*, 39th Cong. 1st Sess., 2459 (1866) (Rep. Stevens): "Some answer, 'Your civil rights bill secures the same things.' That is partly true, but a law is repealable by a majority. And I need hardly say that the first time that the South with their copperhead allies obtain the command of the Congress it will be repealed"; 1095 (Rep. Hotchkiss): "Let that amendment stand as a part of the organic law of the land, subject only to be defeated by another constitutional amendment. We may pass laws here to-day, and the next Congress may wipe them out. Where is your guarantee then?"; 2462 (Rep. Garfield); 2498 (Rep. Broomall).

46. Berger, *Government by Judiciary*, 23.

47. Ibid.; *Congressional Globe*, 39th Cong., 1st Sess., 2883 (1866) (Rep. Latham).

48. *Congressional Globe*, 39th Cong., 1st Sess., 2896 (1866) (Sen. Howard).

49. Ibid. at 1291.

accordance with the Constitution."[50] Bingham, as we will see shortly, had already introduced the first version of the Fourteenth Amendment into the House on February 26, 1866. He, too, saw the necessity of "constitutionalizing" the substance of the Civil Rights Act.

THE FOURTEENTH AMENDMENT: FIRST VERSION

The principal framers of the Fourteenth Amendment are generally thought to be Representative John Bingham of Ohio and Senator Jacob Howard of Michigan. Bingham was a member of the Joint Committee on Reconstruction and the principal author of Section 1 of the Fourteenth Amendment (with the exception of the Citizenship Clause[51]); Senator Howard was also a member of the Joint Committee on Reconstruction and spoke for the committee in presenting the amendment to the Senate. It is almost certain that Howard was one of the principal authors of the Citizenship Clause that was eventually ratified.[52] Michael Kent Curtis rightly remarks that "the views of Bingham and Howard . . . are entitled to very great weight" in uncovering the intentions of the framers of the amendment. "Indeed," Curtis continues, "some say that the intention of the legislature 'may be evidenced by the statements of leading proponents.' The intent, once found, 'is to be regarded as good as written into the enactment.'"[53] As Abraham Lincoln said more succinctly in his first inaugural, "the intention of the law-giver is the law."[54]

On February 26, 1866, Representative Bingham introduced the first version of the Fourteenth Amendment:

> Congress shall have power to make all laws which shall be necessary and proper to secure to the citizens of each State all privileges and immunities of citizens in the sev-

---

50. Ibid. at 2896.

51. See Bingham's statement on March 31, 1871, in debate over the Enforcement Bill: "I had the honor to frame . . . the first section [of the Fourteenth Amendment] as it now stands, letter for letter and syllable for syllable . . . save for the introductory clause defining citizens." *Congressional Globe*, 42nd Cong., 1st Sess., Appendix, 83 (1871) (Rep. Bingham).

52. *Congressional Globe*, 39th Cong., 1st Sess., 2768–69 (1866) (Sen. Wade); with 2869, 2890 (1866; Sen. Howard). See Edward J. Erler, "Citizenship," in *The Heritage Guide to the Constitution*, ed. David F. Forte and Matthew Spalding, 493 (Washington, DC: Regnery, 2014); and Edward J. Erler, Thomas West, and John Marini, *The Founders on Citizenship and Immigration* (Lanham, MD: Rowman & Littlefield, 2007), ch. 2.

53. Michael Kent Curtis, *No State Shall Abridge: The Fourteenth Amendment and the Bill of Rights* (Durham, NC: Duke University Press, 1990), 120, quoting Berger, *Government by Judiciary*, 136–37. Curtis and Berger, of course, have diametrically opposed views of what constitutes the original intent of the framers of the Fourteenth Amendment. Berger denies that there was ever any intention of making the Bill of Rights applicable to the states. Curtis (rightly, in my view) makes an impressive case that the framers of the Fourteenth Amendment intended the amendment to incorporate the Bill of Rights. See also Bryan H. Wildenthal, "Nationalizing the Bill of Rights: Revisiting the Original Understanding of the Fourteenth Amendment in 1866–67," *Ohio State Law Journal* 68, no. 6 (2007).

54. Abraham Lincoln, *The Collected Works of Abraham Lincoln*, ed. Roy P. Basler (New Brunswick, NJ: Rutgers University Press, 1953), IV:251.

eral States, and to all persons in the several States equal protection in the rights of life, liberty, and property.[55]

Bingham made reference to the Privileges and Immunities Clause of Article 4 and the Fifth Amendment, stating that "the amendment proposed stands in the very words of the Constitution of the United States as it came to us from the hands of its illustrious framers. Every word of the proposed amendment is to-day in the Constitution of our country, save the words conferring the express grant of power upon the Congress of the United States."[56] Had an express power been conferred on Congress in the original Constitution "to enforce these requirements of the Constitution in every State," Bingham alleged, "that rebellion, which has scarred and blasted the land, would have been an impossibility."[57] Hitherto, Bingham stated, the "great provisions of the Constitution, this immortal bill of rights embodied in the Constitution, rested for its execution and enforcement . . . on the fidelity of the States."[58] State officers—legislative, executive, and judicial—were obliged by the express language of the Supremacy Clause of the Constitution to uphold their oaths to support the Constitution, an obligation that was superior to their obligation to support state laws and state constitutions. These state officers, Bingham said, obviously failed in their sworn obligations and continued to do so. The Supremacy Clause is the constitutional warrant for the power of Congress to enforce those obligations upon the states.

Representative Andrew Rogers, Democrat of New Jersey, immediately rose to reply to Bingham's short introduction to the amendment, taking an extreme states' rights position. "When sifted from top to bottom," he said, the proposed amendment "will be found to be the embodiment of centralization and the disfranchisement of the States of those sacred and immutable State rights which were reserved to them by the consent of our fathers in our organic law."[59] Privileges and immunities in the Constitution, Rogers alleged, had been construed by both state and federal courts to exist "in a qualified sense, and subject to local control, dominion, and the sovereignty of the States. But this act of Congress," he continued,

> proposes to amend the Constitution so as to take away the rights of the States with regard to the life, liberty, and property of the people, so as to enable and empower Congress to pass laws compelling the abrogation of all the statutes of the States which makes a distinction, for instance, between a crime committed by a white man and a crime committed by a black man, or allow white people privileges, immunities, or property not allowed to a black man.[60]

For all his pious imprecations, there is no doubt that Rogers misrepresented the federal relationship in the Constitution as it was understood by the framers.

---

55. *Congressional Globe*, 39th Cong., 1st Sess., 1034 (1866) (Rep. Bingham).
56. Ibid.
57. Ibid.
58. Ibid.
59. *Congressional Globe*, 39th Cong., 1st Sess., appendix, 133 (1866) (Rep. Rogers).
60. Ibid. at 134.

However much hyperbole Rogers displayed in putting states' rights at the center of the American constitutional system, he was correct in suspecting that an essential change in the federal relationship was contemplated by the proposed amendment.

This was confirmed on February 28, 1866, when Representative Frederick Woodbridge, Republican of Vermont, mounted a spirited reply to Rogers. He emphasized that "the object of the proposed amendment" was to give "the power to Congress to enact those laws which will give to a citizen of the United States the natural rights which necessarily pertain to citizenship." "It is intended," Woodbridge continued, "to enable Congress to give to all citizens the inalienable rights of life and liberty, and to every citizen in whatever State he may be that protection to his property which is extended to the other citizens of the State."[61]

Woodbridge ended with two rhetorical questions and a declaration.

> Is there anything which interferes with the sovereign power of a State that adheres to a republican form of government? Is there not rather in this a tendency to keep the States within their orbits, and by what the gentleman from New Jersey would call "the organic law," insure and secure forever to every citizen of the United States the privileges and blessings of a republican form of government? There is nothing more, there is nothing less, in this proposition.[62]

The Republican Guarantee Clause was frequently used throughout the debates to argue that the federal government had an obligation to protect fundamental rights, including the franchise, for all state citizens.

Bingham expressed his wholehearted agreement with the sense of purpose and urgency that Woodbridge ascribed to the proposed amendment, adding that it "is simply a proposition to arm the Congress of the United States, by the consent of the people of the United States, with the power to enforce the bill of rights as it stands in the Constitution today. It 'hath that extent—no more.'"[63] Bingham's use of an enigmatic (and no doubt ironic) quote from Shakespeare's *Othello* should have alerted the defenders of states' rights and any others who opposed changes in the federal relationship to his true intentions.

On May 10, 1866, Bingham introduced the final version of Section 1 that eventually became the Fourteenth Amendment (with the exception of the Citizenship Clause). It read,

> No State shall make or enforce any law which shall abridge the privileges or immunities of citizens of the United States; nor shall any State deprive any person of life, liberty, or property without due process of law; nor deny to any person within its jurisdiction the equal protection of the laws.[64]

---

61. *Congressional Globe*, 39th Cong., 1st Sess., 1088 (1866) (Rep. Woodbridge).
62. Ibid.
63. *Congressional Globe*, 39th Cong., 1st Sess., 2543 (1866) (Rep. Bingham).
64. Ibid. at 2542.

Section 5 of the proposed amendment stated, "The Congress shall have power to enforce by appropriate legislation the provisions of this article." Bingham repeated his oft-expressed reasons why an amendment of this nature was required: to give Congress a power that they had not hitherto possessed, which was to "protect by national law the privileges and immunities of all the citizens of the Republic and the inborn rights of every person within its jurisdiction whenever the same shall be abridged or denied by the unconstitutional acts of any State."[65] This version of the Fourteenth Amendment is much more explicitly a restriction directed at the states. The Citizenship Clause had not yet been added to Section 1, so Bingham was not able to take advantage of the fact that the new Citizenship Clause, when it was finally added, made U.S. citizenship primary and state citizenship secondary, thus reversing the previous understanding of the relation of state and federal citizenship.[66] This would remove any doubt that the privileges or immunities that attached to federal citizenship were primary as well, thus giving the federal government the primary responsibility for their protection.

Bingham's final defense of the amendment was spirited but, compared to his previous speeches, rather tepid. He may have been so confident of victory that he decided to refrain from saying anything unnecessarily provocative. This stands in stark contrast to his defense of the first version of the amendment, when he insisted against his states' rights tormentors that the right of revolution should be made the principle of Reconstruction. On February 28, 1866, Bingham had remarked, as we have already seen,

> As the whole Constitution was to be the supreme law in every State it therefore results that the citizens of each State, being citizens of the United States, should be entitled to all the privileges and immunities of citizens of the United States in every State, and all persons, now that slavery has forever perished, should be entitled to equal protection in the rights of life, liberty, and property.[67]

In addition to declaring the Constitution the supreme law of the land, Article 6 of the Constitution offers "a further security for the enforcement of the Constitution,

---

65. Ibid.

66. In his response to President Johnson's veto of the Civil Rights Act, Senator Lyman Trumbull on April 4, 1866, noted that while the president did not object to the provision of the bill conferring citizenship on the newly freed slaves as "persons born in the United States," he did see fit to warn the Congress that it had no power to confer state citizenship; that power, the president said, rests exclusively with the states. To counter the president, Trumbull cited Chief Justice John Marshall's opinion in *Gassies v. Ballon* (1832), where the Court held that "[a] citizen of the United States, residing in any State of the Union, is a citizen of the State." 31 U.S. (6 Pet.) 761, 762 (1832) (Marshall, C. J.). Despite the Supreme Court's ruling, the prevailing practice was that every citizen of a state was automatically considered a citizen of the United States. The president accurately stated the practice but, as Trumbull pointed out, was mistaken about the law (*Congressional Globe*, 39th Cong., 1st Sess., 1756 [1866]).

67. *Congressional Globe*, 39th Cong., 1st Sess., 1090 (1866) (Rep. Bingham). The germ of the final version of the Fourteenth Amendment is easily recognizable in this statement. Bingham's February 28 speech was reprinted as a pamphlet titled "One Country, One Constitution, and One People" and widely distributed. See *McDonald v. Chicago*, 561 U.S. 742, 829 fn 10 (2010) (Thomas, J., concurring in part, concurring in the judgment).

and *especially of this sacred bill of rights*, to all the citizens and all the people of the United States."[68] Legislative, executive, and judicial officers, both in the states and in the country at large, were required to take an oath to uphold the Constitution. And, Bingham added,

> is it surprising that the framers of the Constitution omitted to insert an express grant of power in Congress to enforce by penal enactments these great canons of the supreme law, securing to all the citizens in every State all the privileges and immunities of citizens, and to all the people all the sacred rights of persons—those rights dear to freemen and formidable only to tyrants—and of which the fathers of the Republic spoke, after God had given them the victory, in that memorable address in which they declared, "Let it be remembered that the rights for which America has contended were the rights of human nature"?[69]

It was remarkable, Bingham declaimed, that the framers, after having acknowledged that the security of these sacred rights of human nature were the principal object of government, would leave "their lawful enforcement to each of the States." What more could have been done, he queried, for the Constitution to secure those sacred rights—the whole panoply of privileges and immunities belonging to federal citizenship, including the provisions of the Bill of Rights? Bingham answered, "The additional grant of power which we ask this day." Were the framers unaware that the Constitution was severely defective without this power? Bingham believed they were in fact intensely aware of this defect but were unable to act because of the presence of slavery. "That grant of power would have been there," he asserted, "but for the fact that its insertion in the Constitution would have been utterly incompatible with the existence of slavery in any State; for although slaves might not have been admitted to be citizens they must have been admitted to be persons. That is the only reason why it was not there."[70] Bingham concluded that there was no reason why the grant could not be given now that slavery had been abolished. A grant of such power now would accord with the original intentions of the framers who had been forced to compromise on the issue of slavery from political necessity.

Bingham proceeded to make not-so-thinly veiled references that the exigencies presented by the preservation of the Union might be considered an aspect of the right of revolution. He boldly paraphrased the Declaration of Independence (following Madison in *Federalist* 43), saying "that the right of the people to self-preservation justifies it; it rests upon the transcendent right of nature, and nature's God," and commented "that the right of revolution is still in the people and has justified their action through all this trial. It is the inherent right of the people. It cannot be taken

---

68. *Congressional Globe*, 39th Cong., 1st Sess., 1090 (1866) (Rep. Bingham) (emphasis added).
69. Ibid. at 1090. The quote is from James Madison, "Address to the States," April 25,1783, in *The Papers of James Madison*, ed. Robert A. Rutland et al. (Chicago: University of Chicago Press, 1962–), 6:493: "Let it be remembered finally that it has ever been the pride and boast of America, that the rights for which she contended were the rights of human nature."
70. *Congressional Globe*, 39th Cong., 1st Sess., 1090 (1866) (Rep. Bingham).

from them."[71] That the Civil War was an act of "self-preservation" authorized by "the transcendent right of nature, and nature's God" meant that it was justified by the principles of the Revolution; in other words, the Civil War was the continuation of the Revolutionary War, this time fought to extend the principle of consent to all of the governed. Thus, as many other members of the Thirty-Ninth Congress understood the matter, the Reconstruction amendments were to be understood as a completion of the principles of the Declaration of Independence, the expression of the ground and principle of the Revolution.[72] This speech must have raised alarm bells among those who still harbored illusions that Reconstruction could be accomplished without any change in the federal relationship.

SENATOR JACOB HOWARD INTRODUCES THE FOURTEENTH AMENDMENT IN THE SENATE

The amendment introduced into the Senate by Jacob Howard on May 23, 1866, still did not contain a Citizenship Clause, and this lacuna was remarked upon by Howard. The first clause of Section 1, he said, "relates to the privileges and immunities of citizens of the United States as such and as distinguished from all other persons not citizens of the United States. It is not, perhaps, very easy to define with accuracy what is meant by the expression, 'citizen of the United States,' although the expression occurs twice in the Constitution."[73] In order "to put the citizens of the several States on an equality with each other as to all fundamental rights," Howard continued, "a clause was introduced in the Constitution declaring that 'the citizens of each State shall be entitled to all privileges and immunities of citizens in the several States.'"[74] The effect of the Privileges and Immunities Clause, according to Howard, was to make the citizens of each state citizens of the United States, who in turn had become citizens of their respective states by "birth or by naturalization. They became such in virtue of national law, or rather of natural law which recognizes persons born within the jurisdiction of every country as being subjects or citizens of that

---

71. Ibid. at 1089.

72. Earlier in a debate about an amendment to allow Congress to set the terms of representation in the states, Bingham made this statement on January 25:

I am for . . . that absolute, eternal verity which underlies your Constitution. The right is the law of the Republic. So it was proclaimed in your imperishable Declaration by the words, all men are created equal; they are endowed by their Creator with the rights of life and liberty; to secure these rights Governments are instituted among men, deriving their just powers from the consent of the governed; and by those other words, these States may do what free and independent States may of right (not *wrong*, but of *right*) do . . . This truth is recognized as distinctly in your Constitution as it is proclaimed in your Declaration (*Congressional Globe*, 39th Cong., 1st Sess., 429 [1866] [Rep. Bingham]).

See the statement of Representative Richard Yates of Illinois, February 19, 1866, debating the Civil Rights Act (*Congressional Globe*, 39th Cong., 1st Sess., Appendix, 99).

73. *Congressional Globe*, 39th Cong., 1st Sess., 2765 (1866) (Sen. Howard).

74. Ibid.

country."[75] Howard admitted that it would be a "curious question" to answer what exactly are "the privileges and immunities of citizens of each of the States in the several States." What is certain, however, is that the framers of the Constitution inserted the Privileges and Immunities Clause into the Constitution for a purpose. Like many other debaters, Howard quoted extensively from *Corfield v. Coryell*, remarking,

> Such is the character of the privileges and immunities spoken of in the second section of the fourth article of the Constitution. To these privileges and immunities, whatever they may be—for they are not and cannot be fully defined in their entire extent and precise nature—to these should be added the personal rights guarantied and secured by the first eight amendments of the Constitution.

Howard then proceeded to list the provisions of the Bill of Rights,[76] lamenting the fact, often expressed by Bingham, that the Constitution, as it presently stood, gave the federal government no power to protect the privileges and immunities of United States citizens from state deprivations. That was the object of Section 5, which gave Congress direct power to enforce the provisions of the amendment.

Howard was even more expansive in his presentation of the second two clauses of Section 1. These clauses, Howard announced, "disable a State from depriving not merely a citizen of the United States, but any person, whoever he may be, of life, liberty, or property without due process of law, or from denying to him the equal protection of the laws of the State." The "any person" language was required because of the unsettled citizenship question. Had the Citizenship Clause that was eventually adopted been part of the original submission, declaring that U.S. citizenship carried with it automatic state citizenship (a reaffirmation of Marshall's opinion in the *Gassies* case), language asserting the primacy of U.S. citizenship would have been sufficient. In any case, Howard was emphatic: "This abolishes all class legislation in the States and does away with the injustice of subjecting one caste of persons to a code not applicable to another. It prohibits the hanging of a black man for a crime for which the white man is not to be hanged. It protects the black man in his fundamental rights as a citizen with the same shield which it throws around the white man."[77]

Howard was quick to deny that any rights or privileges and immunities of U.S. citizenship included the right of suffrage. He expressed his preference that newly freed slaves should be enfranchised but realized that it was politically inexpedient to advocate such a measure under the circumstances. Howard expressed a confident opinion, however, that in the not-too-distant future, public opinion would eventually realize the importance of Madison's statement of "the vital principle of free government that those who are to be bound by the laws ought to have a voice in making them" was no less true of black citizens than of white citizens.[78] Madison's statement

---

75. Ibid.
76. Ibid.
77. Ibid. at 2766.
78. Ibid. at 2767. Howard is quoting James Madison, "Notes on Suffrage," *Letters and Other Writings of James Madison* (Philadelphia: J.B. Lippincott & Co., 1865), 4:25.

was, in fact, a concise statement of the rule of law that rested on the consent of the governed: those who are subject to the law must participate in the making of the law. Howard counseled patience, urging a statesmanlike approach: Don't refuse to accept the genuine good that is available now because it is not the complete good. The complete good will be attainable only in the future when public opinion is willing to accept the justice of black suffrage. Public opinion, as we have discussed, sets the limits of republican statesmanship; it can lead but not defy public opinion. Howard's advice was prophetic. The time between 1866 and the ratification of the Fifteenth Amendment in 1870 was, in political terms, a veritable blink of the eye.[79]

Senator Wade of Ohio suggested on May 23, 1866, that given the importance of Section 1's guarantee of privileges or immunities to U.S. Citizens, it was imperative that a "strong and clear" definition of citizenship be added to the amendment. He suggested "persons born in the United States or naturalized by the laws thereof."[80] Howard responded on May 30, 1866, with a proposal that was drafted in the Joint Committee and became the first sentence of the Fourteenth Amendment as finally adopted: "All persons born in the United States, and subject to the jurisdiction thereof, are citizens of the United States and of the States wherein they reside."[81] States no longer had any pretense to controlling who became citizens of a state. Federal citizenship was primary and state citizenship derivative. State citizenship was no longer a prerogative of the much-diminished state sovereignty after the adoption of the Fourteenth Amendment.

We remember House Speaker Schuyler Colfax's ex cathedra statement before the opening session of the Thirty-Ninth Congress advocating, as a condition of reentry into the Union for the states previously in rebellion, "that the Declaration of Independence must be recognized as the law of the land, and every man, alien and native, white and black, [must be] protected in the inalienable and God-given rights of life, liberty, and the pursuit of happiness." After the passage of the Fourteenth Amendment in the Senate on June 8 and the House on June 13, Colfax made another ex cathedra statement in a speech at Indianapolis on August 7, 1866. Colfax praised "Abraham Lincoln, that great and good man—would to God he were to-day in the Presidential chair." "But while he is gone," Colfax lamented, "and although God buries his workman, his work still goes on, and we are to finish the work that Abraham Lincoln began." Colfax quoted Section 1 of the Fourteenth Amendment and remarked, "I stand by every word and letter of it. It's going to be the gem of the

---

79. The Fifteenth Amendment was ratified on February 3, 1870. On March 30, there was a march in Washington to commemorate the event. President Ulysses Grant, addressing the procession, remarked, "There has been no event since the close of the war in which I have felt so deep an interest as that of the ratification of the fifteenth amendment to the Constitution by three-fourths of the States of the Union. I have felt the greatest anxiety ever since I have been in this house to know that that was to be secured. It looked to me as the realization of the Declaration of Independence" ("Speech," April 1, 1870, in *The Papers of Ulysses S. Grant*, ed. John Y. Simon (Carbondale: Southern Illinois University Press, 1995), 20:137. I owe this reference to David Sonenstein, Esq.

80. *Congressional Globe*, 39th Cong., 1st Sess., 2768–69 (1866) (Sen. Wade).

81. *Congressional Globe*, 39th Cong., 1st Sess., 2890 (1866) (Sen. Howard).

Constitution, when it is placed there, as it will be, by this American people. I will tell you why I love it," the Speaker continued,

> It is because it is the Declaration of Independence placed immutably and forever in our Constitution. What does the Declaration of Independence say?—that baptismal vow that our fathers took upon their lips when this Republic of ours was born into the family of nations. It says that all men are created equal, and are endowed by their Creator with certain inalienable rights, among which are life, liberty and the pursuit of happiness; *and that to secure these rights governments were instituted among men.* That's the paramount object of government, to secure the right of all men to their equality before the law. So said our fathers at the beginning of the Revolution. So say their sons to-day, in this Constitutional Amendment, the noblest clause that will be in our Constitution.[82]

Colfax was here confirming that the vision he had set into motion as the supervening principle for the debates in the Thirty-Ninth Congress had been a grand success. It was a vision that he had carried forth on behalf of Abraham Lincoln. But to say that the Declaration had become a part of the Constitution through the language of Section 1 of the Fourteenth Amendment was not only accurate but also profound. This was indeed Abraham Lincoln's vision, as it was the ultimate vision of the founders. Colfax recognized the Fourteenth Amendment—as Lincoln certainly would have—as the ultimate completion of the founding. But the translation of principle into practice would require statesmanship of another order. Without the completion of the principle, there could be no demands made that practice should conform to principle. This was the heart of Abraham Lincoln's statesmanship. It was necessary to establish the principle first and then enforce the principle as fast as circumstances permitted. As Lincoln might have said, the thought is always the father to the deed—"last is act, first is thought." Once the principle has been established, then moral demands can be made in the name of principle, and opinion can be made to conform. As Lincoln always insisted, the Declaration is "the father of all moral principle."[83]

THE *SLAUGHTERHOUSE CASES* AND THE FAILURE OF JUDICIAL STATESMANSHIP

The Supreme Court's first effort at interpreting the Fourteenth Amendment represented a massive failure to understand the intentions of its framers. Justice Samuel Miller, who wrote the opinion for a 5-4 majority, denied that the Fourteenth Amendment was intended to work any fundamental change in the federal

---

82. "Speech of Hon. Schuyler Colfax," *Cincinnati Commercial,* August 9, 1866, 2. See *Congressional Globe,* 39th Cong., 1st Sess., Appendix 103, 106, 100 (1866) (Sen. Yates); *Congressional Globe,* 39th Cong., 1st Sess., 2691 (1866) (Sen. Poland).
83. Abraham Lincoln, "Speech at Chicago," July 10, 1858, *Collected Works of Abraham Lincoln,* II:499.

relationship. Subjecting the states "to the control of Congress," Miller argued, by placing "the entire domain of civil rights heretofore belonging exclusively to [the states] . . . radically changes the whole theory of the relations of the state and Federal governments to each other and of both these governments to the people."[84] Absent any clearly expressed language in the amendment, such a constitutional revolution, Miller concluded, was unwarranted. He further argued that the language of the amendment clearly only intended to protect the privileges or immunities of citizens of the United States and not citizens of the several states. The power of the states to protect the privileges and immunities of their own citizens remained undisturbed by the amendment. In general, Miller declared,

> we do not see in [the Reconstruction] Amendments any purpose to destroy the main features of the general system. Under the pressure of all the excited feeling growing out of the war, our statesmen have still believed that the existence of the states with powers for domestic and local government, including the regulation of civil rights, the rights of person and of property, was essential to the perfect working of our complex form of government, though they have thought proper to impose additional limitations on the states, and to confer additional power on that of the nation.[85]

As we will see shortly, the "additional limitations on the states" were few, and the "additional power" conferred on the nation insignificant. Throughout his opinion, Justice Miller professes to follow the intentions of the framers of the Fourteenth Amendment. It is difficult to fathom, however, how Miller arrived at the conclusion that there was no change in the federal relationship with respect to the status of state and federal citizenship, that a kind of dual citizenship had been created where the states and the federal government possessed equal powers to protect privileges or immunities that fell within their respective spheres.

Justice Miller notes that the first section of the Fourteenth Amendment, "to which our attention is more specially invited," provides, for the first time, a definition of citizenship for both the United States and the states. Prior to the passage of the Fourteenth Amendment, "it had been said by eminent judges that no man was a citizen of the United States except as he was a citizen of one of the states composing the Union. . . . Whether this proposition was sound or not had never been judicially decided."[86] Miller insists, however, that the definition of citizenship in the Fourteenth Amendment maintains a clear "distinction between citizenship of the United States and citizenship of a state." It is possible for "a man to be a citizen of the United States without being a citizen of a state, but an important element is necessary to convert the former into the latter. He must reside within the state to make him a citizen of it, but it is only necessary that he should be born or naturalized in the United States

---

84. *Slaughter-House Cases*, 83 U.S. (16 Wall.) 36, 78 (1873) (Miller, J.).
85. Ibid. at 81.
86. Ibid. at 72–73. It is curious that Justice Miller did not acknowledge Chief Justice Marshall's opinion in *Gassies v. Ballon* (1832) upholding the proposition that U.S. citizenship carries automatic state citizenship. See *supra* note 66.

to be a citizen of the Union."[87] This distinction between the two citizenships leads Miller to conclude, "It is quite clear, then, that there is a citizenship of the United States and a citizenship of a state, which are distinct from each other and which depend upon different characteristics or circumstances in the individual."[88] What Miller does not mention, however, was that the Fourteenth Amendment entirely reversed the federal relationship in regard to citizenship. Every United States citizen was automatically a citizen of the state where he resided. The states thus had no role or agency in determining who became citizens. This change was necessary because states could otherwise circumvent federal protection for privileges or immunities by withholding state citizenship from the newly freed slaves, thus preventing them from becoming citizens of the United States. It is a simple matter to conclude that this fundamental change in the status of citizenship and its implications for the federal relationship meant that the privileges or immunities attached to U.S. citizenship became primary and those attached to state citizenship, derivative. This was indeed a fundamental change in the federal relationship and one that was clearly anticipated by the Republican leaders in the Thirty-Ninth Congress. Republicans knew that without federal enforcement and a constitutional mandate for enforcement, the Southern states would not honor their commitment to protect the privileges or immunities or the "life, liberty, and property" of the newly freed slaves who had now become state citizens by virtue of their U.S. citizenship and residence. There can hardly be any doubt about the framers' intentions in this regard.

Raoul Berger comments, "The notion that by conferring dual citizenship the framers were separating . . . rights of a citizen of the United States from those of a State citizen not only is without historical warrant but actually does violence to their intentions."[89] Justice Miller, however, would have us believe that nothing essential had changed. All of the privileges and immunities described in the *Corfield* case still belonged in the realm of state privileges and immunities. We learned from our reading of the debates, however, that those privileges and immunities specified in Justice Washington's decision were widely understood by the leading Republicans in the Thirty-Ninth Congress to be those belonging to U.S. citizenship, to which we may add all of the provisions of the Bill of Rights, which were understood to be constituent elements of the privileges or immunities of federal citizenship. Justice Miller ignored or misconstrued the most revealing evidence of the framers' intentions because it brought to light what a revolution in the federal relation the Reconstruction Amendments were intended to produce. Even a casual reading of the debates by the most careless reader would easily reveal Miller's misrepresentations.

In Justice Miller's scheme of dual citizenship, it becomes merely a matter of determining the privileges or immunities that belong to federal citizenship and those that attach to state citizenship. As it turns out, federal privileges or immunities, as

---

87. Ibid. at 73–74.
88. Ibid. at 74.
89. Berger, *Government by Judiciary*, 46.

recounted by Miller, are relatively insignificant, while the bulk of privileges and immunities belong exclusively to the citizens of the several states. Federal privileges or immunities include some that are explicit in the Constitution and some that are only implied. Miller doesn't attempt to list them all, but he gives examples: the right to travel to the seat of government to assert a claim against the government and to demand care and protection for "life, liberty, and property" when on the high seas or within the jurisdiction of foreign governments are implied rights; the right of peaceable assembly and petition for redress and habeas corpus are guaranteed by the Constitution; there is a privilege and immunity to use navigable waters of the United States, however much those waters might penetrate into the territory of the several states; a right conferred by the Fourteenth Amendment to become a citizen of a state by residence; and all rights conferred by the Thirteenth and Fifteenth Amendments. All other privileges or immunities mentioned in *Corfield*, including (but not mentioned by Miller) the right to reside in a state for "professional pursuits," belong to state citizenship and do not implicate the privileges or immunities of U.S. citizenship.[90]

Miller concluded that none of the claims asserted in *Slaughterhouse* implicated any of the privileges or immunities of federal citizenship. The regulation of slaughterhouses as here specified by "the legislature of Louisiana is, in its essential nature, one which has been up to the present period in the constitutional history of this country, always conceded to belong to the states, however it may now be questioned in some of its details."[91] The statute in question granted a twenty-five-year monopoly to operate the only slaughterhouse in New Orleans, although butchers were permitted by law to slaughter at the facilities for a "reasonable fee." "The wisdom of the monopoly granted by the legislature," Miller conceded, "may be open to question, but it is difficult to see a justification for the assertion that the butchers are deprived of the right to labor in their occupation." There is no bar to such legislation in the Louisiana Constitution, and as to the U.S. Constitution, there is no privilege or immunity of federal citizenship that has been violated. As to the claim of a violation of "equal protection of the laws" that the states must accord to all "persons," the "history" and "pervading purpose" of the Reconstruction Amendments make it doubtful "whether any action of a state not directed by way of discrimination against the negroes as a class, or on account of their race, will ever be held to come within the purview of this provision. It is so clearly a provision for that race and that emergency, that a strong case would be necessary for its application to any other."[92]

Raul Berger points to the massive contradiction in Justice Miller's opinion. He quotes Miller as saying, "'The existence of laws in the States where the newly emancipated negroes resided, which discriminated with gross injustice and hardship against them as a class, was the evil to be remedied'—that is the Black Codes."[93] Thus, the

---

90. Ibid. at 75–80.
91. Ibid. at 62.
92. Ibid. at 81.
93. Berger, *Government by Judiciary*, 47, quoting *Slaughterhouse Cases*, 83 U.S., at 81.

"one pervasive purpose," Berger notes, continuing to quote Miller, was "protection of the newly-made freeman and citizen from the oppression of those who had formerly exercised unlimited dominion over him."[94] Berger comments that "when Miller held that 'the citizen of a State' must look to the State for protection, he aborted what he himself had declared to be the 'pervading purpose': to protect the Negro from the 'evil' of the Black Codes, Codes that handed the Negro back to their oppressors."[95] Berger similarly detected a fatal error in Miller's equal protection reasoning:

> Paradoxically, Justice Miller was ready to protect Negroes from "gross injustice and oppression" by resort to the equal protection clause. How, one wonders, did "equal protection" escape the blight that struck down "privileges or immunities"? It equally "degrad[ed] the State governments by subjecting them to the control of Congress"; it too constituted a "great departure from the structure and spirit of our institutions."[96]

The same questionable reasoning that drove Miller's argument in deciding the privileges or immunities issue was also used in his equal protection argument. Miller's privileges or immunities argument became authoritative, but no one seemed to notice that Miller's due process and equal protection arguments suffered from the same fatal weakness. Nevertheless, equal protection, along with due process, became the focus for substantive rights, although it is abundantly clear that the framers intended privileges or immunities to be the focus.

JUSTICE JOSEPH BRADLEY'S DISSENT IN THE *SLAUGHTERHOUSE CASES*

The majority decision in the *Slaughterhouse Cases* rendered the Privileges and Immunities Clause of the Fourteenth Amendment, in the words of Justice Stephen Field's acerb dissent, "a vain and idle enactment, [that] accomplished nothing, and most unnecessarily excited Congress and the people on its passage."[97] Michael Kent Curtis accurately characterizes Justice Miller's majority opinion as "a strange reading of the language of the Fourteenth Amendment" because by its convoluted reasoning "the

---

94. Ibid.
95. Ibid. at 48, quoting *Slaughterhouse Cases*, 83 U.S., at 75.
96. Ibid., quoting *Slaughterhouse Cases*, 83 U.S., at 78.
97. *Slaughterhouse Cases*, 83 U.S. (16 Wall.) 36, 96 (1873) (Field, J., dissenting). It is odd that arguments for privileges or immunities were abandoned so easily. Miller had mentioned that his list was suggestive and not exhaustive, at 79. Miller also noted that the "right to peaceably assemble and petition for redress of grievances" were privileges or immunities of United States citizenship, possibly suggesting that other provisions of the Bill of Rights were also among the privileges or immunities incorporated into Section 1. There was considerable evidence from the debates that this was in fact the intention of the framers of Section 1 of the Fourteenth Amendment. Perhaps the move to abandon privileges or immunities and concentrate on equal protection and due process was too precipitous. An attempt to expand what Miller had indicated was only a preliminary list of privileges or immunities of U.S. citizenship might have been a more logical and promising reaction to *Slaughterhouse*.

fundamental rights of American citizens were left to the protection of the states."[98] Curtis almost needlessly remarks that "Miller's reading also flew in the face of legislative history," commenting that Republicans of the Thirty-Ninth Congress argued that fundamental rights were privileges and immunities that states could not abridge. "These absolute rights," Curtis rightly notes, "had other incidental rights connected with them, and Congress had power to enforce protection of such civil rights. Justice Miller turned the plan for the Fourteenth Amendment on its head."[99] In support of his observation that Congress had the power to enforce the rights that attached to U.S. citizenship, Curtis cited a speech by Representative William Lawrence of Ohio before the House on April 7, 1866. Lawrence quoted the Declaration of Rights of 1774 and the Declaration of Independence, along with legal commentaries and case reports, concluding,

> It has never been deemed necessary to enact in any constitution or law that citizens should have the right to life or liberty or the right to acquire property. These rights are recognized by the Constitution as existing anterior to and independently of all laws and all constitutions. . . . There are certain absolute rights which pertain to every citizen, which are inherent, and of which a State cannot constitutionally deprive him. But not only are these rights inherent and indestructible, but the means whereby they may be possessed and enjoyed are equally so.

As if anticipating the *Slaughterhouse* decision, Lawrence concludes,

> It is idle to say that a citizen shall have the right to life, yet to deny him the right to labor, whereby alone he can live. It is a mockery to say that a citizen may have a right to live, and yet deny him the right to make a contract to secure the privilege and rewards of labor. It is worse than mockery to say that men may be clothed by the national authority with the character of citizens, yet may be stripped by State authority of the means by which citizens may exist.[100]

Justice Joseph Bradley's dissent in the *Slaughterhouse Cases* is almost an exact reprise of Representative Lawrence's speech in the House of Representatives, which was, I believe, an authentic account of the intent of the framers of the Fourteenth Amendment. Bradley, like Lawrence, cites the Declaration of Rights of 1774 for the recognition that "taxation without representation is subversive of free government" because it is taking property without consent. This, Bradley says, was "the origin of our own revolution." Bradley next quotes

> the Declaration of Independence, which was the first political act of the American people in their independent sovereign capacity, [and] lays the foundation of our national existence upon this broad proposition: "That all men are created equal; that they

---

98. Curtis, *No State Shall* Abridge, 175.
99. Ibid., 176.
100. *Congressional Globe*, 39th Cong. 1st Sess., 1833 (1866) (Rep. Lawrence).

are endowed by their Creator with certain inalienable rights; that among these are life, liberty, and the pursuit of happiness."

Here, Bradley notes, the rights to life, liberty and the pursuit of happiness are "equivalent" to the rights of life, liberty and property.[101] Bradley duly explains that "these are fundamental rights which can only be taken away by due process of law, and which can only be interfered with, or the enjoyment can only be modified, by lawful regulations necessary or proper for the mutual good of all; and these rights, I contend, belong to the citizens of every free government."[102]

But there are other rights that serve as a necessary means to equal protection of the fundamental natural rights to life, liberty, and property. If the end, fundamental natural rights, deserves protection, then the means necessary to secure those ends deserve the same protection. Justice Bradley quoted the ubiquitous *Corfield* opinion and concluded that the privileges and immunities set out there were those of U.S. citizens even before the "late amendments" and belonged to them "whether they were citizens of any state or not." "And," he continued, "none is more essential and fundamental than the right to follow such profession or employment as each one may choose, subject only to uniform regulations equally applicable to all."[103]

Bradley concluded that the state issuance of an exclusive monopoly was not a proper "police regulation . . . within the power of the legislature." Rather, he contended, "the granting of monopolies, or exclusive privileges to individuals or corporations, is an invasion of the right of others to choose a lawful calling, and an infringement of personal liberty" in violation of the Due Process Clause. This was a matter of the rights of U.S. citizenship and the protection of those rights extended by the Fourteenth Amendment. Thus, Bradley reasoned,

> for the preservation, exercise and enjoyment of these rights the individual citizen, as a necessity, must be left free to adopt such calling, profession or trade as may seem to him most conducive to that end. Without this right he can not be a free man. This right to choose one's calling is an essential part of that liberty which it is the object of government to protect; and a calling, when chosen, is a man's property and right. Liberty and property are not protected where these rights are arbitrarily assailed.[104]

The choice of an occupation is an act of freedom, and once the choice is made, it becomes a part of one's property. This chain of reasoning is straight out of Madison's essay "Property," where, as we have seen, he had written,

---

101. It is doubtful, as Berger argues, that Bradley narrowed the phrase "pursuit of happiness" to mean *only* the "right to property." Since Bradley includes "the right to follow [a] . . . profession or employment" as an aspect of the right to property, he did not consider "property" a narrow concept, as Berger seems to think (*Government by Judiciary*, 33).

102. *Slaughterhouse Cases*, 83 U.S. (16 Wall.) 115–16 (1873) (Bradley, J., dissenting).

103. Ibid. at 119.

104. Ibid. at 116.

That is not a just government, nor is property secure under it, where arbitrary restrictions, exemptions, and monopolies deny to part of its citizens that free use of their faculties, and free choice of their occupations, which not only constitute their property in the general sense of the word; but are the means of acquiring property strictly so called.[105]

As in Lawrence's account, fundamental rights are natural rights that exist prior to government. Government is created to secure those rights that it does not create. Privileges and immunities are the incidental rights that attach to citizenship, and they are the means by which natural rights are secured within the confines of civil society. These are frequently described as civil rights—the positive laws that are necessary to secure natural rights.

THE DECLARATION, DUE PROCESS, AND EQUAL PROTECTION IN SOME LATER CASES

As late as 1897, the Supreme Court was still quoting the Declaration in its opinions as authority for due process and equal protection decisions, while references to "privileges or immunities" had almost disappeared or were relegated to afterthoughts. A notable example is *Gulf, Colorado, & Santa Fe Railway Co. v. Ellis* (1897).[106] At issue in this case was a Texas law that allowed the recovery of attorneys' fees from railroad companies without reciprocal recovery rights from the parties suing the railroad. The law singled out railroad companies and applied to no other citizens or corporations. Although the Gulf, Colorado, & Santa Fe Railway Company alleged the law was a deprivation of property without due process and a violation of equal protection of the laws, both violations of the Fourteenth Amendment, the Court decided only on equal protection grounds.

Justice David Brewer wrote for the majority,

> While good faith and a knowledge of existing conditions on the part of a legislature is to be presumed, yet to carry that presumption to the extent of always holding that there must be some undisclosed and unknown reason for subjecting certain individuals or corporations to hostile and discriminating legislation is to make the protecting clauses of the 14th Amendment a mere rope of sand, in no manner restraining state action.[107]

The State of Texas had argued that the power of classification was a matter of state power and did not fall within the scope of the Equal Protection Clause. Justice Brewer answered that it was not the intent of the Fourteenth Amendment to withdraw the power of the state to engage in classification—only the power to engage in arbitrary classifications (that is, those classifications that do not serve as a reasonable

105. James Madison, "Property," *Papers of James Madison*, 14:267.
106. *Gulf, Colorado, & Santa Fe Railway Co. v. Ellis*, 165 U.S. 150 (1897).
107. Ibid. at 154.

means to the ends or purposes for which the law was enacted). Under the guarantee of equal protection, classifications could not be made arbitrarily. "The state may not say," Brewer insisted,

> all white men shall be subjected to the payment of the attorneys' fees of parties success-
> fully suing them, and all black men not. It may not say that all men beyond a certain
> age shall be alone thus subjected or all men possessed of a certain wealth. These are
> distinctions which do not furnish any proper basis for the attempted classification. That
> must always rest upon some difference which bears a reasonable and just relation to the
> act in respect to which the classification is proposed, and can never be made arbitrarily
> and without such basis.[108]

In a remarkable conclusion, Brewer brings the argument to first principles:

> The first official action of the nation declared the foundation of government in these
> words: "We hold these truths to be self-evident, that all men are created equal, that they
> are endowed by their Creator with certain unalienable rights, that, among these are life,
> liberty, and the pursuit of happiness." While such declaration of principles may not have
> the force of organic law, or be made the basis of judicial decision as to the limits of right
> and duty, and while in all cases reference must be had to the organic law of the nation for
> such limits, yet the latter is but the body and letter of which the former is the thought
> and the spirit, and it is always safe to read the letter of the Constitution in the spirit of
> the Declaration of Independence. No duty rests more imperatively upon the courts than
> the enforcement of those constitutional provisions intended to secure that equality of
> rights which is the foundation of free government.[109]

Justice Brewer's argument here is consistent with those we have seen in the debates in the Thirty-Ninth Congress. In 1878, the four organic laws of the United
States had entered the United States Code as a preface to the code but not yet as a
separate title. A separate title, "The Organic Laws of the United States," was added
in 1926.[110] Still, it is true, as Brewer states, that even after the Declaration became
the first of the organic laws of the United States in Title I of the United States Code,

---

108. Ibid. at 155.
109. Ibid. at 159–60.
110. Today, both the Declaration and the Constitution, along with the Articles of Confederation and
the Northwest Ordinance, are included in Title I of the United States Code as "The Organic Laws of
the United States." For the history of how the organic laws entered the code, see Richard H. Cox, *Four
Pillars of Constitutionalism: The Organic Laws of the United States* (Amherst, NY: Prometheus Books,
1998), 9–71. Understood as the completion of the principles of the Declaration, the first organic law of
the United States, a serious argument can be made that the Reconstruction Amendments—particularly
the Thirteenth Amendment—are unrepealable provisions of the Constitution. As we have already seen,
even unanimous consent is bound by the requirements of natural law and can only approve what is right
and just by nature. As Lincoln would frequently express it in his inimitable way, the people do not have
a right to do wrong (see *Collected Works of Abraham Lincoln*, III:315 and VIII:152). Abraham Lincoln
never described the Declaration as organic law, always reserving that term exclusively for the Constitution
(*Collected Works of Abraham Lincoln*, III:100; III:496; IV:264; IV:426; IV:281).

no judicial decision could be based directly on the Declaration. But Brewer's point was that the text of the Constitution was to be understood in terms of the principles of the Declaration that had been incorporated into the Constitution. Equal protection was certainly one of those principles. Equal protection of the laws, as we have already discussed ad nauseam, is intrinsic to social compact and entered into the organic law of the Constitution through that fundamental understanding of the foundation of "right and justice" at the heart of the rule of law. Brewer's description of the relation of the Declaration and the Constitution is reminiscent of nothing so much as Lincoln's description of the Declaration as "*the* word, '*fitly spoken*' which has proved an 'apple of gold' to us. The *Union* and the *Constitution* are the *picture* of *silver*, subsequently framed around it. The picture was made, not to *conceal*, or *destroy* the apple; but to *adorn*, and *preserve* it. The *picture* was made *for* the apple— *not* the apple for the picture." Lincoln's imagery is made more compelling by his clear reference to the biblical passage in Proverbs 25:11.

What is also notable is the extent to which Brewer adheres to the arguments of Justice Patterson in *Vanhorne's Lessee v. Dorrance* and Justice Chase's opinion in *Calder v. Bull*. Both justices argued that interpretations of the Constitution must always be guided by first principles, meaning that the Court's primary role in the constitutional separation of powers was to defend the fundamental rights of life, liberty, and property against legislative encroachment. Hamilton had argued in the *Federalist*, an argument repeated by Marshall in *Marbury*, that courts are "to be considered as the bulwarks of a limited Constitution against legislative encroachments" (78:468). This was the view of Justices Patterson and Chase that was adopted here by Justice Brewer.

Scarcely eight years after Brewer's opinion, the Supreme Court handed down its decision in *Lochner v. New York*, a decision that quickly became the bête noire of Progressivism. Justice Rufus Peckham, writing for a 5-4 majority, refused to defer to the decision of the New York legislature to regulate the number of hours bakers could work and the conditions under which they could ply their profession. The law was justified as a measure to protect the health of bakers, who were said to be subject to particularly unhealthy working conditions. It was not a law to protect the safety or health of the public at large, which would clearly have fallen within the state's police powers; rather, it was an attempt to regulate the health of individual bakers and therefore was not obviously within the purview of state power.

The majority decision struck down the New York law as a violation of the Fourteenth Amendment because it interfered with "liberty of contract," which the Court said was part of the "liberty" protected by the Due Process Clause. Bakers as a class were fully capable of negotiating for wages, hours, and working conditions, and the legislation limiting hours was a violation of their liberty of contract, a substantive due process right of the Fourteenth Amendment. That right was protected from "unreasonable, unnecessary, and arbitrary interference with the right of the individual to his personal liberty, or to enter into those contracts in relation to labor which may

seem to him appropriate or necessary for the support of himself and his family."[111]
Thus, what the framers of the Fourteenth Amendment thought was one of the privileges or immunities of U.S. citizenship that no state could violate, the right to labor
and choose an occupation, was now incorporated into the Due Process Clause as an
aspect of "personal liberty" or "the liberty of contract." A privilege or immunity of
the Fourteenth Amendment, as a result of the *Slaughterhouse Cases*, had now been
transmogrified into a "substantive due process" right.

The kind of social regulation that was exemplified by the New York law, osten-
sibly for the health of bakers, was championed by Progressives and their allies, and
they made opposition to *Lochner* a cause célèbre. So distraught were Progressives at
the Supreme Court's decisions upholding individual liberties against intrusive social
legislation from both state and federal legislation that a future Supreme Court justice
and leading Progressive, Felix Frankfurter, called for the repeal of the Due Process
Clause of the Fifth Amendment and the Due Process and Equal Protection Clauses of
the Fourteenth Amendment. In an unsigned editorial published in the *New Republic*,
October 1, 1921, Frankfurter wrote that the right to freedom of contract has been the

> doctrine which the Supreme Court has used as a sword with which to slay most impor-
> tant social legislation and to deny the means of freedom to those least free. To invoke
> it is to indulge in sterile abstractions and cruelly to shut one's eyes to cases like Lochner
> v. New York. . . . An informed study of the work of the Supreme Court of the United
> States will probably lead to the conclusion that no nine men are wise enough and good
> enough to be entrusted with the power which the unlimited provisions of the due pro-
> cess clauses confer. We have had fifty years of experiment with the Fourteenth Amend-
> ment, and the centralizing authority lodged with the Supreme Court over the domestic
> affairs of forty-eight widely different states is an authority which it simply cannot dis-
> charge with safety either to itself or to the states. The due process clauses ought to go.[112]

Two years earlier, Frankfurter had complained of the "nullification of state action
based on eighteenth century conceptions of 'liberty' and 'equality,'"[113] clearly conceptions that fueled the irrational mania displayed by the Court for individual liberty. As
every informed Progressive seemed to know in the early twentieth century, individual
rights and liberties had been rendered obsolete by the Progressive forces of history.
The founders glibly spoke of "the rights of human nature" without realizing that the
"human nature" they mistakenly believed to be permanent was actually part of an
evolutionary process. The idea of unchanging "nature" was simply an affectation of
the eighteenth century. The rights that were thought to belong to individuals because
of that nature were also subject to evolutionary change, a change that was dictated by
the ever-evolving needs of society. History had thus revealed the superiority of social
over individual rights. When there was a conflict between a claim of social justice

---

111. *Lochner v. New York*, 198 U.S. 45, 56 (1905) (Peckham, J.).
112. Felix Frankfurter, "The Red Terror of Judicial Reform," *New Republic*, October 1, 1924, 113. See
Bernstein, *Rehabilitating Lochner*, 44.
113. Felix Frankfurter, "Child Labor and the Court," *New Republic*, July 26, 1922, 248–49.

and individual rights, there could be no historical justification to choose the rights of individuals over the needs of society—the rights of individuals must give way to the welfare of the whole of society.

By the time Frankfurter reached the Supreme Court in 1939, the goal of Progressivism had been achieved. The Due Process Clauses, of course, had not been repealed, but the Supreme Court had reverted to the position of legislative deference that had been advocated by the *Slaughterhouse* majority. What is more, the Court had adopted the Progressive view that individual rights must be subordinated to the welfare of the community. In *West Coast Hotel v. Parrish* (1937), the Court took up the question of whether the State of Washington's minimum-wage law for women violated the liberty of contract component of the Due Process Clause of the Fourteenth Amendment. In executing a volte face from the Court's previous line of decisions, Chief Justice Charles Evans Hughes, writing for a 5-4 majority, noted,

> The Constitution does not speak of freedom of contract. It speaks of liberty and prohibits the deprivation of liberty without due process of law. In prohibiting that deprivation the Constitution does not recognize an absolute and uncontrollable liberty. Liberty in each of its phases has its history and connotation. But the liberty safeguarded is liberty in a social organization which requires the protection of law against the evils which menace the health, safety, morals and welfare of the people. Liberty under the Constitution is thus necessarily subject to the restraints of due process, and regulation which is reasonable in relation to its subject and is adopted in the interests of the community is due process.[114]

The chief justice expressed in this short paragraph the essence of Progressivism. Liberty has its "phases," "history," and "connotation," all determined by the requirements of "social organization." The degree to which the "interests of the community" require the subordination of liberty is "due process." Individual rights—those fundamental rights that were constantly referred to in the debates in the Thirty-Ninth Congress—are no longer the focal point of the Fourteenth Amendment. They have been eclipsed by the evolving needs of society. Liberty has its phases! The "phase" (or historical epoch) where liberty was identified with individual natural rights, especially the comprehensive right to property—the "right that includes all other rights"—had now reached its conclusion. The primary purpose of government in the current "phase" was not the protection of rights and liberties but the security of the welfare of the community, which required the redistribution, not the protection, of property.

THE *KELO* DECISION AND THE POST-CONSTITUTIONAL STATE

Nearly thirty years ago, a constitutional scholar applauded the "demise of property as a formal constitutional limit." A new view of the right to property had, in this

---

114. *West Coast Hotel v. Parrish*, 300 U.S. 379, 391 (1937) (Hughes, C. J.).

author's opinion, begun to replace the old constitutionalism of the inviolable and sacred right to property. Indeed, this new conception of property "requires incursions on traditional property rights. What once defined the limits to governmental power becomes the prime subject of affirmative governmental action."[115] The object or purpose of governmental action should be the various kinds of "redistribution" that characterize the "regulatory welfare state."[116] And, this commentator concludes, "once redistribution can be held out as a public purpose, it is difficult to see how lines can be drawn defining some redistribution as, in principle, too much or the wrong kind."[117] This view of the redistributionist state is premised on the discovery that the right to property is not, as Madison and the framers believed, a natural right, but merely a "social construct."[118] As such, it has no greater value than any other social construct. And like any mere construct, it is not limited by "deeply problematic" notions of "natural rights" or "limited government."[119] "It is now widely accepted," this prognosticator concludes, "that property is not a limit to legitimate governmental action, but a primary subject of it."[120]

In 1990, when these views were published, they seemed wildly inflated—mere wishful thinking on the part of an intellectual searching for "a new conceptual framework."[121] The Supreme Court's decision in *Kelo v. City of New London* (2005), however, translated the far-fetched dreams of a redistributionist intellectual into a reality. Although not entirely unexpected, the Court's decision was nevertheless shocking for its shoddy and dishonest reasoning. Its saving grace was that it has forced us to think once again about why the right to property is essential to the maintenance of limited government; in other words, it forces us to reexamine—and to reaffirm—what the founders and the framers of the Fourteenth Amendment understood: the prevention of tyranny, which in our immediate situation means the tyranny of the administrative state, depends upon the defense of the right to property as the comprehensive natural right.

Kelo represents the reductio ad absurdum of the Supreme Court's Takings Clause jurisprudence. The Court's opinion translated the right to private property into a doctrine of public trust, where the right to property is considered only a conditional right. Property is now held on the condition that no one else can use the property in a manner that better serves a public purpose. The right to private property has actually been abolished since holding property on terms and conditions is not any part of the understanding of the natural right to property. It does, however, meet the requirements of the feudal understanding of property that, as we have seen, Blackstone says was a necessary legal fiction adopted by the English common law. But as

115. Jennifer Nedelsky, *Private Property and the Limits of American Constitutionalism: The Madisonian Framework and Its Legacy* (Chicago: University of Chicago Press, 1990), 262.
116. Ibid., 251.
117. Ibid., 262–63.
118. Ibid., 255.
119. Ibid., 266.
120. Ibid., 231.
121. Ibid., 261.

we have also seen, this fiction was emphatically rejected by the founders when they grounded the natural right to property on the truth of natural right and discarded the fiction of feudal tenures.

In 1990, the city of New London was designated a "distressed municipality" by the State of Connecticut, and state and local officials were prompted to target the city for "economic revitalization." The city used the New London Development Corporation, a private nonprofit organization, to formulate economic redevelopment plans. It received money from two state bonds issued to support its planning activities, one for $5.35 million and another for $10 million. By February 1998, the corporation had persuaded the Pfizer Corporation to build a research facility on the New London waterfront, adjacent to the Fort Trumbull peninsula area, which was the focus of the city's redevelopment efforts. Claire Gaudiani, described as "the civically prominent president of Connecticut College,"[122] had been tapped to lead the corporation's efforts. It was well known that the Pfizer Corporation, located just across the river from New London, was searching for a new location, and Gaudiani decided to make a move on behalf of the development corporation. She succeeded in having her husband, a high-ranking employee of Pfizer, appointed to the corporation board and was also instrumental in recruiting George Milne, another high-level Pfizer executive and the one who would decide on Pfizer's new location, as a board member.[123] Professor Ilya Somin reports that "Pfizer representatives did indeed demand the redevelopment plan and its associated takings as a quid pro quo for its agreement to build a new headquarters in New London."[124] The integrated redevelopment plan covered ninety acres of property in the Fort Trumbull area and included commercial (office space, a hotel, and a new residential community) as well as noncommercial facilities such as a museum, a state park, and marinas. Most of the private homeowners in the Fort Trumbull area willingly sold their property, but nine owners, including Susette Kelo, challenged the corporation's attempt to take their property by eminent domain because the taking was intended to serve a public purpose—economic development—and therefore did not meet the "public use" requirement of the Fourteenth Amendment. Somin comments,

> Most of the specific facilities that Pfizer wanted built could probably have been constructed without eliminating all the houses in the area. But [New London Development Corporation] and Pfizer officials also believed that it was essential to wipe out all the existing buildings for aesthetic reasons. David Burnett, a high-ranking Pfizer employee and husband of Claire Gaudiani, told a reporter that the houses had to be destroyed because "Pfizer wants a nicer place to operate," and "we do not want to be surrounded

---

122. Julia D. Mahoney, "*Kelo's* Legacy: Eminent Domain and the Future of Property Rights," *Supreme Court Review* (2005): 107.

123. See Jeff Benedict, *Little Pink House: A True Story of Defiance and Courage* (New York: Grand Central Publishing, 2009), 24–29.

124. Ilya Somin, *The Grasping Hand:* Kelo v. City of New London *and the Limits of Eminent Domain* (Chicago: University of Chicago Press, 2015), 16.

by tenements." Gaudiani herself stated that the houses had to be knocked down because otherwise they would have looked "ugly and dumb."[125]

Throughout the proceedings, however, there were no allegations that the Fort Trumbull properties were blighted or anything but typical, well-maintained, middle-class homes. A casual observer might be excused for thinking that the fix was in and that the homeowners were at the mercy of an overbearing redevelopment agency that was doing the bidding of a large corporation. Even though the development corporation was willing to pay just compensation for the takings, the question was whether the takings could be justified to benefit a private corporation that would arguably contribute to a "public purpose" but not provide "public use." Surely there was a conflict of interest involved here, or at least the appearance of one. Professor Somin, not one to shy from criticism where it is justified, nevertheless treats the issue of conflict and the development corporation with uncharacteristic delicacy. "It is extremely difficult," he says, "to divine their subjective motivations with any certainty." Somin believes that Gaudiani genuinely thought she was acting for the public good. "But," Somin says,

> it is nonetheless problematic that a city redevelopment plan that was closely based on Pfizer's demands was produced by an agency headed by the wife of a high-ranking Pfizer employee and including a Pfizer executive on its board. At the very least, this created a potential conflict of interest. And even if Gaudiani and Milne genuinely believed they were acting in the public good, it is hard not to wonder whether their perception of where the public good lies was affected by their respective connections to Pfizer.[126]

We are compelled to draw the curtains on these unsavory scenes of private peculation because the Supreme Court assured all interested parties that no conflict of interest or appearance of conflict was in play. Since the redevelopment plan was "well integrated," the Court reasoned, all private interests would have been transformed to serve public purposes by the comprehensive character of the plan. In the Court's view, there was a kind of Kantian categorical imperative involved—the universal or comprehensive eliminates the private, or somehow translated private interest into public purpose or public good. But even the most casual observer can see that the language of "integration" and "comprehensiveness"—terms redolent of the administrative state—cannot disguise the fact that in the *Kelo* case, private interests were aggrandized under the guise that greater benefits would accrue to the public. In fact, greater benefits were never realized and the property taken by eminent domain was never developed. Nevertheless, according to the Court, the plan survived the "meaningful rational basis" review that is required by the Public Use Clause.

The question posed by Justice Stevens's majority opinion was "whether a city's decision to take property for the purpose of economic development satisfies the 'public

---

125. Ibid., 17.
126. Ibid.

use' requirement of the Fifth Amendment."[127] Stevens argued that a narrow or literal reading of the "public use" requirement had been abandoned long ago by the Court because "it proved to be impractical given the diverse and always evolving needs of society." We recognize here, of course, the language of Progressivism that exposed itself in the *West Coast Hotel v. Parish* case quoted earlier. In light of these "evolving needs," the Court was compelled to understand "public use" in terms of the more expansive concept of "public purpose." Not only was "public purpose" a broader interpretation, it was also, according to Stevens, a "more natural interpretation."[128] It is not entirely clear what Justice Stevens meant by "more natural," but, as Justice Thomas pointed out in his dissent, the conflation of "public use" and "public purpose" is hardly a natural reading since it contravenes both the text and the spirit of the Constitution.

Two Polar Propositions and the Nether World of Public Purpose

Justice Stevens nevertheless insists that the Fifth Amendment still sets limits to what can be demanded by government to meet the evolving needs of society. "It has long been accepted," Stevens notes, "that the sovereign may not take the property of A for the sole purpose of transferring it to another private party B, even though A is paid just compensation." It is also "equally clear," the justice continues, "that a State may transfer property from one private party to another if future 'use by the public' is the purpose of the taking." Justice Stevens is quick to add, however, that neither of these "two polar propositions" disposes of the case at hand. The city of New London "would no doubt be forbidden from taking petitioners' land for the purpose of conferring a private benefit on a particular private party."[129] The New London economic plan did, of course, take property from A and transfer it to private party B. But in an argument that seems to be unparalleled in the annals of constitutional reasoning, Justice Stevens argued that since the "the identities of those private parties were not known when the plan was adopted," it is "difficult to accuse the government of having taken A's property to benefit the private interests of B when the identity of B was unknown."[130] Justice Stevens would thus rewrite the famous dictum that everyone seems to concede is the de minimus foundation of takings jurisprudence: No governmental agency may use eminent domain proceedings to take property from private party A for the benefit of private party B unless the identity of private party B has not been determined at the time of the taking. However this bowdlerized version of the old—and justly celebrated—dictum is parsed, the fact that private party B will be known only at some future date does not lessen the fact that property has been transferred to a private party who will benefit from the government taking. The fact that the person is unknown at the

---

127. *Kelo v. City of New London*, 545 U.S. 469, 477 (2005) (Stevens, J.).
128. Ibid. at 479.
129. Ibid. at 477.
130. Ibid. at 478, n. 6.

time of the taking—but it is known that *some* private person will benefit from the taking—does not transform the private party into a public entity. This argument is remarkable enough on its own terms, but, as Justice Kennedy pointed out in his concurring opinion, "the identity of *most* of the private beneficiaries were unknown at the time the city formulated its plans."[131]

With respect to the second "polar proposition," only a part of the New London economic redevelopment area was reserved for "future use by the 'public.'" Economic development, not public use, was the overwhelming "purpose of the taking."[132] Thus, from Justice Stevens's point of view, the *Kelo* case existed somewhere in a nether universe bounded by the "two polar propositions"—one of which was substantially redefined into an absurd proposition, the other a palpable rewriting of the text of the Constitution. Justice Stevens's polar propositions provide no realistic limits to a takings jurisprudence that seeks to accommodate itself to the constantly evolving needs of society. The only constant in this universe is change or evolution—hardly the grounds for a takings jurisprudence or any other jurisprudence. Since the "needs of society" are constantly evolving, it is difficult to discern what precise role the text of the Constitution plays in a judiciary inspired by Progressivism other than as a pretext for adding the slightest patina of legitimacy to progressively evolving social constructions.

Legislative Deference and Judicial Standards

To bolster his argument for the first "polar proposition," Justice Stevens cited *Calder v. Bull*, the case we discussed *in extenso* at the beginning of this chapter. What we learned from Justice Samuel Chase's opinion in *Calder* was his hostility to the idea of "legislative deference" in matters involving property rights, insisting that all legislative acts touching on the rights of property be subjected to strict scrutiny. Justice Stevens seems to have missed this aspect of Chase's opinion because he relies almost entirely on legislative deference in reaching the result in *Kelo*. "For more than a century," Stevens writes, "our public use jurisprudence has wisely eschewed rigid formulas and intrusive scrutiny in favor of affording legislatures broad latitude in determining what public needs justify the use of the takings power."[133] Justice William O. Douglas, writing for a unanimous Court in *Berman v. Parker* (1954), marked the culmination of a trend toward legislative deference that had been developing since *West Coast Hotel*. "Subject to specific constitutional limitations," Douglas intoned,

> when the legislature has spoken, the public interest has been declared in terms well-nigh conclusive. In such cases the legislature, not the judiciary, is the main guardian of the public needs to be served by societal legislation. . . . This principle admits of no exception merely because the power of eminent domain is involved. The role of the

---

131. Ibid. at 493 (emphasis added).
132. Ibid. at 477.
133. Ibid. at 545.

judiciary in determining whether that power is being exercised for a public purpose is an extremely narrow one.[134]

For Justice Douglas, the Takings Clause does not represent a constitutional limitation on governmental power. Indeed, as we will see, the doctrine of legislative deference converts what the framers intended to be a limit on government into a grant of power.

This view was confirmed by Justice Sandra Day O'Connor thirty years later in *Hawaii v. Midkiff* (1984). After quoting *Berman*, Justice O'Connor helpfully concluded that "the 'public use' requirement is thus coterminous with the scope of a sovereign's police powers."[135] With this grand *ipse dixit*, the Court extended its regime of legislative deference to the point of reductio ad absurdum. One commentator aptly described it as "supine deference."[136]

Midkiff involved state land redistribution legislation, the Hawaii Land Reform Act of 1967, "which created a mechanism for condemning residential tracts and for transferring ownership of the condemned fees simple to existing lessees." The putative purpose of the legislation was to overcome "concentrated land ownership" that the state legislature had determined was "responsible for skewing the State's residential fee simple market, inflating land prices, and injuring the public tranquility and welfare."[137] The Ninth Circuit Court of Appeals had earlier found the scheme to be unconstitutional, describing it as a "naked attempt on the part of the state of Hawaii to take the private property of A and transfer it to B solely for B's private use and benefit."[138] Judge Arthur Alarcon distinguished the situation in *Midkiff* from *Berman*. In *Berman*, there was a "transformation from slum to healthy thriving community" that, according to Judge Alarcon, "represents a change in the use of the land." The mechanism employed in the Hawaii Land Reform Act, however, "will result in no change in use of the property. The property . . . is currently used for residential purposes. After condemnation it will be used for residential purposes. . . . [This results in] simply different forms of *private* use."[139] The difference was that in *Berman* the government took actual possession of the condemned property. Thus, the court concluded, "the key in *Berman* is the intermediate step in which the property was transferred from the private owner to the government for a public purpose." The Hawaii plan, however, provided for the transfer from private parties to private parties without the "intermediate step in which the government holds the property for the accomplishment of a public purpose. The lessee simply retains possession of residential property throughout the condemnation process until he receives fee simple title." This result, according to the court, was not authorized by *Berman*: "Nothing

---

134. *Berman v. Parker*, 384 U.S. 26, 32 (1954) (Douglas, J.).
135. *Hawaii Housing Authority v. Midkiff*, 467 U.S. 229, 240 (1984) (O'Connor, J.).
136. James W. Ely Jr., "'Poor Relation' Once More: The Supreme Court and the Vanishing Rights of Property Owners," *2004–2005 Cato Supreme Court Review* (Washington, DC: Cato Institute, 2005), 62.
137. *Hawaii Housing Authority v. Midkiff*, 233 (O'Connor, J.).
138. *Midkiff v. Tom*, 702 F.2d 788, 798 (1983).
139. Ibid. at 796–97.

in *Berman* permits the lessee of property to take ownership of that property from the owner involuntarily through condemnation proceedings. Nothing in *Berman* would provide, as does the Hawaii Land Reform Act, the lessee of condemned property with greater rights to that property than the owner."[140]

Justice O'Connor disagreed. She argued that the Supreme Court had never struck down an exercise of state eminent domain power where the use of that power was "rationally related to a conceivable public purpose."[141] "Regulating oligopoly and the evils associated with it," she asserted, "is a classic exercise of a State's police powers." Whether the redistributionist scheme invented by the legislature would actually achieve its purpose was not a proper part of the Court's consideration. It was enough that the Hawaii legislature could have believed that the act would promote its objectives. No proof that the legislature actually did believe that the means were calculated to secure the end was necessary. Even if the legislature did not articulate a rational ground or basis for its actions, if there was, in the Court's own imagination, a possible argument to support the legislation—even though the argument was unknown to the legislature—then the rational relation requirement would be satisfied.

In response to Judge Alarcon's attempt to distinguish the *Berman* holding, Justice O'Connor merely noted, "The Act advances it purposes without the State's taking actual possession of the land. In such cases, government does not itself have to use property to legitimate the taking; it is only the taking's purpose, and not its mechanics, that must pass scrutiny under the Public Use Clause."[142] This is a remarkable assertion: only the purpose of the taking is subject to the Public Use Clause scrutiny, not the means. The Court's deference to legislative determinations as to what constitutes a "public purpose" is almost unlimited, and the means chosen by a legislature to accomplish a putative public purpose will receive no scrutiny. The ends justify almost any means.

Even though Justice O'Connor had argued for the broadest possible legislative deference in *Midkiff*, by the time of the *Kelo* decision she had become alarmed that the "distinction between private and public use of property" had been abandoned by the majority. "Under the banner of economic development," O'Connor warned, "all private property is now vulnerable to being taken and transferred to another private owner so long as it might be upgraded—i.e., given to an owner who will use it in a way that the legislature deems more beneficial to the public—in the process."[143] It is difficult—if not impossible—to understand why Justice O'Connor did not see the *Kelo* majority opinion as the fruit of her own labor in *Midkiff*.

Justice Stevens Reconsiders His *Kelo* Opinion

In 2011, nearly eighteen months after his retirement, Justice Stevens gave a speech reflecting on his opinion in *Kelo*. After remarking that his opinion for the majority

140. Ibid. at 797.
141. *Hawaii Housing Authority v. Midkiff* at 241.
142. Ibid. at 467.
143. Ibid. at 494.

was "the most unpopular opinion that I wrote during my thirty-four year tenure on the Supreme Court," he confessed that he had incorrectly assumed that "the case required us to construe the 'Takings' or 'Public Use' Clause of the Fifth Amendment to the Constitution." What Justice Stevens alleges he had discovered in the meantime was that the Takings Clause of the Fifth Amendment has never been held to be a restriction upon state activities. The case that is usually cited as having "incorporated" the Takings Clause and made it binding on the states through the Fourteenth Amendment is *Chicago, B. & Q. R. Co. v. Chicago* (1897). But Stevens notes that this case never mentions the Fifth Amendment and speaks only of the right to property as a takings issue in terms of due process protection against state action. As Stevens says, "neither that case nor any later Supreme Court case with which I am familiar explained how or why the Takings Clause might have been made applicable to the states."[144] Thus, the justice concluded, *Kelo* should have been decided as a "substantive due process" case under the Fourteenth Amendment and not as a Takings Clause case under the Fifth and Fourteenth Amendments.

The property owners contesting the eminent domain actions of the City of New London would have been better served had they argued for a substantive due process right to "home ownership" as a liberty interest to forestall the city's action. This would be similar to the "liberty of contract" cases where a substantive due process right was asserted against legislative attempts to regulate wages, hours, and working conditions. But, of course, Stevens knows that *Lochner* was interred many years ago, and the chance that it could have been disinterred in *Kelo* to vindicate the rights of home-ownership was far-fetched—or rather, utterly impossible.

Stevens's public return to his handiwork in *Kelo*, while not unprecedented, is unusual. He is correct that *Chicago, B. & Q. R. Co. v. Chicago* doesn't mention the Fifth Amendment, but it clearly uses takings language in paraphrasing the amendment. Justice John Harlan, writing for the majority, noted, "If compensation for private property taken for public use is an essential element of due process of law as ordained by the 14th Amendment, then the final judgment of a state court, under the authority of which the property is in fact taken, is to be deemed the act of the state within the meaning of the Amendment."[145] This was the language of "incorporation" or "selective incorporation" before it became a routine part of the Court's lexicon. But the Court here clearly considered all the elements of the Fifth Amendment's Takings Clause to be part of the Due Process Clause of the Fourteenth Amendment. It is odd that Justice Stevens missed this essential point of Justice Harlan's opinion.

Justice Stevens also mentions "the famous quotation from Justice Chase's opinion in *Calder v. Bull* that states 'a law which takes property from A and gives it to B . . . is against all reason and justice'" and comments that "while the Justices in *Kelo* agreed that this common law rule is an element of the due process that

---

144. Justice John Paul Stevens, "*Kelo*, Popularity, and Substantive Due Process," *Alabama Law Review* 63, no. 5 (2012): 941, 946.
145. *Chicago, B. & Q. R. Co. v. Chicago*, 166 U.S. 226, 235 (1897) (Harlan, J.).

the Fourteenth Amendment mandates, the precise dimensions of that rule are not defined in the Constitution's text. The rule is an aspect of substantive due process that had been explicated through a process of common law case-by-case adjudication."[146] It is again odd—not to say disingenuous—that Justice Stevens insists that the rule is not a part of the text of the Constitution when he knows that "public *purpose*" is a complete bowdlerization of the text. What is even more disingenuous is that Justice Chase did not consider his now famous dictum a "common law rule" but, as we have seen, something that was intrinsic to social compact and therefore essential to the natural right and natural law understanding of the right to property. It could not be a part of a common law rule that evolved on a case-by-case basis or a right that evolved to meet the changing needs of society because, in Chase's understanding and the understanding of the founders, this principle that rested at the core of the *natural right to property* derived from human nature, a nature that itself did not evolve but was permanent and fixed.

Justice Stevens's second thoughts about his *Kelo* opinion are entirely fanciful. The result would not have been different had it been decided as a "substantive due process" case. What Justice Stevens thought was embarrassing about his majority opinion was, in fact, not an embarrassment—the Takings Clause had in fact been incorporated. What was truly embarrassing about his opinion was his support for the transmogrification of "public use" into "public purpose" by his wholly misleading and dishonest example of the "two polar opposites." His second thoughts did nothing to relieve that embarrassment—which Justice Thomas justly ridiculed as transforming the Public Use Clause into the "Diverse and Always Evolving Needs of Society Clause."[147]

Justice Clarence Thomas Dissents

Justice Thomas argues that "the most natural reading of the [Takings] Clause is that it allows the government to take property only if the government owns, or the public has a legal right to use the property, as opposed to taking it for any public purpose or necessity whatsoever."[148] He notes, however, that "our current Public Use Clause jurisprudence . . . has rejected this natural reading of the Clause." Justice Thomas accuses the Court of "blindly" adopting "with little discussion of the Clause's history and original meaning" a "modern interpretation" that rests on the legislative deference articulated in *Berman* and *Midkiff*. This leaves the Takings Clause without a "doctrinal foundation" and renders the "public purpose standard" incapable of "principled application." This is, needless to say, a severe—if entirely just—indictment of the majority opinion.

---

146. Stevens, "*Kelo*, Popularity, and Substantive Due Process," 948.
147. *Kelo v. City of New London* at 506.
148. Ibid. at 508.

Legislative deference has forced the Court to concede second-class status to the right to property. Justice Thomas points out that

> it is most implausible that the Framers intended to defer to legislatures as to what satisfies the Public Use Clause, uniquely among all the express provisions of the Bill of Rights. We would not defer to a legislature's determination of the various circumstances that establish . . . when a search of a home would be reasonable. . . . Yet today the Court tells us that we are not to "second-guess the City's considered judgments" when the issue is, instead, whether the government may take the infinitely more intrusive step of tearing down petitioners' homes. Something has gone seriously awry with this Court's interpretations of the Constitution. Though citizens are safe from the government in their homes, the homes themselves are not. Once one accepts, as the Court at least nominally does, that the Public Use Clause is a limit on the eminent domain power of the Federal Government and the States, there is no justification for the almost complete deference it grants to legislatures as to what satisfies it.[149]

Professor Somin explains why the right to property was banished, as it were, from the privileged status occupied by other fundamental rights in the Bill of Rights. "The Progressives," he writes, "were hostile to judicial protection for property rights because they believed it impeded effective economic planning and was a tool that the wealthy wielded to protect their economic interests at the expense of the poor."[150] Justice Thomas sees a perverse irony at work here. Urban redevelopment programs which take property for "public purpose," he notes,

> fall disproportionately on poor communities. Those communities are not only systematically less likely to put their lands to the highest and best social use, but are also the least politically powerful. If ever there were justification for intrusive judicial review of constitutional provisions that protect "discrete and insular minorities" [citing *U.S. Carolene Products* (1938)], surely that principle would apply with great force to the powerless groups and individuals the Public Use Clause protects. The deferential standard this Court has adopted for the Public Use Clause is therefore deeply perverse.[151]

We might add that the deferential standard is not only "perverse" but also a violation of the rule of law that we have identified throughout as the "equal protection of equal rights." The founders considered the security of the right to property as the principal purpose of government and the most comprehensive right possessed by human beings by nature. No one can fail to see that a doctrine of legislative deference with respect to the right to property means that all other rights included in the right to property will similarly be at risk. As Justice Thomas suggests, Progressivism must be countered by a resort to first principles.

---

149. Ibid. at 517–18.
150. Somin, *The Grasping Hand*, 56.
151. *Kelo v. City of New London* at 521–22.

FEUDALISM AND THE ADMINISTRATIVE STATE: GOVERNMENT AS "UNIVERSAL LANDLORD"

Sir William Blackstone observed that the prescriptive right to property found in the English common law had evolved in opposition to the feudal idea of property. Blackstone, however, admitted that an important aspect of the feudal law remained active in the common law, conceding that it was a "necessary fiction" that the king was "the universal landlord" of all the lands in his kingdom and that all property was a "gift" of the king held on terms and conditions of feudal services.[152] This fiction was too transparent to last forever, and the contests between the crown and Parliament gradually eroded the idea that the king's title to the kingdom was that of the first occupier—or, more accurately, the last conqueror. But the development of the English right to property, as Blackstone made clear, proceeded as exceptions to or limitations on the king's original right as proprietor and not from natural right.

We have already seen how Blackstone was rejected in favor of Locke by the American founders. The legal fiction of feudal tenures, having been driven out at the founding, however, seems to have insinuated its way back into our concept of property rights through the development of our takings jurisprudence—this time with the administrative state serving in the stead of the king. Professor Dennis Coyle writes,

> The liberal vision of the founders that private property would provide the independence and responsibility on which to anchor democracy has been obscured by the growth of the state during the twentieth century. A more hierarchical perspective, that possession of private property is encumbered by obligations to the state, has gained prominence. . . . Landowners are becoming "stewards" who hold their property rights at the pleasure of the state.[153]

Professor Coyle has ferreted out some revealing passages from legal scholars advocating a return to features of the feudal system. "Within the traditions of property law," one luminary scolded, "there is nothing particularly radical in visualizing land being owned by the sovereign and being channeled out again to persons who would hold it only as long as they performed the requisite duties which went with the land."[154] Indeed, Coyle notes, "arguments for the feudal-like encumbrance of private property have been heard throughout this [twentieth] century." He quotes a legal scholar who wrote in 1938 that "in [the] case of feudalism it is regrettable that there could not have been preserved the idea that all property was held subject to

---

152. William Blackstone, *Commentaries on the Laws of England* (1765–1769; repr., Chicago: University of Chicago Press, 1979), II:51.
153. Dennis J. Coyle, *Property Rights and the Constitution: Shaping Society Through Land Use Regulation* (Albany: State University of New York Press, 1993), 213–14.
154. E. F. Roberts, "The Demise of Property Law," *Cornell Law Review* 57 (1971): 43, quoted in Coyle, *Property Rights and the Constitution*, 217.

the performance of duties—not a few of them public."[155] These remarks were writ-ten at a time when the advocates of the administrative state were confident that they would prevail in the re-founding of the American system of politics—transforming the regime from one that protected individual rights and liberties to one in which public welfare and the redistribution of property was the primary object of govern-ment. This same scholar expressed surprise that the principles of the founding had been so robust: "The perdurance of assumptions of natural rights has been extremely striking," he argued, especially since "the Constitution's guarantee of both property and liberty began with individualism and natural law as a background." The "per-durance" is surprising because the progress of science—especially evolutionary sci-ence—has disproven the existence of the idea of nature and natural law that inspired the founders' view of natural rights. It was this background that forced the framers to accept the negative idea of "the state as a policeman. That is the general background of the asserted rights to 'life, liberty, and the pursuit of happiness.' More positive conceptions of liberty enriched by state action belong to recent, non-individualistic times. They could not have occurred or appealed to our self-reliant ancestors."[156]

In oral argument before the Supreme Court, the lawyer representing the City of New London, Wesley Horton, was questioned sharply by Justices O'Connor and Scalia. Justice Scalia asked Horton whether his understanding was that the Takings Clause allowed the confiscation of the property of those who paid fewer taxes to transfer to those who would develop the property in a way that produced more tax revenues. "That would be a public use, wouldn't it?" Justice Scalia queried. Before Horton could answer, Justice O'Connor intervened, saying, "For example Motel 6 and the city thinks, well, if we had a Ritz-Carlton, we would have higher taxes. Now, is that okay?" Horton replied, "Yes, Your Honor. That would be okay . . . because otherwise you're in the position of drawing the line." Justice Scalia must have been startled by Horton's answer. He again asked, "Let me qualify it. You can take from A to give to B if B pays more taxes?" Horton: "If it's a significant amount." Justice Scalia: "You accept that as a proposition?" Horton: "I do, Your Honor."[157] This ex-change should have ended New London's chances of prevailing in the case. Horton later said, however, that this was the point in the argument when he knew that he had won the case.[158]

Justice Thomas in his *Kelo* dissent noted that the Court has consistently refused to adopt any "heightened form of review" in matters involving the determination of what constitutes "public purposes." The Court will instead indulge the greatest possible deference to legislative bodies. "Still worse," Thomas wrote, "it is backwards to adopt a searching standard of constitutional review for nontraditional property

155. Francis S. Philbrick, "Changing Conceptions of Property in Law," *University of Pennsylvania Law Review* 86 (1938): 710, quoted in Coyle, *Property Rights and the Constitution*, 217.
156. Philbrick, "Changing Conceptions in Property in Law," 716.
157. Transcript of the oral argument in *Kelo v. City of New London*, February 22, 2005, 29–31, www .supremecourt.gov/oral_arguments/argument_transcripts/2004/04-108.pdf.
158. See Somin, *Grasping Hand*, 33–34.

interests, such as welfare benefits, while deferring to the legislature's determination as to what constitutes a public use when it exercises the power of eminent domain, and thereby invades individuals' traditional rights in real property."[159] Thomas cited *Goldburg v. Kelly* (1970)[160] as a case that applied a higher standard of review for nontraditional property interests. In *Goldburg*, the Court held that the Fourteenth Amendment's Due Process Clause required that welfare recipients "be afforded an evidentiary hearing *before* termination of benefits."[161] Justice Brennan argued that "such benefits are a matter of statutory entitlement for persons qualified to receive them. . . . The constitutional challenge cannot be answered by an argument that public assistance benefits are a 'privilege' and not a 'right.'"[162] And in a helpful footnote, Justice Brennan explained, "It may be realistic today to regard welfare entitlements as more like 'property' than as 'gratuity.'"[163] Thus, Brennan concluded, "important governmental interests"—a standard of heightened judicial scrutiny—are served by a constitutional requirement of "a pre-termination evidentiary hearing." What are the "important governmental interests" that trigger this heightened judicial solicitude? Brennan was effusive: "Welfare, by meeting the basic demands of subsistence, can help bring within the reach of the poor the same opportunities that are available to others to participate meaningfully in the life of the community. At the same time, welfare guards against the societal malaise that may flow from a widespread sense of unjustified frustration and insecurity."[164]

Justice Hugo Black, in dissent, noted the majority's untenable assumptions about the right to property:

> The Court . . . in effect says that failure of the government to pay a promised charitable installment to an individual deprives that individual of *his own property*, in violation of the Due Process Clause of the Fourteenth Amendment. It somewhat strains credulity to say that the government's promise of charity to an individual is property belonging to that individual when the government denies that the individual is honestly entitled to receive such a payment.[165]

Black suggested that the majority had created a property right in the redistribution of wealth—that is, a right to property in the property of others.

Justice Thomas's complaint is clearly on point. The Court has created a higher level of scrutiny—important governmental interests—to test welfare payments than it accords to the right to property under eminent domain proceeding. Eminent domain takings are accorded minimum rationality—or imaginable rationality—in the Court's "supine deference" to legislative determinations. The different standards of

---

159. *Kelo v. City of New London* at 518.
160. *Goldberg v. Kelly*, 397 U.S. 254 (1970).
161. Ibid. at 260 (emphasis added).
162. Ibid. at 262.
163. Ibid. at n. 8.
164. Ibid. at 397.
165. Ibid. at 275.

deference extended to welfare rights—those rights that form the core of the administrative state—and the rights of real property indicate that property rights are no longer understood as essentially private rights. If the administrative state is primarily an agent for the redistribution of property, then the conclusion is inevitable that ultimately all property—at least *in potentia*—belongs to government. The redistribution takes place on terms and conditions set by government itself. The right to property has therefore become merely a conditional right—property is held in public trust. The individual must justify his public trust by showing that no one else can use his property in a manner that better serves a public purpose, even if it means only generating more tax revenue. In short, government has become, once again, the universal landlord. Having expelled feudalism at the founding, it has returned with a vengeance in a new form, disguised as a force serving the public good, or the continually evolving needs of society, but still working in the interests of the ruling classes, now known as the minions of the administrative state.

Conclusion

The Administrative State and Post-constitutionalism: The Demise of the Right to Property

"The unregulated life is not worth living (with Apology to Socrates)."

—Anonymous

I began this book by attempting to articulate an argument that, for the founders, the right to property was the central idea and purpose that animated limited government. It was the comprehensive right that was expressed as "the pursuit of happiness." "As a man is said to have a right to property so he has a property in his rights" is the illuminating summary penned by James Madison in 1792. I tried to make the argument that the founders understood "the pursuit of happiness" as both a right and a moral obligation. Today, we hear from our most progressive thinkers that too much emphasis is placed on property rights at the expense of human rights, whereas we believe we have demonstrated that the founders thought that the right to property was properly understood as the comprehensive human right. The protection of individual rights has been replaced by the welfare of the community as the end, or purpose, of government. The welfare of the community, of course, demands the subordination of rights and liberties to this greater good. The preservation of property was once believed to be the principal object of social compact, but under a new historical dispensation that informs our current social construct—or, if you will, our new social compact—redistribution of property is the principal object of government. This is the new ground and foundation of justice.

The old social compact resulted in inequality because it allowed natural talents and abilities to express themselves in unequal ways. Nature, we are assured, distributes talents and abilities arbitrarily. No one is responsible for his own talents and abilities because no one is responsible for his own creation; everyone receives talents and abilities from the lottery of nature—nature is arbitrary. Those who receive natural advantages—intelligence, industry, ambition, beauty, strength, social or moral capacity, or a host of other distinctions—do not merit them because they have done nothing to deserve them. It is impossible to know why some are lucky in the lottery of nature and others are not. Redistribution will correct this arbitrariness and make the results equal and therefore just. Perhaps in a bolder future, lobotomies or other more advanced scientific procedures will correct the lottery of nature in more direct and permanent ways. But for now, the equalization of results—the redistribution of property—will have to serve. It will be incomplete justice because it is only a correction of nature, not the conquest of nature.

It is true that the founders believed that nature or natural right provided permanent and unchanging standards of justice, but evolutionary science has revealed that history, not nature, is the primary force of human experience. Speaking of the rights of individuals was always anti-communitarian. It set the individual and egoism against the community and the common good. The language of individual rights reminds us of the "different and unequal faculties" for acquiring property that Madison spoke of in *Federalist* 10; these faculties produce not only different kinds of property but also unequal amounts of property. These results would seem to be "according to nature." But if equality of results has become the measure of justice, the only way to achieve justice is to employ human art to rectify the arbitrariness of nature. Unequal results will have to be redistributed to those "less fortunate in the lottery of nature" or even in the "lottery of life." Equality of opportunity—which preserves both the equality and the inequality of nature—must give way to equality of result if there is to be genuine justice, and genuine justice is a correction of nature, not a standard of nature. Nature can no longer be regarded as the "unchanging ground of changing experience"[1] because in a world of constant change and evolution there is nothing permanent except change itself. But, of course, it is only by reference to the unchanging that change can be understood. Without the unchanging, the only alternative is positivism and nihilism.

The idea that there was such a thing as unchanging human nature was challenged by Progressivism, the movement that paved the way for the eventual emergence of the administrative state and what is known today as "post-constitutionalism." Social construction, not the objective reality of a created universe governed by the "Laws of Nature and of Nature's God," is the touchstone of reality that dominates our most advanced and sophisticated thinkers today. But this socially constructed universe is dominated by historicism, nihilism, and positivism, all merging to form what might be loosely called "post-modernism." These different strands of modernity have resulted from what the most profound political philosopher of the twentieth century called the "self-destruction of reason," the "inevitable outcome of modern rationalism as distinguished from premodern rationalism."[2]

---

1. Harry V. Jaffa, *A New Birth of Freedom: Abraham Lincoln and the Coming of the Civil War* (Lanham, MD: Rowman & Littlefield, 2000), 84, 101–2, 104; Harry V. Jaffa, *American Conservatism and the American Founding* (Durham, NC: Carolina Academic Press, 1984), 175.

2. Leo Strauss, *Liberalism Ancient and Modern* (New York: Basic Books, 1968), 257; Harry V. Jaffa, *Original Intent and the Framers of the Constitution: A Disputed Question* (Washington, DC: Regnery, 1994), 317.

What Madison and the founders understood—and we seem to have forgotten—is that without protection for diverse and unequal faculties for acquiring property, there will be no individual liberty or political liberty. This is the reason that Madison said in *Federalist* 10 that the protection of these faculties was "the first object of government." We recall Jefferson's remarks in "A Bill for Establishing Religious Freedom" that the metaphysical ground of religious and political liberty was the fact that "Almighty God hath created the mind free." Madison's statement in *Federalist* 10 has the same meaning. The fact that the mind has been created free—that is, with diverse and unequal faculties—is the ground of political liberty and must be protected by government as the source of liberty. Individual liberty and political liberty are both grounded in reason and revelation. But if we are willing to sacrifice liberty for the welfare of the community, as the imperative of the administrative state suggests we must do, then, I say, we should do so with our eyes wide open. The founders were convinced that the welfare of the community was best protected by promoting liberty.

The American founding, we have argued throughout, was an exception to this steady and unrelenting march of modernity, a safe haven in which both reason and revelation were defended against the corrosive influences of modernity. The principles of the founding received their greatest challenge in that great contest for America's soul that we know as the Civil War. Without the Declaration, Lincoln argued, America would lose its soul—its animating principles. In 1859, Lincoln wrote, "It is now no child's play to save the principles of Jefferson from total overthrow in this nation."[3] Those principles were saved by the Civil War and Reconstruction, but the restoration lasted only a short time before it was overwhelmed by Progressivism, the latest iteration of modernity that had its roots in Rousseau and Hegel and eventuated in the post-modernism of Heidegger and his epigones.

Woodrow Wilson was the best known of the Progressives. He was utterly contemptuous of the idea that political liberty could be grounded in the "Laws of Nature and of Nature's God." The laws of nature had been exposed by Darwinism as hopelessly outmoded: "Liberty fixed in an unalterable law," Wilson wrote, "would be no liberty at all."[4] In the eyes of Wilson and the Progressives, the laws of nature were the source of tyranny because they were unalterable and permanent, creating the illusion that they were immune to the irresistible forces of progressive history and the evolution of science. As one latter-day epigone of Wilson expressed it, "no man who is as well abreast of modern science as the Fathers were of eighteenth-century science believes any longer in unchanging human nature."[5] The only principle of liberty that can be recognized within the Darwinian universe is the freedom to change or progress, a freedom that has no particular end or purpose. But as anyone can see,

3. Abraham Lincoln, "Letter to Henry L. Pierce and Others," April 6, 1859, in *The Collected Works of Abraham Lincoln*, ed. Roy P. Basler (New Brunswick, NJ: Rutgers University Press, 1953), III:376.
4. Woodrow Wilson, "Constitutional Government," in *The Papers of Woodrow Wilson*, ed. Arthur S. Link (Princeton, NJ: Princeton University Press, 1966–), 4:172.
5. Richard Hofstadter, *The American Political Tradition* (New York: Vintage, 1948), 16–17.

under this principle of freedom it is impossible to distinguish between freedom and necessity—or, considered properly, between freedom and the tyranny of necessity. It may be, as one of Wilson's bolder contemporaries phrased it, simply that every living organism—and Wilson understood the political community to be a "living organism"—is moved by "will to power" and that liberty exists only to the extent that organisms can "discharge their strength." It is obvious that in a universe governed by necessity, there is no ground for morality or moral choice.

The permanent order presided over by the laws of nature, however, provides the basis for a moral order that is grounded in both reason and revelation. The idea that scientific evolution or value relativism resting on historicism, nihilism, and positivism can substitute for morality has driven Progressivism for well over a century. It has undermined the basis for morality by denying that reason or revelation can inform moral questions. Reason cannot settle value disputes because questions of value are not amenable to rational discourse; questions of value are simply idiosyncratic preference, ultimately rooted in sub-rational passions. As for revelation, religion has been revealed to be mostly irrational superstition that people cling to when confronted with complex issues beyond their comprehension. Needless to say, Progressivism has succeeded in ridiculing reason and revelation as grounds of morality but has not succeeded in refuting either reason or revelation as the ground of private or public morality by reasonable arguments.

The Declaration offers a reasoned ground for morality rooted in a permanent order derived from the principles of human nature. Modernity, however, offers a deceptive liberation from the constraints of nature. For the Progressives, freedom exists only to the extent that humans can be liberated from the false notion that nature or God imposes moral constraints on behavior. As Wilson implied, a freedom according to the laws of nature is no freedom: only liberation from nature and God is genuine freedom. Wilson's contemporary, Nietzsche, wrote about "the invincible Society of Assassins," an eleventh-century Islamic sect he described as "that order of free spirits *par excellence*," whose motto was "Nothing is true, everything is permitted." Nietzsche comments, "Here we have real freedom, for the notion of truth itself has been disposed of."[6] Truth, like the laws of nature and God, also imposes moral constraints. Where there is no truth, freedom is indistinguishable from nihilism, and freedom is also indistinguishable from slavery.

Today many scholars argue that we operate in a post-constitutional era where the imperatives of the administrative state have replaced the formalism of the Constitution. It was the deliberate purpose of Progressivism to undermine the constitutional structures of limited government that led to the emergence of this post-constitutional era and the creation of the administrative state whose single-minded purpose seems to be to magnify its power and extend its reach into every aspect of American life. This is an intrinsic feature of a system where administration and regulation replace politics as the ordinary means of making policy.

---

6. Friedrich Nietzsche, *The Birth of Tragedy and the Genealogy of Morals*, trans. Francis Golffing (Garden City, NY: Doubleday, 1956), essay 3, sec. 24, 287.

Thirty-five years ago, an intrepid supporter of the administrative state saw the first glimmers of the rapidly approaching new dawn of the post-constitutional era when he confidently wrote,

> The growth of administrative lawmaking over the half-century since the New Deal has been fueled by fundamental political and cultural currents that the law is powerless to reverse and to which it must accommodate itself.
>
> The existence of a sprawling administrative bureaucracy with broad powers to make law should no longer be regarded as an open constitutional question. It is constitutional fact. It must become one of the fundamental premises from which our reasoning about constitutional structure and relationships begins. In this sense, the rise of administrative lawmaking, although accomplished gradually and without benefit of a formal amendment to the Constitution, now constitutes an amendment to the Constitution de facto. The changes in structure and working relationships which are hinted at by the term "the administrative state" are at least as fundamental as any of the changes in governmental institutions that have been embodied in constitution amendments during the twentieth century.[7]

Scarcely a year after this article was published, the Supreme Court handed down its decision in *Chevron, U.S.A. v. Natural Resources Defense Council* (1984). In this case, which still serves as the Supreme Court's authoritative ruling on Congress' constitutional authority to delegate lawmaking power to administrative agencies, the greatest latitude was extended both to Congress and to administrative agencies. Indeed, one prominent commentator has said that the opinion in *Chevron* has achieved the status of quasi-constitutional text.[8] *Chevron* thus serves as the epitome of how the post-constitutional administrative state evolved, not by constitutional authority but by constitutional indirection and subterfuge. Congress' authority to delegate is broad, the Court noted, and administrative agencies have wide discretion in interpreting their lawmaking mandates. The Court averred,

> While agencies are not directly accountable to the people, the Chief Executive is, and it is entirely appropriate for this political branch of the Government to make such policy choices—resolving the competing interests which Congress itself either inadvertently did not resolve, or intentionally left to be resolved by the agency charged with the administration of the statute in light of everyday realities.[9]

When an agency construes a statute, "if the intent of Congress is clear, that is the end of the matter; for the court as well as the agency, must give effect to the unambiguously expressed intent of the Congress." On those frequent occasions when "the statute is silent or ambiguous with respect to the specific issue, the question for the

---

7. E. Donald Elliott, "*INS v. Chadha*: The Administrative Constitution, the Constitution, and the Legislative Veto," in *The Supreme Court Review, 1983*, ed. Philip B. Kurland et al. (Chicago: University of Chicago Press, 1994), 125, 174.

8. Cass R. Sunstein, "*Chevron* Step Zero," *Virginia Law Review* 92, no. 2 (April 2006): 188.

9. *Chevron U.S.A. v. Natural Resources Defense Council*, 467 U.S. 837, 865–66 (1984) (Stevens, J.).

court is whether the agency's answer is based on a permissible construction of the statute."[10] The Court itself is ambiguous as to whether Congress' silence or ambiguity in legislation means that "Congress has *explicitly* left a gap for the agency to fill" and that this constitutes a "delegation of authority to the agency to elucidate a specific provision of the statute by regulation."[11] The Court concedes, as it must, that the delegation is "implicit rather than explicit." In any case, "such legislative regulations are given controlling weight unless they are arbitrary, capricious, or manifestly contrary to the statute," and the Court may not substitute its own construction for any reasonable one "made by the administrator of an agency."[12] This is deference in the extreme. If Congress can delegate by its silence and ambiguity, then the delegation is uncontrollable and the Court's attempts to impose reasonable constraints seem to ring hollow. Deference to administrative agencies by the Congress and the courts has become routine since *Chevron*, and questions of Congress' power to delegate authority to administrative agencies are widely considered to have been rendered moot by the imperatives of the administrative state.[13]

Since the *Chevron* decision, the administrative state's authority to act on delegated power has become as extensive as it is ill defined. Courts routinely interpret ambiguous legislative language, implicit language, or even legislative silence as a delegation of power.[14] In 2013, the Supreme Court extended the *Chevron* doctrine to include an administrative agency's power to define its own jurisdictional reach. Justice Scalia, writing for the majority in *City of Arlington, Texas v. F.C.C.*, noted that "*Chevron* is rooted in a background presumption of congressional intent: namely, 'that Congress, when it left ambiguity in a statute' administered by an agency, 'understood that the ambiguity would be resolved, first and foremost by the agency, and desired the agency (rather than the courts) to possess whatever degree of discretion the ambiguity allows.'"[15] And according to Justice Scalia, for *Chevron* purposes, there are no statutory distinctions between "jurisdictional questions" that would not warrant deference and non-jurisdictional questions that would. The distinction, Justice Scalia avers, is simply "a mirage" that deserves no judicial cognizance. Under *Chevron*, therefore, the FCC can define the limits of its own jurisdiction as long as it doesn't do so in a wholly arbitrary and capricious way.[16]

Chief Justice Roberts's dissent in *Arlington* seems almost quaint in this post-constitutional era. The chief justice observes, invoking the famous passage in

---

10. Ibid. at 842–43.
11. Ibid. at 843–84 (emphasis added).
12. Ibid.
13. Two years after *Chevron*, Justice Byron White, in his dissenting opinion in *Bowshear v. Synar*, 478 U.S. 714, 761 (1986), acknowledged "the advent and triumph of the administrative state and the accompanying multiplication of the tasks undertaken by the Federal Government."
14. For a general overview, see Kenneth R. Mayer, *With the Stroke of a Pen: Executive Orders and Presidential Power* (Princeton, NJ: Princeton University Press, 2001), 44–50.
15. *City of Arlington, Tx. v. F.C.C.* 133 S. Ct 1863, 1868 (2013) (Scalia, J., quoting *Smiley v. Citibank (South Dakota), N.A.*, 517 U.S., 735, 740–41 [1996]).
16. Ibid.

Marbury v. Madison that "it is emphatically the province and duty of the judicial department to say what the law is," that "the rise of the modern administrative state has not changed that duty," pointing out that even the Administrative Procedure Act "instructs reviewing courts to decide 'all relevant questions of law.'"[17] Later in his dissent, Roberts refers to the "separation of powers" that is "firmly rooted in our constitutional structure" and that obliges "the Judiciary not only to confine itself to its proper role, but to ensure that the other branches do so as well."[18] There is no doubt that the delegation doctrine authorized by *Chevron* violates the separation of powers as originally understood by the framers. In Article I of the Constitution, "All Legislative Powers herein granted" are vested exclusively in the Congress. Neither the courts nor the executive have express or implied powers to legislate. The delegation of lawmaking power by Congress subverts one of the important purposes of the separation of powers: fixing responsibility for the actions of those who occupy constitutional offices. If the legislative branch is allowed to delegate lawmaking power to other branches or agencies, it can easily avoid or deflect its responsibilities. We know from our experience with the administrative state that fixing responsibility for lawmaking, administration, and adjudication has become increasingly difficult. Can there be any doubt that, from the point of view of the framers, the delegation of vague, imprecise, and ambiguous lawmaking power to executive agencies violates not only separation of powers but also every idea of the rule of law? This is certainly the thrust of the argument in *Marbury* that Chief Justice Roberts uses to buttress his case against the administrative state. But the chief justice's argument seems almost hopelessly anachronistic: a constitutional argument made in a post-constitutional era. It is certainly true that if constitutionalism is ever to be restored, it will be with arguments like those advanced by the chief justice and other like-minded, original intent jurisprudes. But constitutional arguments seem to have little weight in the post-constitutional era, where the administrative state steadily and inexorably extends its reach and power, insinuating itself into every nook and cranny of American life, all the while receiving the imprimatur of the courts and the most advanced constitutional scholars.

One of the powerful vehicles the administrative state has discovered for magnifying its power and influence in the post-constitutional world has been the creation of a regulatory regime that is openly hostile to property rights. The American people seem to have an inordinate attachment to property rights, and their stubborn unwillingness to subordinate this attachment to the evolving needs of the community stands as a barrier and a rebuke to the administrative state. Environmental regulations, wetlands regulations, historic preservation, endangered species regulation, and a myriad of other ways in which property is taken by regulation are used by the administrative state to force private property into public service. Private property

---

17. Ibid. at 1880 (Roberts, C. J., dissenting) (quoting *Marbury v. Madison*, 5 U.S. [1 Cranch] 137, 177 [1803]).
18. Ibid. at 1886.

owners should be doing this voluntarily to serve the public good, but their intransigence still needs to be disciplined by government administrators. The days when private rights trump the needs and desires (whether real or imagined) of the community seem to be gone—or almost gone. One of the authors we quoted in the last chapter, writing in the 1930s, was baffled that people were still clinging to the notion of individual rights that prevailed at the founding. He seemed confident that the epoch of individual rights was about to close forever. Yet the idea of individual rights still lingers almost eighty years later, although it is everywhere under attack and may have retreated behind its last defensive ramparts. The assaults on the right to property have been vigorous, as I believe the *Kelo* case surely indicates. The assaults on liberty—particularly freedom of speech and free exercise of religion, to say nothing of the right to keep and bear arms—are now frequent, especially on university campuses, which provide the training in diversity and political correctness that fuels the administrative state. The framers knew that once the battle for the right to property was lost, once government had become the "universal landlord," we would be fighting a rear-guard action to protect the bundle of essential rights associated with the right to property. We should have taken alarm when the Supreme Court executed the de facto amendment of the Fifth Amendment, substituting "public purpose" for "public use." But this was an "amendment" that was approved by the dominant forces of Progressivism and the historicism and positivism it represented. It was this transmogrification of the Constitution that paved the way for the administrative state and post-constitutionalism. Now that we have conceded the high ground that all our rights are derived from the "Laws of Nature and of Nature's God," we have conceded our most powerful defense. The post-constitutional world leaves us without a Constitution—or a Declaration of Independence.

Appendix

Professor Thomas G. West has written recently that Jefferson and Madison do not represent the founders' view on religious liberty and the rights of conscience. According to Professor West, Jefferson presented an "extreme position," and "Madison was one of the few who endorsed" his extremism. Both "may have made . . . intemperate claims under the influence of their strong anticlerical bias."[1] Jefferson, in particular, made contradictory statements about religion that undermine any claims that his views should be regarded as authoritative. Professor West thus seems to agree with a prominent public intellectual who famously stated that Jefferson never wrote anything worth reading on religion.[2] Professor West adds the father of the Constitution and the Bill of Rights to this condemnation.

What has provoked the ire of Professor West is the fact that Jefferson and Madison do not seem to allow for government support of religion. Both opposed a proposal to tax Virginia citizens to support teachers of Christian religion as a violation of religious liberty and the rights of conscience. Professor West argues, however, that government should support religion because morality, good order, good manners, and decency depend on religious instruction. Government support of religion can be accomplished, West maintains, without violating religious freedom or the rights of conscience. A tax to support Christianity does not force anyone to worship in any

---

1. Thomas G. West, *The Political Theory of the American Founding: Natural Rights, Public Policy, and the Moral Conditions of Freedom* (New York: Cambridge University Press, 2017), 204.
2. Irving Kristol, in *The Spirit of the Constitution: Five Conversations*, ed. Robert A. Goldwin and Robert S. Licht (Washington, DC: AEI Press, 1990), 81. See Harry V. Jaffa, "The Decline and Fall of the American Idea: Reflections on the Failure of American Conservatism," in *The Rediscovery of America: Essays by Harry V. Jaffa on the New Birth of Politics*, ed. Edward J. Erler and Ken Masugi (Lanham, MD: Rowman & Littlefield, 2019), 145–209.

particular manner or to embrace any particular religion or compel anyone to believe anything that would violate rights of conscience.

Professor West supports his view by pointing to religious establishment in the states as a better example of what the founding era believed was government's role in promoting good order and morality. Established religion in Massachusetts was upheld in a famous decision, *Barnes v. Inhabitants of First Parish in Falmouth* (1810),[3] written by Chief Justice Theophilus Parsons, who, West says, presented an "unanswerable" "argument for the harmony of natural rights and government support of religion." The Massachusetts Constitution of 1780 allowed townships to establish by majority rule not just Christianity in general but any sect of Protestant Christianity and to impose a mandatory tax to support the public teaching of the precepts and maxims of the chosen religion to all the people in the parish. No one was required to attend any religious instruction not approved by his conscience or that in any way interfered with his religious freedom. Parsons argued, "The object of free civil government is the promotion and security of the happiness of the citizens," and this can only be produced "by the knowledge and practice of our moral duties, which comprehend all the social and civil obligations of man to man, and of the citizen to the state. If the civil magistrate in any state could procure by his regulations a uniform practice of these duties, the government of that state would be perfect."[4]

But civil government is defective, the chief justice avers; civil power needs the assistance of "some superior power" that "might cooperate with human institutions, to promote and secure the happiness of the citizens, so far as might be consistent with the imperfections of man."[5]

The Christian religion, Parsons contends, has long been "promulgated, its pretensions and excellences well known, and its divine authority admitted. This religion was found to rest on the basis of immortal truth; to contain a system of morals adapted to man, in all possible ranks and conditions, situations and circumstances." And it is this religion—"as understood by Protestants"—that tends "to make every man submitting to its influence, a better husband, parent, child, neighbor, citizen, and magistrate." It was for this reason that "the people established" the Protestant religion "as a fundamental and essential part of their constitution."[6] Parsons points out that the Massachusetts Constitution also secures the "liberty of conscience, on the subject of religious opinion and worship, for every man, whether Protestant or Catholic, Jew, Mahometan, or Pagan."[7]

The part of the decision that Professor West touts as an "unanswerable" argument proving the harmony of natural rights and government support for religion resides in this passage:

3. 6 Mass. 401 (1810).
4. Ibid. at 404–5.
5. Ibid. at 406.
6. Ibid. at 407.
7. Ibid.

If any individual can lawfully withhold his contribution because he dislikes the appropriation, the authority of the state to levy taxes would be annihilated. . . . The great error lies in not distinguishing between liberty of conscience in religious opinion and worship, and the right of appropriating money by the state. The former is an unalienable right; the latter is surrendered to the state, as the price of protection.

Thus, the "unanswerable" argument of Parsons is that a compulsory tax to support an established religion levied on all citizens is a tax indistinguishable from any other tax. Parsons does recognize the "liberty of conscience in religious opinion and worship" as "an unalienable right," by which we presume he means a "natural right," but he does not identify "the right of appropriating money by the state" as a natural right belonging to government, as he certainly could not. In the face of this conflict between "unalienable" natural rights belonging to individuals and an alienable positive right of the state, on what ground does the positive right prevail or even have equal status? And how can this be described as "harmonizing" natural rights with government support for religion? As it stands, Parsons's decision is merely an *ipse dixit*. A compulsory tax to support a religion—even one particular sect—that one cannot in conscience support is surely a violation of an unalienable natural right. A tax to support municipal services *is* different! A compulsory tax to support a particular religion is in a different class and implicates the foundations of both religious liberty and the rights of conscience in a way that no other tax does.

In addition to the fact that Parsons in *Barnes* ignores blatant invasions of fundamental natural rights, he seems oblivious to the fact that those invasions depend "exclusively on the will of a majority," which in this case is obviously a majority faction depriving a minority of its natural rights of conscience. Parsons seems to be under the impression that unchecked majority will is the ordinary course of democratic politics, that the protection of minority rights is not a natural law restraint upon majority rule. For democracy to succeed, however, the minority must be willing to accept the decisions of the majority; at the same time, the majority must be willing to rule in a manner that is consistent with the rights and liberties of the minority. This was the major problem that faced the framers of the Constitution: how to avoid majority faction. If religion is allowed to become an issue in ordinary politics and the majority is called upon to decide matters of religion, no member of the minority would or could acquiesce to a majority decision if it involved a matter of religious conscience. Questions of religion cannot be resolved by democratic politics because there is no ground for compromise. Religious questions are intractable; they are politically irresolvable. The very basis for democracy is dissolved when religious questions intrude on democratic politics. Without separation of church and state, democracy is impossible. Sooner or later, majorities and minorities will form exclusively along sectarian lines.

One of the objections made against the compulsory tax to support teachers of Protestantism was that Christianity did not look to temporal power for its promulgation but sought to reign solely in the hearts and souls of men. But Parsons rejects this biblical injunction, saying that the teaching of Protestant Christianity is so congenial and beneficial to civil society that the state of Massachusetts "has wisely taken care" that its precepts be taught. "And," Parsons contends,

> from the genius and temper of this religion, and from the benevolent character of its Author, we must conclude that it is his intention that man should be benefited by it in his civil and political relations, as well as in his individual capacity. And it remains for the objector to prove, that the patronage of Christianity by the civil magistrate, induced by the tendency of its precepts to form good citizens, is not one of the means by which the knowledge of its doctrines was intended to be disseminated and preserved among the human race.[8]

Thus Parsons indulges some creative theology in order to justify upholding the compulsory tax against a claim that it violates the natural rights of conscience. The Author of our "benign religion" did not want to promulgate his teachings by temporal power but insisted that his kingdom is not of this world. Parsons insists, however, that we will not receive the civil and political benefits of this benign religion if we don't make it of this world. But every reader of the New Testament knows that worldly concerns corrupt true religion, and Parsons's reasoning is a prime example of how that corruption takes place under the cloak of the best of intentions. Anyone who reads Parsons's opinion without the predisposition to believe it to be "unanswerable" will also realize how it corrupts civil power by ignoring the dangers of tyranny in the amalgamation of church and state.

Professor West also quotes a New Hampshire Supreme Court opinion from 1803 with evident approval to buttress Parsons's assertion: "The situation of the taxpayer who resents funding someone else's religion," West recounts, "'is precisely the same as it is in other civil concerns of the state. The minority are compelled to pay for instructions in learning, though they may be of opinion that the schoolmaster chosen by the majority neither promotes learning nor good manners, but the contrary.'"[9] Professor West agrees with the New Hampshire court that a tax to support teachers of Protestant religion is no different than any other tax; the minority is often compelled to pay taxes to support measures that they don't approve. The New Hampshire Constitution, however, had a strong statement regarding the separation of church and state, mandating that it

> wholly detaches religion, as such, from the civil State. By the mixture of civil and spiritual powers, both become polluted. The civil uses religion for an engine of State to support tyranny, and the spiritual becomes invested with the sword of the civil magistrate to persecute. Under our Constitution there is no such union, no such mixture.[10]

Despite this ringing endorsement of separation, the state supreme court did not regard the tax to be enough of a "mixture of civil and spiritual powers" to be a viola-

---

8. Ibid. at 410–11.
9. West, *Political Theory of the American Founding*, 207 (quoting from *Muzzy v. Wilkins* 1 Smith [N.H.] 1 [1803]).
10. Quoted in *Muzzy v. Wilkins* 1 Smith (N.H.) 9 (1803).

tion of the constitution. But, of course, it is difficult to fathom how this mandatory tax did not entrench upon the rights of conscience, which we have seen Madison in the essay "Property" describe as the "most sacred of all property." It is simply incorrect to say that a tax to support one religion is the same as any other tax. A tax to support a religion not endorsed by one's own conscience directly assaults the free exercise of religion and the rights of conscience, both essential natural rights, the protection of which is essential to constitutional government.

Professor West can cite all the state-established religions he wants and the arguments given to support those establishments, but the American Revolution was intended to promote change, in both opinion and practice, and not to ratify circumstances as they existed at the time of the Revolution. The states were not the standard bearers for republican government during the founding era. We have only to recall Madison's statement in *Federalist* 10: "Our governments are too unstable, that the public good is disregarded in the conflicts of the rival parties, and that measures are too often decided not according to the rules of justice and the rights of the minor party, but by the superior force of an interested and overbearing majority" (72). This was majority faction, and it was this disregard of the public good and private rights in the states that led to the Constitutional Convention. The states could hardly be said to represent the standard for religious freedom as it was understood by the founders. The strong statement of separation quoted above from the New Hampshire Constitution represented widespread sentiment on the subject of religious liberty, but, as the New Hampshire Supreme Court decision illustrated, states were too often willing to violate their own constitutions, frequently sacrificing the rights of minorities to majority factions. The majority of state constitutions, for example, had provisions calling for separation of powers, but in almost all of the states these provisions were routinely violated, leading to legislative dominance that worked the will of majority factions.[11] The states were hardly a model of stable republican government, and the Constitutional Convention was a revolutionary appeal to the people to find a stable basis for justice and the common good—most particularly, protections for the free exercise of religion and the rights of conscience.

Jefferson and Madison correctly argued, as did the New Hampshire Constitution, that a mixture of church and state was harmful to both. Politics are corrupted by spiritual power, and religion is corrupted by the admixture of political authority. There is no biblical support for religious establishment; in fact all evidence points in the opposite direction. Harry Jaffa rightly notes,

America was founded upon the wise conviction that to make a state officially Christian would defeat the ends of Christianity. This conviction was fortified by the devastation wrought upon Christian civilization by the internecine wars and persecutions of Christian states in the centuries preceding the American Revolution. These wars and persecutions,

11. Edward S. Corwin, "The Progress of Constitutional Theory between the Declaration of Independence and the Meeting of the Philadelphia Convention," in *American Constitutional History: Essays by Edward S. Corwin*, ed. Alpheus T. Mason and Gerald Garvey (New York: Harper & Row, 1964), 4–9.

waged in the name of Christian truth, were in their own way every bit as cruel as those waged in the name of atheistic ideologies in the 20th century. The memory of the wars of religion was still fresh in the minds of both Madison and Jefferson, who led the movement—supported by George Washington—for disestablishment in Virginia.[12]

How did the Christianity that presided over the wars of religion become the Christianity that supported the separation of church and state of the American Founding? We saw in chapter 2 that the Protestant theologians of the founding era accepted the idea that reason and revelation were the twin pillars of Christian doctrine and that religious liberty and political liberty depended upon the separation of church and state. This was, in large part, a legacy of Locke, whom the Protestant ministers had studied and frequently referred to in their sermons. Locke's *Reasonableness of Christianity* presented a reading of the New Testament that was non-sectarian within Protestantism. When Jefferson referred in his first inaugural to an America "enlightened by a benign religion," he meant primarily the religion that had been taught to American theologians by Locke's *Reasonableness of Christianity* and *A Letter Concerning Toleration*. They supported religious freedom and the rights of conscience, considered them natural rights, and supported the separation of church and state as a political doctrine required by both reason and revelation. This was the accommodation between theology and politics that allowed the American experiment in republican government to proceed unencumbered by theological-political disputes. Jefferson and Madison worked diligently to prevent the revival of those disputes that would have made the American founding less successful, if not altogether impossible.

Professor West cites two passages from Jefferson's *Notes on the State of Virginia* that he contends prove that Jefferson's confusion on the issue of government and religion is irredeemable. In the first, Jefferson infamously remarked, "It does me no injury for my neighbor to say there are twenty gods or no god. It neither picks my pocket nor breaks my leg." The second statement, Professor West argues, is a stark contradiction of the first: "Can the liberties of a nation be thought secure," Jefferson wrote, "when we have removed their *only* firm basis, a conviction in the minds of the people that these liberties are of the gift of God?"[13] West believes the two passages show hopeless confusion on Jefferson's part: the presence of the atheist is a matter of indifference, but liberties are secure only with the conviction that they are the gift of God. How did Jefferson miss this obvious confusion in passages separated only by a few paragraphs?

We remember the argument from Locke's *A Letter Concerning Toleration* that government can deal with issues of civil goods but not with matters of the soul or opinions with respect to religion. Locke, however, argues that atheists do not have to be tolerated because their presence will tend to undermine the morality that is derived from observance of religion. Jefferson, however, argues here that both the

12. Jaffa, "Decline and Fall of the American Idea," 168.
13. Ibid., 205. The quotations are from Thomas Jefferson, *Notes on the State of Virginia*, in *Jefferson: Writings*, query xvii, 285; query xviii, 289.

atheist and the polytheist are to be tolerated, even though both adhere to views that
are not only false but also harmful to republican government. From the point of view
of the theology of the Declaration, atheism and polytheism are irrational. Atheism
would ultimately mean that all law is positive, having no transcendent source or
ground in God's eternal law. The Declaration clearly relies on a creator ("all men are
created equal") and a creation that is intelligible, of which human beings form part
of an ordered whole. And, as every reader of Plato's *Euthyphro* knows, polytheism
leads to the untenable conclusion that the world is made up of only fighting gods
(much like Oliver Wendell Holmes's "fighting faiths," or, in contemporary parlance,
"competing value systems"). Rational monotheism and revealed monotheism in the
Declaration are in complete agreement in rejecting both atheism and polytheism. Yet
Jefferson's hatred of sectarian tyranny was so thoroughgoing that he thought it better
to tolerate those few who adhered to such beliefs rather than to allow government to
engage in coercion by disabling such persons with civil or criminal penalties. Private
instruction from fellow citizens and the gentle persuasion of community opinion
would be a more effective way of bringing to "true religion" those who could not be
authentic republican citizens because they believed in polytheism or did not believe
their "rights come from the hand of God."

Jefferson concluded his statement in *Notes on the State of Virginia*: "Reason and
free inquiry are the only effectual agents against error. Give a loose to them, they will
support the true religion."[14] A fuller statement of this principle had been made in "A
Bill for Establishing Religious Freedom," where Jefferson said, in addition, "Truth is
great and will prevail if left to herself . . . she is the proper and sufficient antagonist
to error, and has nothing to fear from the conflict unless by human interposition
disarmed of her natural weapons, free argument and debate; errors ceasing to be
dangerous when it is permitted freely to contradict them."[15] This is a statement,
Professor West claims, that Jefferson knew was false. As proof that Jefferson knew
that the statement was false, West cites a highly selective quotation from Jefferson's
second inaugural to this effect: Jefferson knew the statement from "A Bill for Establishing Religious Freedom" was false, "otherwise he would not have praised the use of
'salutary coercions of the law' to punish 'false and defamatory publications,' as he did
in his Second Inaugural."[16] A full quotation of the second inaugural shows, however,
that Jefferson's remarks were in full agreement with his earlier statement:

> No interference is here intended, that the laws, provided by the State against false and
> defamatory publications, should not be enforced; he who has time, renders a service to
> public morals and public tranquility, in reforming these abuses by the salutary coercions
> of the law; but the experiment is noted, to prove that, since truth and reason have main-
> tained their ground against false opinions in league with false facts, the press, confined
> to truth, needs no other legal restraint; the public judgment will correct false reasonings

14. Jefferson, *Notes on the State of Virginia*, query xvii, 285.
15. Jefferson, "A Bill for Establishing Religious Freedom," in *Jefferson: Writings*, 347.
16. West, *Political Theory of the American Founding*, 207.

and opinions, on a full hearing of all parties; and no other definite line can be drawn between the inestimable liberty of the press and its demoralizing licentiousness. If there be still improprieties which this rule would not restrain, its supplement must be sought in the censorship of public opinion.[17]

Jefferson clearly regrets the abuse of freedom of the press, in which newspapers had routinely engaged in not only slander of private reputations but also seditious libel, and he supported prosecutions as provided by the laws in the several states. The experiment of individual prosecutions was time consuming and inefficient. The best remedy for "false opinions in league with false facts" was free argument and debate and "the censorship of public opinion." Jefferson, it seems, did not know his argument in "A Bill for Establishing Religious Freedom" was false—indeed, he believed it to be true, as his remarks in his second inaugural confirm (unless he was merely repeating what he knew to be false). He did, of course, take particular delight in seeing his political enemies prosecuted in state courts,[18] but public morality and tranquility were still best served by free argument and debate and public censorship.

There is one statement of Jefferson's on religion that Professor West does find worth reading. In his first inaugural, Jefferson praised, as we have already seen, American laws as "enlightened by a benign religion, professed, indeed, and practiced in various forms, yet all of them inculcating honesty, truth, temperance, gratitude, and the love of man." West concludes that this is evidence that Jefferson "however grudgingly is compelled to admit that government has an interest in promoting religious opinions that favor liberty."[19] Jefferson, however, doesn't say anything here about government "promoting religious opinions." In fact, the conclusion of the paragraph from which West quotes has this statement: "A wise and frugal Government, which shall restrain men from injuring one another, shall leave them otherwise free to regulate their own pursuits of industry and improvement, and shall not take from the mouth of labor the bread it has earned. This is the sum of good government, and this is necessary to close the circle of our felicities."[20] This is Jefferson's inimitable description of limited government. It is beyond imagination that Jefferson could have contemplated measures that would have included a tax to support teachers of the Christian religion. Rather, the morality and virtues embraced by the "benign religion" praised by Jefferson are taught by all the religious sects that inhabit the United States. There would be no need of government support when religions are already promoting the morality necessary to support liberty and free government.

In October 1800, on the eve of the young nation's first crisis election, Jefferson received a letter from Benjamin Rush, an active and prominent member of the founding generation whom no one would accuse of "anticlerical bias." Rush wrote,

17. Thomas Jefferson, "Second Inaugural," in *Jefferson: Writings*, 522.
18. See Leonard W. Levy, *Jefferson and Civil Liberties: The Darker Side* (New York: Quadrangle, 1973 [orig. pub. 1963]), 60ff.
19. West, *Political Theory of the American Founding*, 205.
20. Thomas Jefferson, "First Inaugural," in *Jefferson: Writings*, 494.

I agree with you . . . in your wishes to keep religion and government independent of each Other. Were it possible for St. Paul to rise from his grave at the present juncture, he would say to the Clergy who are now so active in settling the political Affairs of the World. "Cease from your political labors your kingdom is not of *this* World. Read my Epistles. In no part of them will you perceive me aiming to depose a pagan Emperor, or to place a Christian upon a throne. Christianity disdains to receive Support from human Governments. From this, it derives its preeminence over all the religions that ever have, or ever Shall exist in the World. Human Governments may receive Support from Christianity but it must be only from the love of justice, and peace which it is calculated to produce in the minds of men."[21]

This statement undoubtedly represents not only the view of Jefferson and Madison but also the view of the American founders to a much greater extent than the opinions drawn from the scattered state cases cited by Professor West. States, of course, were allowed to retain established religions after the ratification of the First Amendment, but the principles of the founding—and the opinions generated by those principles— would eventually erode any support for government involvement in religion. I say there can be little doubt that Locke, Jefferson, Madison, Rush, the Reverend West, and a host of others already discussed represent more accurately the authentic views of Protestant Christianity than any of the representations of Theophilus Parsons.

Tocqueville is justly praised for celebrating voluntary associations in America. There is virtually no political or social cause, he argued, that doesn't have an association dedicated to its betterment. Tocqueville, of course, is also famous for remarking, "Religion, which, among Americans, never mixes directly in the government of society, should therefore be considered as the first of their political institutions; for if it does not give them the taste for freedom, it singularly facilitates their use of it."[22] Tocqueville likewise reports, as if to confirm Jefferson's observation in his second inaugural,

I interrogated the faithful of all communions. . . . I found that all these men differed among themselves only on details, but all attributed the peaceful dominion that religion exercises in their country principally to the complete separation of church and state. I do not fear to affirm that during my stay in America I did not encounter a single man, priest or layman, who did not come to accord on this point.[23]

As Harry Jaffa cogently notes, "Tocqueville's celebration of the role of voluntary associations in American democracy has its foundation in the idea of limited government. But limited government has its origin in the doctrine of religious liberty."[24]

21. Benjamin Rush, letter to Thomas Jefferson, October 6, 1800, in *The Papers of Thomas Jefferson*, ed. Julian P. Boyd et al. (Princeton, NJ: Princeton University Press, 1950–), 32:205.
22. Alexis de Tocqueville, *Democracy in America*, ed. and trans. Harvey C. Mansfield and Delba Winthrop (Chicago: University of Chicago Press, 2000), vol. 1, pt. 2, ch. 9, 280.
23. Ibid., 283.
24. Jaffa, "Decline and Fall of the American Idea," 185; and Harry V. Jaffa, "The American Founding as the Best Regime," in *The Rediscovery of America*, 127–28.

This is the true gloss on Jefferson's first inaugural and "A Bill for Establishing Religious Freedom" as well as Madison's *Memorial and Remonstrance*. Government support for religion would be an entrenchment on limited government. It would also undermine the morality that it would attempt to support because benign religion associated with government would not remain benign. Locke, Jefferson, and Madison were well aware of this impending danger, as were most of the founders.

It is certainly possible to share Professor West's despair at the precipitous decline of morality in modern America. But it is disingenuous to place the blame—or any part of the blame—on a lack of government support for religion. There is no doubt that the influence of religion on morality, especially the ethics and morality needed to sustain republican government, has reached a very low point of declension. Mainstream churches have abandoned the teaching of morality in favor of one form or another of liberation theology. The decline in the political principles of the founding and the moral principles taught by religion in American churches have gone hand in hand, both under assault by radical modernity in its various guises, historicism, positivism, and nihilism. The principles of the American founding and the religion of the founding stood together against the tides of radical modernity that inundated Europe. After the Civil War, radical modernity came to American shores through the works of Rousseau and Hegel and found willing adherents in Progressivism and its successor movements.

It is wrong to blame the separation of church and state for the demise of religion when, in fact, it was the source of religion's strength in America, as Tocqueville so adeptly pointed out. If America's first principles can ever be revitalized, it will take place alongside the revitalization of the morality of the "true religion" that was defended by the theologians and clergy of the founding era. Government support for religion today would just add one more tool to the regulative arsenal of the administrative state. Allow churches to be drawn into the impetuous vortex of the administrative state, and they will be coopted and corrupted more than they already have been by the insidious forces of modernity. The restoration of America's first principles that relied on reason and revelation is the primary task facing Americans today—it is not to magnify the power and extend the reach of the administrative state.

Index